Bullets, Bandages
and Beans

Also by Alexander F. Barnes
and Peter L. Belmonte

*United States Army Depot Brigades
in World War I* (McFarland, 2022)

Bullets, Bandages and Beans

United States Army Logistics in France in World War I

ALEXANDER F. BARNES *and*
PETER L. BELMONTE

McFarland & Company, Inc., Publishers
Jefferson, North Carolina

LIBRARY OF CONGRESS CATALOGUING-IN-PUBLICATION DATA

Names: Barnes, Alexander (Alexander F.), author. | Belmonte, Peter L., author.
Title: Bullets, bandages and beans : United States Army logistics in France in World War I / Alexander F. Barnes and Peter L. Belmonte.
Other titles: United States Army logistics in France in World War I
Description: Jefferson, North Carolina : McFarland & Company, Inc., Publishers, 2023 | Includes bibliographical references and index.
Identifiers: LCCN 2023028896 | ISBN 9781476690582 (print) ∞
ISBN 9781476650302 (ebook)
Subjects: LCSH: United States. Army. Services of Supply. | United States. Army. American Expeditionary Forces. | World War, 1914–1918—Logistics—United States. | United States. Army—Supplies and stores. | Argonne, Battle of the, France, 1918. | World War, 1914–1918—Campaigns—Meuse River Valley.
Classification: LCC D570.75 .B37 2023 | DDC 940.4/36—dc23/eng/20230711
LC record available at https://lccn.loc.gov/2023028896

BRITISH LIBRARY CATALOGUING DATA ARE AVAILABLE

ISBN (print) 978-1-4766-9058-2
ISBN (ebook) 978-1-4766-5030-2

© 2023 Alexander F. Barnes and Peter L. Belmonte. All rights reserved

No part of this book may be reproduced or transmitted in any form or by any means, electronic or mechanical, including photocopying or recording, or by any information storage and retrieval system, without permission in writing from the publisher.

Front cover images: Services of Supply monument at Tours image (courtesy of the American Battle Monuments Commission); truck-loading scene. As the St. Mihiel and Meuse-Argonne offensives proceeded, the requirement for supplies of all types grew even larger. This photograph was taken at one of the large supply points near a railhead and designated for vehicle tires. Of note here are the many varied uniforms, rubber boots, coats and hats of the soldiers and their POW coworkers. (Author collection)

Printed in the United States of America

McFarland & Company, Inc., Publishers
Box 611, Jefferson, North Carolina 28640
www.mcfarlandpub.com

American author and poet Ruth Wright Kauffman
wrote an article in April 1919 intending to let
the homefolks know how their boys were holding up
in the transit camps in France as they waited to cross
the Atlantic to return to their homes.
In it, she recounted a story she had heard in which
a father had written his son who was serving in the
combat-weary 42nd "Rainbow" Division: "My boy,
you do not know what a wonderful opportunity
it has been for you to live through this war."
The soldier's reply was short:

> My dear father;
> A hell of a lot you know about it.
>
> Affectionately,
> Bob

The authors would therefore like to dedicate this book
to their children and their children's children
in the sincere belief that while we may not always
see things in the same light or from the same perspective,
the affection will always remain.

And a special dedication to Oliver Michael Barnes:
8 February 2021–10 February 2021.
I know we'll meet again some sunny day

Table of Contents

Acknowledgments ix
Preface 1

1. The Plan and the Failed First Efforts 7
2. The Ships and the Ports 28
3. Transit Camps and a Marine Brigade 43
4. New Leadership and Support to Combat Divisions 58
5. The Hospitals and the Flu 86
6. Working on the Railroad 106
7. Service Organizations: The Red Cross and the "Seven Sisters" 116
8. Biographies 131
9. Unique Events and the Problem with Prisons 141
10. The Central Records Office and the Postal Express Service 177
11. Closing the Accounts: Postwar SOS Operations and the U.S. Third Army 188

Chapter Notes 207
Bibliography 217
Index 223

Acknowledgments

Any work of this scope obviously requires the help and support of many people. We would like to thank the following folks for the use of their family photographs, private collections and other information: John Adams-Graf, Brennan Gauthier, Jim and Peg Peck, Eric Queen, Charles G. Thomas, and Jeff T. Giambrone.

There were also a number of people who encouraged us and lent their unique talents to helping us tell the story of the soldiers, civilians and Marines of the Services of Supply. They include Steve Girard, Rogier van de Hoef, Rob Dalessandro and Mike Shipman at the American Battle Monuments Commission, MG (Ret.) Ken Bowra, MG Timothy P. Williams, MG James Ring, Ms. Harlow Sullivan, MAJ Kevin Hoffman, CPT Ulyana Pivovarova, Capt. Josh McAnnally, SSG Aaron Edgerton, the Honorable Joan E. Shkane, Richard Killblane and Ewalina Arvan, who cheerfully translated the Polish/Russian letter of Private Stanley Nasilowski to his friend Helen Bialkoswka.

We also extend our thanks to Chris Garcia at the Virginia War Museum who lent his expertise on the AEF in general and the 42nd Division in particular, Jesse Smith at the Virginia War Memorial, Dr. John Metz and Dale Neighbors at the Library of Virginia and Luther Hanson at the U.S. Army Quartermaster Museum. Thanks also go to Brian Grogan, Alison Hutton and Kevin Born who helped make sure the pictures and images were of the highest quality possible.

The authors would also like to recognize the hardworking volunteers and maintenance crew at the Virginia Army National Guard Headquarters who work diligently to preserve and protect U.S. and Virginia military history: COL (Ret.) James Ebertowski, COL (Ret.) Steven Bourgeois, LTC (Ret.) Tom Michels, LTC (Ret.) Forrest Malcomb, CW4 (Ret.) USN John Perdue, CSM (Ret.) Cheyenne Johnson, MSG (Ret.) Craig Jewell, SSG (Ret.) Andre Williamson, GS15 (Ret.) Brian Wood, our Chinook pilot Doug Weiser, our combat engineer Jim McClure and our jack of all trades Jacob G. Gray.

Acknowledgments

A number of photographs and historical documents included are courtesy various governmental, military or historical organizations. Without their generosity, this work would not be complete. These include the Library of Congress; the Library of Virginia; the National Archives; the U.S. Army Quartermaster Museum; the U.S. Marine Corps History Division; and the Virginia National Guard Historical Collection.

To all of you, again we say thank you; we truly hope we met your expectations.

Preface

> He encouraged and directed subordinates to go directly to the source of supply, information, and authority ... he wanted results; and he got them.[1]

There's an old saying: "Before you embark on a journey of revenge, dig two graves"; the implication is that you can go on such a journey, but there are consequences. Writing about the U.S. Army logistics effort and the Services of Supply (SOS) in World War I is much like that. You can do it but, like revenge, there are some real consequences. You have to be prepared to sift through mountains of paperwork, reams of documents and a seemingly endless bookshelf of official reports. The SOS was only in operation for a little more than two years, 17 months during the war and the eight or nine months after the war that were needed to support the troops as they were sent back to the States as well as to shut down the organizations and facilities of the American Expeditionary Forces (AEF). During that short period there were more than 600,000 American soldiers in France working in the SOS as well as thousands of French and British women, German prisoners of war (POWs), and a large number of Asian laborers and drivers.

This was a period when Allied propaganda was telling the world that "ten thousand American soldiers arrive in France every day." Left unsaid was that "someone" had to feed, shelter, pay, clothe, equip and move those soldiers as well as tend to their physical, moral, mental and spiritual health while integrating them into combat units that would provide them with the tools, weapons and ammo needed for combat. And that "someone" was the Services of Supply.

As authors, our goal is guide you on a journey of exploration and discovery. To do so we will introduce you to some members of the SOS and let them tell you in their own words what they thought and what they knew. We have consciously made an effort not to correct their spelling or grammar unless absolutely necessary to your understanding. During the course of researching this book we found a collection of more than a hundred letters from an Ohio soldier who trained as an infantryman but spent the war building barracks in the transit camps and watching the nearby trains carry other soldiers to and from combat. While he was a steady writer with fairly clear handwriting, he didn't believe in using commas or periods. Each letter became a single sentence. Interestingly, after we read dozens of his letters, the flow actually started to make sense. We have spared you that experience, but in the pages that follow you will get a sense of his opinions on the war, the French, working in the SOS, and Germans.

Wearing a satisfied smile for a job well done, a Services of Supply (SOS) engineer poses for a portrait with the American flag and his gas mask after the war is over (John Adams-Graf Collection).

In these pages you'll read about a variety of interesting units: salvage squads, postal units, garden service companies, and even a coffee roasting plant. Perhaps most anomalous are the pioneer infantry regiments. These men were not quite engineers and not quite infantry. While some indeed saw combat, others toiled away in the SOS performing such unglamorous but necessary duties as operating a stone quarry and crushing plant, issuing ammunition, working on water supply infrastructure, and serving as stevedores. *C'est la guerre.*

So if studying and presenting a history of the SOS is such a daunting task, why do it? The overarching answer lies in the fact that the history of the American military in the 20th and 21st centuries has been one of ensuring that "bullets, bandages and beans" make it to where they are most needed. Even the phrase remains in common use among logisticians and operational planners when developing mission support plans. Sometimes they are successful and other times not. The U.S. Army's struggle to deliver gasoline to the forces breaking out of Normandy in 1944 or to provide sufficient anti-tank weapons to American soldiers in Korea in June 1950 are examples of failure. Examples of success also abound as when the U.S. Air Force was able to drop bridge sections to Marines fighting their way from the Chosin Reservoir in Korea or the massive supply build-up for Operation Desert Storm.

One of the many African Americans assigned to the Services of Supply, this soldier takes a break from work to enjoy a cigar and to pose for the camera (John Adams-Graf Collection).

On a personal level, our answer is deceptively simple: we found the people involved and their stories compelling. Together we have written three other World War I books, one about foreign-born soldiers in the U.S. Army, one about baseball and

GENERAL PERSHING SAYS:

"I want the S. O. S. to know how the First Army appreciates the prompt response made to every demand for men, equipment, supplies and transportation necessary to carry out the recent operations. Hearty congratulations. The S.O.S. shares the success with us."

A period postcard with the words of AEF Commander General John J. Pershing thanking the workers of the Services of Supply for their efforts in support of the "recent operations." His public gratitude was well deserved (private collection).

soldiers, and one a very complex history of the two million soldiers in the U.S. Army who trained for war but never left the States. As we worked together to research and write those books, we often found other stories and events that we knew were worthy of being told. Men and women who were black, brown, or white; American, French, German, Russian or British; soldiers, sailors, Marines or civilians; volunteers, draftees or prisoners; college-educated or illiterate, world-wise or naïve, native-born or foreign-born, all served in the SOS and all deserve to be remembered. Those seeking information on the total tonnage of cargo discharged at the port of Brest in August 1918 should look elsewhere. Instead this book will focus on the people who made that cargo discharge happen and what the cost was to them. Bless them all.

Equally important, this journey through the American logistics system of 1917 to 1919 in France will show how and where mistakes were made and if they were corrected or not. Any organization of this size is bound to have some interesting characters, and the reader will meet a number of them. After the war some will go on to greater fame, and one will even become the vice president of the United States. Others will return home and fade quietly into the background. Some will go to prison.

It is time, then, to turn the page and start a trip through a fascinating period where many countries looked to America to end the war and, as President Woodrow Wilson promised, to "make the world safe for Democracy." Brave words from a country that didn't really know how it was going to get its soldiers to the war or how it was going to feed them once they were there. Let's go!

1

The Plan and the Failed First Efforts

> The cause for the crisis was clear: the French simply were overwhelmed with the demands of the growing American presence in France, and their domestic supply organization was breaking down under the pressure.[1]

Getting to and into the war in Europe involved almost overwhelming logistical planning and execution. Just transporting the Army and Marine units to France was a major effort. German U-boats were patrolling the Atlantic and had devastated the shipping capabilities of England and France since 1914. After arriving in France in 1917 with a small headquarters contingent, AEF commander General John J. Pershing waged a continuous struggle against his French, British and Italian counterparts who wanted to use the U.S. soldiers and Marines as piecemeal replacements in their decimated armies. Mindful of the terrible casualty rates of the European allies in their trench warfare, Pershing insisted that the U.S. soldiers would serve and fight as an independent American force under American commanders.

The constant negotiation with the British for shipping space led Pershing to compromise to the degree that he later assigned some his soldiers to train and serve with the British army, but always as complete infantry brigades and divisions. He also "loaned" the provisional African American 93rd Division to the French. The urgency for getting troops to France and into combat increased when Russia, suffering massive defeats and internal dissent leading to the communist revolution, signed the Treaty of Brest-Litovsk in March 1918 and dropped out of the war. This released a number of German and Austrian divisions to join their comrades in France and Italy to fight on the Western Front starting in the spring of 1918.

While all the political battles over the creation of an independent

U.S. Army were being fought, the first AEF logisticians in France were struggling with mighty problems of their own. Aware of the distances between staging and depot locations and the need to avoid entangling the AEF's support operations with those of the British and French armies, the men responsible for sustaining the force developed a support plan based on their doctrinal training. The U.S. Army Field Service Regulations of 1914 carefully defined the doctrine and organizational structure for supporting a deployed force. Under this guidance, the U.S. effort was divided into two large parts: the *Zone of the Interior* (meaning the continental United States) and the *Theater of Operations* (the location where the deployment would take place). The Theater of Operations was divided again into two parts: *the Forward Zone*, where combat operations took place, and *the Rear Zone*, where logistics support was concentrated.

Uncle Sam and the Marquis de Lafayette shake hands as the United States joins the war on the Allies' side. Unfortunately, by this time France had little to give to the arriving soldiers except some weapons, training instructors and moral support. Other matériel such as food, clothing, horses, vehicles, fuel and even locomotives would have to be shipped from the States (Library of Congress).

The focus of this book will be on the "Rear Zone" which was tasked to serve as the logistics pipeline to receive, stage, maintain and transport all forms of support needed by the combat units. The Rear Zone was divided again into *Base Sections*, the *Intermediate Section* and the *Advance Section*.

1. *The Plan and the Failed First Efforts* 9

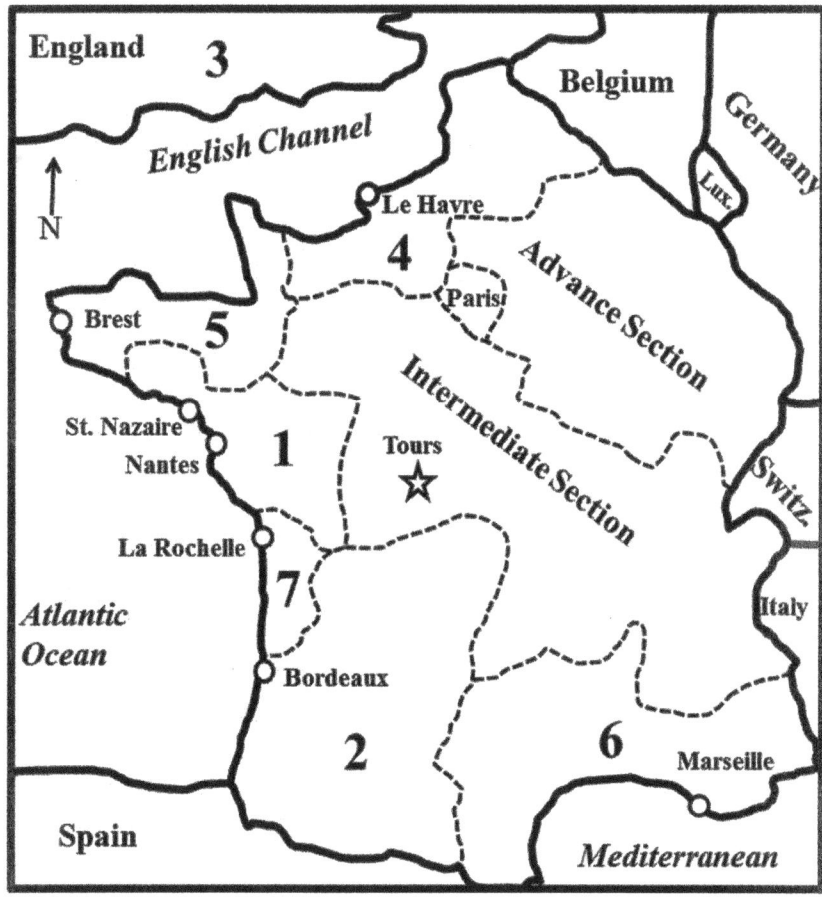

An important graphic for understanding the SOS support to the AEF, this map shows clearly the geographical layout in France and Britain. It also shows how each of the seven Base Sections had a waterport complex to facilitate unit/equipment arrivals and their onward movement and the central location of the SOS HQ at Tours (U.S. Army).

Each Base Section had at least one seaport and contained hospitals, facilities for receiving and equipping inbound soldiers, and some depot and maintenance facilities. The Intermediate Section was responsible for receiving, storing and issuing supplies sent to it from the Base Sections. It was also responsible for forwarding supplies and equipment to the Advance Sections in response to their requirements or as part of pre-determined needs based on operation and troop strength. The Advance Section was responsible for further breaking down the supplies into shipments of a size that could be delivered and then transporting them forward to the rear areas of the combat units. At that point, the logisticians assigned to the armies, corps or divisions would take responsibility for delivery to their supported units.

Under these guidelines, the supplies and equipment would arrive in France and be discharged from the ships. The cargo and equipment would then be sorted at locations close to the ports. It would then either be stored or transported further inland to storage and transshipment sites in the Intermediate Section. There it could be reconfigured for delivery to the Advance Section and on to the training areas or the rear boundaries of the combat units. Following the doctrinal construct for U.S. Army operations, this entire functional structure was called the Lines of Communication or simply the LOC.[2]

Headquarters for the LOC was first established in Chaumont and co-located with the AEF headquarters. The LOC Headquarters was later moved to Tours as part of the overall reorganization of logistics support to the AEF. Because of the use of many northern French ports by the British Expeditionary Forces (BEF) operating in Flanders, the western coast of France would be the main arrival area for soldiers and supplies coming from the States. Soon the port complexes and their associated ship loading and discharge operations, maintenance, transportation and supply support activities were designated as Base Sections and given a number. In time, each of these sections also became what could be considered full-service depots with salvage, supply issue, cold storage, maintenance, and butchery and bakery facilities as well as hospitals and remount facilities.

The Base Sections were:

Base Section Number 1. This section was centered on the ports of St. Nazaire and Nantes. Nantes was a shallow draft port and could not handle as much traffic as St. Nazaire. More than 3,000 U.S. soldiers, many of them African Americans, were employed as stevedores in these ports. St. Nazaire was capable of handling large numbers of animals being shipped from the States to the section's remount station which employed eight remount squadrons. The large Savenay hospital complex, located in Section Number 1, cared for the most seriously wounded soldiers who would require transportation back to the United States. A short distance from St. Nazaire, the AEF established a supply depot that by the end of the war employed more than 8,000 soldiers and several thousand French civilians and German prisoners of war. The 19th Engineer Regiment, a standard gauge railroad unit stationed nearby, reassembled the locomotives that had been shipped to the port in "knocked down" or disassembled condition.[3]

1. The Plan and the Failed First Efforts

Base Section Number 2. This section encompassed the area around the port of Bordeaux and was the largest of the Base Sections. It included large forested areas so most of the AEF's lumbering operations and sawmills were located there. A number of rail spurs were built to allow traffic from the port to avoid passing through the city itself. Since it was located some distance from the front, there were several large hospitals, recreation sites and training areas established in the section as well as a main storage depot at St. Sulpice. At first, the section staff struggled to get cargo offloaded from the ships and moved away in a timely manner. The weight of the cargo being discharged onto the wharves was causing them to sink into the Gironde River. Over time it improved with help from the engineers.[4]

Base Section Number 3. This section was located on the southern coast of Britain but, in reality, the entire island was Base Section Number 3. This included large rest camps at Southampton, Winchester and Romsey. There were depots as far away as Swansea in Wales and many U.S. Army Air Service camps. The Air Service maintained a large presence in Britain with 32 aero service squadrons, 31 aero squadrons, eight aero construction squadrons, 13 repair squadrons and many smaller related organizations. The part of the operation that did not involve the Air Service was the reception, resting and onward transportation to France of the

African American stevedores unload sugar at the port of Bordeaux in Base Section Number 2 in March 1918. It is interesting to note that the cargo ship *Woonsocket*, on the right of the photograph, has been armed with cannons to protect it from German subs and surface raiders (U.S. Army Quartermaster Museum).

soldiers who arrived in British ports.[5]

Base Section Number 4. Section 4 was centered on the port of Le Havre and operated facilities in Rouen and Calais. Le Havre served as the reception station for U.S. soldiers transiting through Britain. Due to its proximity to the front lines behind the British army, a large number of hospitals were established in this section, some of them dedicated to serving sick and wounded British soldiers. Several of the locations in this base section took on much greater significance in the Second World War. These included such places as Dunkirk, Caen, Calais and the Normandy coast.

Base Section Number 5. This section was the area around the port of

In another part of Bordeaux, a mixed group of black and white stevedores are unloading a vessel. Harbord and Pershing's first visit to Bordeaux was not a particularly pleasant one as they saw too many men sitting around watching others work. This and the previous photograph give some evidence of that. The U.S. Army commander of the port was relieved immediately after the visit (U.S. Army Quartermaster Museum).

1. The Plan and the Failed First Efforts 13

Brest. Although the French navy had been reluctant at first to share the port, they gave way and soon the largest of the troop transport vessels, such as the USS *Leviathan* and USS *Kroonland*, were discharging thousands of Doughboys. Although a deep-water port, Brest did not have the capability to dock such large ships, so the troops had to be brought ashore in smaller vessels. During most of the war this was a minor inconvenience but, at the height of the 1918 flu and pneumonia epidemics, it would have deadly implications for sick soldiers having to make this extra trip in bad weather. On one visit to the port late in the war, the commander of the SOS recounted that he saw 35,000 soldiers brought ashore in a single day. They marched to the nearby reception and transit camp while simultaneously 18,000 men from a previous convoy were loaded onto trains and dispatched from the camp.[6] It was an amazing accomplishment by any standard in any military operation of the 20th century. As in Base Section Number 4, this section also contained cities and areas of great importance to the next war: Cherbourg, Sainte-Mère-Église and Brest. Some of the senior artillerymen of the 29th Infantry Division who supported the assault on Brest in 1944 must have had strong memories of their training nearby in 1918.

Base Section Number 6. This section was centered on the large French Mediterranean port of Marseilles. Located almost 900 miles further from the East Coast of the United States than the other French ports, it was primarily used for freight shipments. Until late in the war enemy submarine activity in the Mediterranean had prevented this port from being of greater use. The Army Service Corps maintained several cement companies in the base section, and a large hospital complex was established in the Riviera.[7]

Base Section Number 7. This was the smallest base section in France and was centered on La Rochelle and the twin ports and railheads at La Pallice and Rochefort. It served as one of the main coal-receiving sections and was the main storage depot for both gasoline and oil.[8] One of the main units in the section was the 35th Engineer Regiment, a railway maintenance shop regiment, responsible for reassembling railcars as they came off the ships.

Base Section Number 8. This base section was centered on the port of Genoa, Italy. It was established to support the U.S. Army's 332nd Infantry Regiment, the Army Ambulance Service and a small Air Service contingent, all of which had been dispatched to bolster Italy's sagging morale. Most of the facilities were in north-central Italy.[9]

Base Section Number 9. This section was established after the war to support the U.S. Third Army on occupation duty in the German Rhineland. The main port was Antwerp, Belgium, but some cargo and passengers also passed though the Dutch port of Rotterdam. There were several military police and transportation units assigned to the section, and a number of soldiers from the 4th Division were dispatched for service in Rotterdam. At the start of the occupation, Antwerp's main purpose was the receipt and onward movement of supplies for the Third Army. It soon also became the main port for the retrograde of selected supply matériel and equipment from the Third Army being sent back to the States. Under the standard U.S. Army water port/terminal unit structure there were several staff sections and personnel assigned to support the Antwerp Military Port Commander. These included soldiers from the Quartermaster Corps, the Motor Transport Service, the Signal Corps, a medical detachment and a military police detachment. The port commander was further supported by a series of finance offices that handled all payments, contracting, and claims. To ensure effective mail service, APO 944 was established at Antwerp and would remain there until mid–1922 when the port and the base section were shut down.[10]

The Intermediate Section. Inland from the base sections was the area that was designated the Intermediate Section. Located primarily west and south of Paris, the Intermediate Section was headquartered at Nevers, also the site of a number of important railroad repair facilities. The most important storage facilities were established in the Intermediate Section and included a large ammunition storage facility at Jonchery and the

Even though the living conditions and the personal washing facilities (as seen here) were fairly crude at the large Gièvres Supply Depot in the Intermediate Section, few soldiers assigned there complained. They were well aware of the conditions further forward and on the front lines (private collection).

large aviation facility at Romorantin. At the latter site airplanes shipped from the United States were reassembled. Also in this section were the large ordnance depot at Mehun and the largest supply depot in the AEF: Gièvres. Gièvres was particularly important because it soon was storing two million gallons of gasoline and was the largest cold storage facility for meat in the world. By the end of the war, Gièvres had "warehouse space for food and clothing enough to supply an army of two million men for thirty days."[11] It had been established close to Tours and the location proved a wise choice for several reasons: close proximity to SOS Headquarters at Tours allowing convenient oversight of the massive operation by the senior SOS leadership; proximity to the main rail lines coming from the base sections at St. Nazaire and Bordeaux; and enough distance from Paris to avoid the road and rail congestion there caused by supply traffic supporting the British and French armies. The initial mission of the Gièvres depot was to receive supplies from the base sections and then forward them to advance depots located behind the U.S. combat divisions. In time, Gièvres covered 12 square miles and required the services of 20,000 soldiers and civilian workers. It had "one hundred and sixty-five Storehouses [with] one hundred and forty-three railroad sidetracks, and gave approximately four million square feet of covered space.... Eighty-five locomotives per day were turned within the engine terminal, and twenty-three hundred [rail]cars per day were handled."[12]

The Advance Section. Located between the Intermediate Section and the front line units was the Advance Section, primarily east of Paris. The largest Advance Section depot was located at Is-sur-Tille; it served as a railroad regulating station because of its proximity to the front lines. It began operations in late 1917 and, by the Armistice one year later, was a large facility with some 3,500 soldiers assigned. Supplies received at this facility were reassembled into issuable sets rather than stored by individual components. This was due partly to the need to send supplies and rations forward in combat-ready sets, and partly to the very real threat of German air raids which could demolish a warehouse thereby creating a major shortage of a single item.

From this central location, the Is-sur-Tille complex shipped to almost 700 locations and supported rail traffic to and from 46 other railheads. As Dr. William Chaikin wrote in "Quartermaster Supply in the AEF, 1917–1918," the

> system was found to work reasonably well for the automatic and constant supply of rations but was too slow to take care of sudden and sporadic demands for other classes of supplies. When troops were withdrawn from the lines it was often for too short a period to enable them to wait for the arrival of refitting supplies.... Accordingly, army supply parks and behind them sub-parks,

dumps, and refilling points, were established to hold a minimum reserve of fast moving items.[13]

These comments would not surprise modern-day logisticians as they, too, struggle with the unexpected supply requirements during deployment operations. Given the number of soldiers in a unit, weapons assigned to the unit, expenditure of ammunition, days in combat, number and type of vehicles, etc., logisticians can estimate the requirements for food, ammunition, fuel and even replacement clothing. These items can then be staged and "pushed" forward to the proper unit. What is so much harder, whether in 1918 or today, are the unexpected supply or repair parts requirements. During the early days of Operation Restore Hope in Somalia in 1992, the unforeseen requirements for replacement HUMMWV windshields and tires due to terrible road conditions caught most U.S. Army logisticians off guard. As a result, the supply chain was quickly filled with these items, causing other items to become lower in priority. The subsequent shortage of the other items would then cause them to rise to a higher priority, pushing something else down the priority scale, creating a vicious circle. It was the same for the AEF in 1917 and 1918.

At the railheads forward of the advance depots, supply and transportation soldiers from the combat or supported units received their supplies. The rule of thumb was that if units were within eight miles of the railhead, the unit's motorized vehicles or horse- and mule-drawn wagons would receive the supplies. Distances greater than eight miles usually required trans-loading to a smaller-gauge railroad or the use of motorized convoys to carry the matériel closer to the unit.

The French-made shoulder patch with the Cross of Lorraine and the letters A S worn on the left sleeve by soldiers assigned to the Advance Section (courtesy Alison Hutton).

1. The Plan and the Failed First Efforts

Problems with the LOC. Despite the adherence to doctrine and the great energy expended by the fledgling logistics operation of the LOC on behalf of the AEF, the early results were dismal. Perhaps the biggest problem lay in the fact that not one leader in the Army had dealt with the requirements generated by the massive size of the U.S. forces involved. The U.S. Army these men had grown up in, and had extensive combat experience with, was based on regimental-sized units. Any one of the new divisions was larger than the entire force deployed to China during the Boxer Rebellion. Adding to that problem was the unfortunate fact that there were very few trained logisticians in the U.S. Army. Until just a few years earlier, unit supply officer was an appointed position and filled by infantry, artillery, engineer or cavalry officers. In October 1917, when Colonel Johnson Hagood, a well-esteemed Coast Artillery officer, received the news that he had been selected to command the Advance Section, he asked what that was. When the officer giving him the assignment replied that he didn't know either, Johnson realized it was going to be a most interesting education.[14] He later wrote of the mismatch of trained officers to duty assignments:

> We had created in France a number of new staff services which had nothing corresponding on the other side [of the Atlantic]—notably the Transportation Department, the Motor Transport Service, the Provost Marshal Service, Construction and Forestry, Gas Service, etc. These services were being operated by men detached from other arms. Officers of the Quartermaster Corps were serving in practically all of the other staff departments and even in [combat units]. On the other hand, a very small number of officers on quartermaster duty belonged to the Quartermaster Corps.[15]

The situation was much the same in transportation units where many of the officers were engineers by training or had come as newly minted officers of the National Army. Underscoring the problem was that many of the officers being assigned to the SOS had failed or underperformed while serving in infantry or field artillery units. Officers who had failed to measure up to the rigorous standards required of them in France were sent to the Classification Depot located in the city of Blois which very quickly became "Blooey" in Doughboy French.

As the commander of the SOS later noted: "All officers who fail at the front are sent back to be utilized in ... the Services of Supply where something can be found for one of almost any profession or trade."[16] He also wrote: "More sad memories cling around the Blois, than any other city used by the American Expeditionary Forces.... For many an American it was the grave of buried ambitions, the temporary home of the hopeless."[17] One such artilleryman sent to Blois for reassignment ended up commanding the Headquarters Guard Company in the District of Paris. While there

Officers and enlisted staff of Base Section Number 2, including a colonel (seated third from left), a chaplain (seated far left) and several infantry and artillery officers. Among the enlisted men standing behind them are a cook wearing a white hat while holding a small dog, a Marine standing in front of the cook and a 33rd Division soldier standing second from the right (private collection).

he was required to sit on court-martials for misbehaving drunken soldiers, conducted a heated exchange of memos with the commander of the Military Transport Corps in the District of Paris about requisitioned trucks that never appeared and investigated the disappearance of the prisoners' money at the Roquette Prison.[18]

With so many officers now faced with learning on the job, it should be no surprise that the operations were plagued with shipping mistakes and confusion over cargo destination and delivery priorities. Early deploying units from the States attempted to bring as much extra equipment as they could, based primarily on what they thought would be needed. Most often they were wrong and wasted valuable cargo space. Making the situation worse, many ships unloaded their cargo at British ports for transshipment to France. The supplies and equipment were then loaded onto trains, moved to English Channel ports and reloaded onto other ships. By the time the equipment was unloaded again in France, everything was mixed together. As a result, "wagon bodies arrived ... with no wheels."[19]

Another problem with the supply system down at the divisional level was the reasonable attempt on the part of some quartermasters to predict what the next "greatly needed" item would be. Army supply regulations of the period were quite clear that no unit was allowed to stock more items than its own transportation assets could carry. The rationale for this is obvious: units needed to be able to load and redeploy themselves on short notice. SOS and corps-level inspectors continued to drive this point home to the divisional staffs and most of them quickly complied with the order. In one notable exception, a divisional supply officer had amassed a very large number of shoes, believing these would soon be needed. When orders came to move the division, the officer was forced to leave behind 8,000 pairs of new shoes. The "shoe mountain" episode served as a teaching point for all, and a very short while later that division also had a new quartermaster. Discussing these early operations, a U.S. First Army after-action report said, "The most serious delays experienced were in the case of articles which would be classified as initial equipment, requisitions for which were submitted to G-1, Second Corps. In no case were these requested supplies ever received."[20]

There were many pressing problems back in the States at the busy training camps and seaports, but they paled in comparison to those exhausting the LOC workers. Of the Allied countries, France in particular was drained after three years of constant warfare. Large portions of the country were either occupied by the German army or devastated by the fighting in trenches that stretched from the English Channel to Switzerland. With the largest portion of their male workforce in military service, the French were struggling to provide food and shelter for their own soldiers, and although they were enthusiastic supporters of the AEF, they had very little left to offer the Americans. It quickly became popular among U.S. Army officers to blame the French for all shortages "as an excuse for their own dereliction or lack of energy."[21] Max Brakebill, a former Hollywood "Laskey Players" motion picture studio employee and California National Guardsman in the 144th Field Artillery Regiment, wrote home, "The women of France deserve a lot of credit. They work like men.... If people in the States could see what France has put up with in the last 4 years they would know what war means."[22]

Most of the soldiers of the AEF did not really know either. Although the United States had declared war in April 1917, Pershing had only four divisions training in France by the end of the year. These were the 1st Division; the 2nd Division, built out of separate Regular Army and Marine Corps units; the 26th Division, organized from the units of the New England National Guard; and another National Guard unit, the 42nd "Rainbow" Division. Except for the 26th "Yankee" Division, these were all composite units built on the fly. The Rainbow Division was the conglomeration of National Guard units from 26 different states. The 2nd Division was a uniquely composite unit with one infantry brigade of soldiers and the other of Marines.

The 41st "Sunset" Division arrived in November 1917 and was composed of National Guard units from Washington, D.C., Washington State, Oregon, Montana, North and South Dakota, Colorado, Idaho, New Mexico, and Wyoming.[23] Almost immediately on arrival, the 41st was converted into the 1st Depot Division and so would never face combat as a unit. This type of conversion became more common in 1918. Many units would undergo the same fate with the decision solely depending on the sequence in which they arrived in France. It was a necessary but inelegant solution. Many of the soldiers in depot divisions were sent out to combat divisions as replacements. Other soldiers who had trained for months as infantrymen became

An African American soldier assigned to the SOS poses for a formal portrait after returning home. He is wearing one of the late-war 1918 wool service coats with hidden pockets. Note that he has managed to retain his campaign hat; for soldiers in the SOS, the nature of their work in engineer and transportation units made the campaign hat more practical headgear than the brimless overseas hat (private collection).

part of the LOC and were now assigned to operate transit camps and supply depots or work as longshoremen.

The winter of 1917–1918 was harsh, both in America and in Europe. Pershing's four intact divisions were suffering as much as the citizens back in the States. In response to a letter complaining of a shortage of shoes for soldiers in the 1st Division, former U.S. president Teddy Roosevelt bought and shipped 200 pairs to his son Archie's regiment. Many other soldiers were still wearing the lightweight summer uniforms in which they had deployed to France. One officer noted that "socks had to do duty as gloves, but there was a shortage of socks. Shoes had to be held together with rags and strings.... There were shortages of nearly everything."[24] It is small wonder that the soldiers in France began to refer to their plight as a "Valley Forge winter."[25]

It was the same in the 42nd Division:

> Inspections revealed that the troops were in a terrible state. The feet of some were almost on the snow-covered ground. Others were without gloves or overcoats. Some wore light B.V.D.'s instead of winter underwear ... groups struggled forward, worn-out shoes tied to packs and feet wrapped in rags and gunny sacking.[26]

Despite the arrival of more American units in France in late 1917 and early 1918, the Doughboys' contribution to the fighting had actually been minimal to this point. Pershing's casualty report to the War Department in April 1918 clearly reflected that. It showed a total of 317 soldiers killed in action, 200 died of accidents and 947 died of disease. Even counting the 118 who died of wounds and an additional 49 fatalities from gas, the total casualty list was less than 2,000 and half were from disease.[27]

Making this minimal combat effort look even worse, the LOC was proving to be the subject of some embarrassing episodes. In the 15 November 1917 memorandum to General Pershing's chief of staff, the commander of the Advance Section reported:

> I am informed a ship lay at one of our base ports in France for forty-two days waiting to be unloaded and costing the government in the neighborhood of ten thousand dollars a day ... at one time ninety percent of all of the transportation of one American division had been borrowed from a French captain.... Not only has the [LOC] failed, so far, to function properly in the supply of our own men but it has so clogged the French railway yards, storehouse and quays, in this section as to cause an official complaint to be made.[28]

Cargo shipments proved to be no end of headaches to the AEF. When the French requested that pig iron be sent from America, it was promptly dispatched and reached France. Unfortunately, the ports had no equipment capable of discharging the heavy bulky metal. The ship, still loaded, was sent back to the States. This ocean-crossing fiasco was repeated several times before the iron was finally discharged in France. A similar incident took place, this time involving 500 tons of frozen beef that had arrived but could not be moved due a shortage of refrigerated rail cars. The on-the-scene response was to ship the beef back to the United States. Fortunately, Hagood was able to intercede and hold the ship in port long enough to get the desperately needed meat offloaded and into the hands of the AEF's quartermasters.[29]

Equally embarrassing was the situation in the 42nd "Rainbow" Division, whose supplies had been haphazardly scattered across a 10-acre field, rendering much of it unserviceable or lost. The division followed this up with another problem. The divisional quartermaster contacted the LOC Chief of Staff with urgent news that the French just informed him that 900 horses were inbound to his location. He had no forage to feed them. The quartermaster asked the LOC to have the shipment stopped but the LOC staff could not help because they could not find out the source of the horses. As a last resort, the 42nd's quartermaster sent his troops out to gather what forage as they could find. In the end it didn't matter as the horses never arrived.[30]

Replacement uniforms were in such short supply that other American soldiers, particularly the U.S. II Corps troops attached to the BEF for training, had to be issued British army tunics, complete with the King's Crown brass buttons. Some problems were self-inflicted, as Hagood later wrote that "General [Francis J.] Kernan [first Commander of the LOC] and I were annoyed beyond all measure by subordinates sending out instructions which were absolutely contrary to his wishes or my own."[31] Causing a great deal of confusion and adding to the problem was the awkward arrangement between the quartermasters of the LOC and the officers of the Transportation Department, a separate organization set up in France with its own command structure. When supplies, for example, forage for horses, were needed by a unit, the request went to the LOC. Quartermasters in the LOC would then determine the location of the forage and turn it over to the Transportation Department. From this point on, the LOC had no visibility of, or control over, the shipment. It was entirely in the hands of the Transportation Department to transport and deliver. Should the train carrying the forage be delayed or set aside awaiting other shipments, the requesting unit would contact the LOC in search of the status of their supplies. The LOC officers would have no idea where the missing shipment might be and could only contact the Transportation Department to request a status. Soon these requests led to heated discussions between the LOC commanding general and the staff of the Transportation Department. While charges and countercharges of "unauthorized meddling"

Barreled Beef

Mess Chuck Beef   Corned Beef   Rolled Boneless Beef

Soaps and Washing Powder

Wool Soap   Swift's Pride Soap   Swift's White Laundry Soap
Maxine Elliott Buttermilk Soap   Raven Tar Soap
Castile   Sunbrite Cleanser
Swift's Pride Washing Powder

What it takes to Feed an Army

This table shows the approximate quantity of the different food articles tabulated to feed 100 men.

Articles	Quantity per 100 Rations (1 meal per 100 men)
Boiled Ham	35 lbs.
Veal Loaf	30 lbs.
Corned Beef	40 lbs.
Dried Beef	30 lbs.
Sausage	35 lbs.
Bacon	25 lbs.
Eggs	17 doz.
Salmon	25 cans
Tomatoes	10 cans
Sauer Kraut	5 gallons
Corn	16 No. 2 cans
Peas	17 No. 2 cans
Asparagus	25 No. 2 cans
Peaches	12 cans
Strawberries	12 cans
Pineapple	12 cans
Apple Butter	7 lbs.
Peanut Butter	5 lbs.
Mince Meat (25 pies)	12 lbs.

The above furnishes an idea of the food requirements for one meal for 100 men. What it would require for 30 days to feed 40,000 men runs into stupendous and interesting figures. We are quoting the approximate requirements for this number of men:

Bacon	180,000 pounds
Flour	1,404,320 pounds
Hard Bread	60,000 pounds
Baking Powder	6,505 cans

From a small booklet titled *Food Specialties of the Army and Navy*, used as a training aid for military cooks, this extract clearly shows the massive quantities of food consumed by the Doughboys in their mess halls and their field kitchens (private collection).

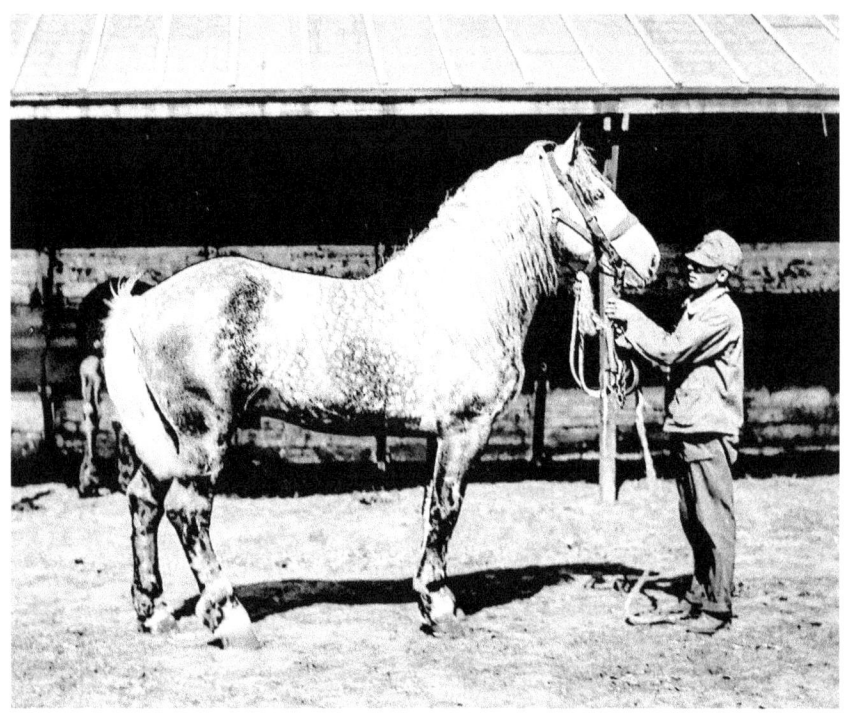

A soldier from the Auxiliary Remount Depot in Base Section Number 1 is placing the bridle on a Percheron horse purchased from the French government in June 1918. Percherons were used mostly as draft animals due to their muscled physique and willingness to work (U.S. Army Quartermaster Museum).

went back and forth, the horses in our example in the divisional areas would go hungry.[32]

Another self-inflicted problem stemmed from the habit of some Army officers bringing too much luggage. In one incident a general officer and his aides arrived in Britain and required two complete trucks to carry all of their suitcases, trunks and baggage. Problems with transportation and motor vehicles continued to be a major concern. A brigade commander in the 26th Division reported, "With traffic cops on every corner of the training camps at home and thousands of cars and trucks in reserve, we were put to the mortification of having to borrow transportation from the British and the French to keep men from starving to death."[33] Major General George Bell, the 33rd Division commander, noted sarcastically on 27 July 1918 that, while the streets of Washington, D.C., were filled with Army and civilian cars, his division did not have a single vehicle capable of driving more than 20 miles without breaking down.[34] Adding to the transportation problems, the motorized divisional supply train units who could have solved, or at least alleviated, some of the problems were pushed further down on the shipping priority list so that more infantry battalions could be shipped. As we will see later, some of these problems were made worse by a compromise made to obtain more transport vessels from the British and French.

What was really needed was a fresh start with a reorganization of the overall logistics effort. But reorganized to what form and at what cost? In February 1918, realizing that the first attempt at a logistics support organization, the LOC, was not working, Pershing tasked the LOC's Chief of Staff, Colonel Hagood, to establish a board and quickly determine a solution to the problems with the LOC. Something had to be done because if the LOC was failing to support the relatively few combat divisions in France, how would it work when the numbers tripled or quadrupled? And there continued to be problems with many of the civilian experts brought into the Army at high ranks due to their experience in industry or their political connections. Hagood later wrote that part of the problem during the early period was that they could not "get the people of the Transportation Department [primarily the ocean shipping and railroad leaders] to consider that they were [now] army officers instead of transportation men dressed up in costume."[35]

Pershing waited impatiently for the results. Among the findings from Hagood and the board were suggestions that the AEF HQ staff sections responsible for Operations (G-3) and for Training (G-5) should remain in the Chaumont General Headquarters while the sections responsible for Personnel Administration (G-1) and Logistics (G-4) should be relocated to an equivalent General Headquarters elsewhere. The staff section responsible for Military Intelligence (G-2) could be split between the two headquarters with focus on their own areas of responsibility.

The Board also recommended transfer of many of the Chiefs of Services (i.e., Quartermaster, Signal, Ordnance, Engineer, Air Service, etc.) from AEF Headquarters to the newly proposed organization. They further proposed that administrative services with responsibility for transportation, supply and procurement also be transferred to the "Services of the Rear" or SOR, the Board's suggested new name for the LOC. Finally, the Board recommended that the Postal Service and many of the administrative services be transferred from the AEF HQ to the SOR and that the SOR should be headquartered, not near Paris, but in the French city of Tours.[36] During the staffing process, however, the suggested new name met with resistance from every direction, and so the board reluctantly suggested that "Line of Communications" be retained as the organizational title. At this point, Pershing himself stepped in and named the new organization the "Services of Supply" or simply "SOS."[37]

Under Kernan's leadership, and with Hagood's skillful assistance, the SOS developed a set of what today would be considered "command philosophies." These included such commonsense dictums as:

1. Rank and authority should not be confused with knowledge. Use of authority was not to outrank the judgement of the man on the job unless it could be proven to be the better course of action.

2. If there was a difference of opinion over a minor matter, it would be resolved at the lowest level possible.

3. No subordinate officer could decide contrary to the guidance of his senior officer until it had been resolved either in person or via telephone, telegraph or letter. While this may sound like common sense, the reader need only review some of the incidents concerning the earlier LOC operations to see why this guidance was included.

4. No order, memorandum or plan could be changed by a staff member until the originating section/officer had reviewed the change and agreed to it. This was another commonsense decree, but necessary nevertheless, as there was often a staff tendency to "improve" guidance or plans and thereby changing the purpose or focus of the plan.

5. There was to be no delay in obtaining General Staff approval to implement projects. If a section chief believed the approval/denial was taking too long, he was authorized to go directly to the SOS Chief of Staff.

6. Bureau chiefs and section commanders were completely responsible for the development and execution of operations within their assigned areas. The vast geographical dispersion of the SOS throughout France and other countries made this decentralization of command responsibility necessary to ensure action was being taken without constantly resorting to higher headquarters for approval.

Although the performance of the SOS continued to slowly improve, especially when compared to the LOC, the increasing workload generated by a rapidly growing AEF was still proving too much.

In June came a new crisis, the German 1918 summer offensive. As the Germans pressed closer to Paris, the AEF took on a much larger share of the fighting and was consuming supplies, ammunition and manpower at almost unsustainable rates. There were now five U.S. divisions serving with the British army and five with the French. Those with the French had proven critical in stopping the German advance. Through their efforts Belleau Wood, Château-Thierry, and the "Rock of the Marne" entered the U.S. military lexicon. By late June, with some of the crisis abated, Hagood decided to visit the front line divisions to get their perspective on the support they were receiving from the SOS. He visited the 2nd, 3rd, 4th and 28th

Divisions near Château-Thierry and the 1st Division near Cantigny. At each stop, senior members of the divisional staff told him they had no major complaints against the SOS. Still believing there was room for improvement, Hagood made a trip to observe the operation of the British logistics system and organization. He also visited the five divisions training with the British: the 27th, 30th, 33rd, 78th and 80th. Again, there were no major complaints other than the Americans struggled to adjust to the British-issued food ration. In particular, they were not thrilled to find that cheese was a major part of a meal rather than just a side dish.[38] In hindsight, it appears Hagood got off easy. He would have heard much stronger sentiments if he had asked some lower-ranking soldiers. A National Guard lieutenant in the 118th Infantry Regiment, 30th Division, wrote about a day-long march with full pack that took place in July 1918. After the strenuous hike, during which only about a third of the men arrived at the finish point to receive their evening meal, he noted the "British had prepared the supper, and if ever insult was added to injury it was done here. We each received a small piece of rabbit, along with a cup of sugarless tea. I know King George's ears must have burned from what we had to say about him and his army."[39]

Despite the high grades the SOS received from the divisions, there was political back-stage maneuvering taking place that would directly impact the SOS. It was rumored that some senior officers serving in the War Department back in the States believed many of the logistics pipeline problems could be solved by them taking direct charge of the operation. They intended to do this through the person of General George Goethals, the officer most responsible for building the Panama Canal. Placing the highly regarded Goethals in Kernan's position in France, in their opinion, would leave Pershing able to concentrate on command and control of the combat divisions. There was one major problem with this theory: Pershing believed that *all* Army and Marine Corps operations and organizations of the AEF in France belonged to him. Moving quickly, before the War Department could send Goethals across the Atlantic, Pershing relieved Kernan and replaced him with the man many believed to be the best general officer in the Army: Major General James G. Harbord.

Pershing handed control of the SOS over to Harbord on 29 July 1918. It was a good decision. And just in time. American soldiers were arriving in ever-increasing numbers. The month in which Harbord assumed command proved to be the busiest month of the war for arriving troops as some 306,000 soldiers were delivered to Europe.[40] Harbord, unhappy at giving up command of the 2nd Division, nevertheless decided to vigorously take on the job of leading the SOS. Before we follow his path, it's important to turn to the problems created by having the Atlantic Ocean between the United States and the AEF in France.

2

The Ships and the Ports

At the beginning the problem was ships.[1] Germany failed when the submarine campaign against transportation failed.[2]

On 28 May 1917, General John J. Pershing left New York City for France on board the USS *Baltic* to establish the advance headquarters for the American Expeditionary Forces (AEF). Accompanying him were 191 soldiers and Marines. Although their departure was considered top secret, one of the coast artillery batteries fired a salute as the ship sailed by. It was an inauspicious start for what many of the Allied leaders from France, Italy and Great Britain hoped would be a fast-rising flood of American soldiers. They were to be very disappointed. Not only was the American Army in 1917 extremely small, fewer than 200,000 soldiers, it was more equipped and trained to fight in the 1898 Spanish-American War than take on the modern, battle-tested Imperial German army in the trenches of France.

Although the United States was beginning to recruit, equip and train a large, more modern army, it would take time and a lot of ships to move it across the Atlantic to France. Unfortunately, as the U.S. Army started to round into size and shape, much of the Allied transportation capability required to move the force was littering the bottom of the ocean. The German navy's surface raiders and submarine fleet had ravaged the shipping fleets of the Allied and neutral countries to the point that, even with a massive shipbuilding program, the Allies could not replace half of their losses. By July 1917, British Admiral Lord Charles Beresford expressed his fears quite clearly by reporting he was

> distressed at the fact that it appears ... impossible to provide enough ships to bring the American Army over ... and, after they are brought over, to supply the enormous amount of shipping which will be required to keep them full up with munition, food and equipment.[3]

The German General Staff agreed completely. In their opinion the American Army would not be able to cross the ocean in sufficient numbers in time to impact the fighting on the Western Front.

2. The Ships and the Ports 29

Transporting the Army. Many American planners also felt that shipping was an insolvable problem. Nevertheless, President Wilson had committed the United States to war. His Secretary of War, Newton Baker, was determined to end the "Great War" by bringing it to a quick and victorious conclusion. Facing him, however, were some harsh truths. The German submarine fleet, although primitive by the standards of the fleet that Germany would field in the Second World War, was proving an effective tool in choking the flow of transatlantic shipping. Another problem for Baker was the American commercial shipping fleet. While large, it was focused almost exclusively on local trade routes on the Great Lakes, in the Caribbean and in coastal waterways, making it almost totally unequipped to move the thousands of soldiers General Pershing needed in France. Perhaps most frustrating of all, what remained of the French and British commercial shipping fleets came with a price tag. The Allied commanders wanted the American Doughboys to fill the manpower gaps that the Germans had ripped in the Allied armies. They were determined to dictate what kind of soldiers and equipment would be transported in their countries' ships and insisted on restricting passage to infantry and machine gun units. This unbalanced approach stood against everything Pershing planned for his army.

Given this list of problems, Secretary Baker could have been forgiven if he were discouraged. Fortunately for the United States, he was made of sterner stuff and decided to attack the problems head on. With the U.S. Navy's assurance that their warships could protect the troop transport ships through the use of convoys and vigorous ant-submarine tactics, Baker checked the first problem off his list.

The Navy proved as good as their word. The majority of the American Navy was transferred to the Atlantic seaboard and careful coordination with the British fleet helped to maximize the number of anti-submarine vessels assigned to convoy protection. It also helped that the Navy had begun conducting "refueling at sea" operations just a few months earlier and was now able to extend the sailing distance of the newer ships in the destroyer fleet.

Baker also knew that Pershing had the complete backing of President Wilson when it came to decisions concerning the Army. Therefore, he left Pershing and his staff to deal with the Allied efforts to piecemeal the American force into their armies. If reduced to shipping only infantrymen, the American Army would end up as a feeder system to the Allied forces. Holding the line against most of the French and British attempts to take over his soldiers, and carefully cooperating at other times, Pershing managed to keep the American Army in one piece as a cohesive fighting force although some of the SOS and combat division replacement

A nice family portrait of a medical corps soldier assigned to the Port of Embarkation Command for the New York area complex. During the final months of the war, the Spanish flu would make working in the ports and transit camps on the East Coast seemingly as dangerous as serving in the trenches on the Western Front (private collection).

2. The Ships and the Ports 31

problems the AEF had later were a direct result of the imbalanced force composition being transported to France.[4]

This left Baker with the lack of transport ships as his biggest problem. Needless to say, he still had other major headaches. One came from the huge amount of rail resources required to move soldiers from their training camps scattered throughout the country to the East Coast ports of embarkation (POE). This proved to be a real challenge as every troop train heading eastward meant one less coal train delivering heating fuel to the large cities of the country. Even nature seemed against Baker as the winter of 1917–1918 proved to be one of the coldest on record.[5]

Yet his truly vexing problem was ships. Those few U.S. ships capable of transatlantic voyages were loaded with soldiers and dispatched to France under the convoy system but at nowhere near the speed or efficiency the other Allies expected or hoped for. The lack of shipping capacity continued to be the chokepoint or bottleneck of the logistical and deployment pipeline. The rapid movement of troops by rail from the camps to the eastern seaboard sometimes compounded the problem. There simply weren't enough ships to get the Doughboys across the Atlantic Ocean, and now thousands of soldiers were being crowded into transit camps near the ports. Adding to the dilemma, winter storms at sea had slowed the departure and passage of the ships that were loaded and under way to France and Britain.

The Germans were well aware of what was going on in the United States and were adding to the problem by aggressively attacking all along the Western Front, threatening to win the war before the Americans could make a difference. Having been victorious against Russia, the Germans were moving their Eastern Front forces westward towards France. Struggling to get the AEF moving towards the front, U.S. Army General Tasker Bliss wrote in exasperation to Secretary Baker that the Army had reached the point "where it is evident that if we do not send enough troops promptly, we must face the probability of losing the insufficient numbers that we may have sent."[6] Bliss had already taken his best shot and attempted to better organize the ports through a centralized embarkation office directly under his control. He had even commandeered the massive German-owned Hamburg American Lines port facilities in Hoboken to serve as a port complex, but it still was not enough.

Borrowed vessels. The Americans needed more ships than were readily available, but where could they come from? Playing the last card in his hand, Baker decided that German ships, interned in U.S. ports since the outset of war, could be used as troopships. This solution turned out, at first, to be more of a challenge than expected. The captains and crews of the captive German ships, correctly fearing that their vessels would be

The USS *Leviathan*, formerly the *Vaterland*, seen here in Brest after making one of her nine voyages to France. This 1919 photograph clearly shows her huge size. Before the war ended, she carried almost 120,000 soldiers to France (private collection).

used against their homeland, had carried out a program of deliberate sabotage soon after they had been impounded. A U.S. admiral later wrote of his personal shock at this effort:

> To a man who really loves his ship, malicious injury to her by her own captain seems almost impossible; but the Teutonic mind is utilitarian rather than sentimental, and so ... the captains of these ships ... set to with sledge and chisel to wreck and destroy.[7]

Fortunately for the United States, the Germans "blundered in the job."[8] The German sailors had underestimated American ship repair skills. Most of the deliberate damage by the crews had been to the vessels' engines. Repair crews set to work, either creating new parts or welding the old parts back into place. Working around the clock and seven days a week, the repairmen brought the ships back on line and made them seaworthy. By the time they were finished the Americans had repaired and placed back into commission some 20 German ships. In most cases, on completion of repair work, the ships were renamed. Some of the larger repaired vessels were:

Original Name	*New Name*
Grosser Kurfust	Aeolus
Kaiser Wilhelm II	Agamemnon
Amerika	America
Neckar	Antigone
Cincinnati	Covington

2. The Ships and the Ports 33

Original Name	New Name
Prinz Eitel Friedrich	DeKalb
George Washington	George Washington
Fredrich der Grosse	Huron
Vaterland	Leviathan
Koenig Wilhelm	Madawaska
Barbarossa	Mercury
Kronprinzessin Cecile	Mount Vernon
Princess Irene	Pocahontas
Hamburg	Powhatan
President Grant	President Grant
President Lincoln	President Lincoln
Rhein	Susquehanna
Kronprinz Wilhelm	Von Steuben[9]

While most of the repair work was performed at the New York City port complex, the ports of Boston, Norfolk and Philadelphia also repaired ships. This program proved to be a major success for the United States and added greatly needed shipping capacity to support the movement of the soldiers to France. Particularly important were the *Leviathan*, noted as the largest ship in the world at the time, the *President Grant* and the *George Washington*. Two other ships were also quite interesting because they had served as surface raiders earlier in the war: the *Prince Eitel Fredrich* and the *Kronprinz Wilhelm*. These two former passenger liners had taken refuge in the Hampton Roads port complex in Virginia and relied on U.S. neutrality to protect them from the British fleet. The 600 officers and crewmen of the two ships had enjoyed a celebrity status in the Virginian port until they were transferred, along with their ships, to Philadelphia. Later, under new names, the ships would contribute to transporting the Doughboys to France.[10]

Another German ship, the *Princess Alice*, impounded in the Philippines, was renamed the *Princess Matoika* and put into service. Very quickly the impounded German ships proved to be worth the efforts made to repair them. Of the 12 ships noted for carrying the most American soldiers to France, the top six were former German vessels. The number of soldiers they transported is staggering: *Leviathan* carried 119,000 soldiers in nine trips, *George Washington* 48,373 in nine trips, *President Grant* 39,974 in eight trips, *America* 39,768 in nine trips, *Agamemnon* 36,097 in 10 trips, and *Mount Vernon* 33,692 in nine trips. These six ships alone

U. S. S. LEVIATHAN
U. S. NAVY ARMED TRANSPORT

Compartment   FRS-3   Located on F deck Amidship

GREEN TICKET

TROOP BILLET

STBD.   N° 140

Deck Space   A-deck

Latrines and Washroom in Compartment   FRS-3

Abandon Ship Mustering Station   No. 12   located A-Deck

(Read orders on other side)

ORDERS STRICTLY ENFORCED

Never touch closed airports and closed water-tight doors.

Keep off life boats and life rafts and don't touch their lashings.

No smoking in bunk compartments.

Never spit on decks—it spreads disease—use the spit kits.

Put all trash in waste cans only—never drop any on decks.

Life preservers must not be used as cushions or pillows—it lessens their buoyancy.

Keep on your compartment's deck space.

Stop violators of these rules at once and turn them over to nearest army officer.

***Don't lose this ticket**—Always carry it with you—you will be required to show it.*

The boarding pass (front and back) for the *Leviathan*. By late 1918, with the onset of the Spanish flu, the warning not to spit on the deck became as critically important as knowing the "abandon ship" mustering station (private collection).

delivered the equivalent of 14 of Pershing's 28,000-man divisions. Only two U.S.-owned ships, both named for U.S. railroads, were in the top 12: *Great Northern*, 28,248 troops in nine trips, and *Northern Pacific*, 20,711 in nine trips.

Despite their German origin, the impounded ships became targets for the German submarines. Of the newly American ships, three were torpedoed. All three were on west-bound return voyages and empty of soldiers. The *Covington* and *President Lincoln* were sunk, and the *Mount Vernon* was damaged but reparable. Another ship, the *Von Steuben*, went on the offensive during a U-boat attack and helped to depth-charge the enemy vessel.

Always seeking to add even more vessels to speed up the deployment of the AEF, Baker directed Herbert Hoover, the Director of Food Administration (and future president of the United States), to hand over to General Bliss some of the vessels being used for subsistence shipments to Europe. Baker also dispatched his staff to investigate means of speeding up the loading and unloading of ships when they were in harbor. He recognized that faster turnaround times could further maximize the tonnage and personnel capacity of the fleet of transport ships. With all of these successes to Baker's credit, it is important to remember that President Wilson had been criticized by pro-war U.S. political leaders for selecting Baker, a well-known pacifist, as his Secretary of War. On the other hand, Baker's selection had been seen favorably by many pacifists or isolationists who strongly opposed America's participation in the European war. They believed Baker would help keep the United States out of the fight. Inopportunely for Baker, the day after he was sworn into office in March 1916, Pancho Villa attacked Columbus, New Mexico. The attack immediately put Baker's personal anti-war beliefs to a difficult test. It didn't get any easier, and by April 1917 the United States was at war with Germany. Even with these challenges, Baker maintained as much as possible his pacifist leanings and wrote "the quickest route to peace is by employing the maximum effort and every possible facility to the fullest extent at the earliest possible moment."[11]

However, until the German ships could be repaired and begin their shuttle to Europe as part of the nation's maximum shipping effort, the situation in France remained bleak. As noted earlier, when Pershing left for France, he was accompanied by barely enough soldiers to hold a decent-sized formation. He was counting on the War Department to start sending him the troops he would need to build his army from the ground up. With each passing week a few more American soldiers appeared in France and were transferred to training facilities where they became acclimatized to France and the dreary European weather. More than one AEF soldier would write home saying that "sometimes it doesn't rain in France."

The 42nd Division was typical of the first units to arrive. Up to that point the arrivals had been few, so many people turned out to see the ships and troops come into the port. One woman wrote that she stood beside

Soldiers of the 42nd "Rainbow" Division crowd the deck of the *President Lincoln* while en route to France in October 1917. Among the very first of the Doughboys to deploy, these soldiers would participate in a number of hard-fought campaigns. The *President Lincoln* was torpedoed by a U-Boat and sunk on a return voyage to the United States in May 1918 (U.S. Navy).

three Y.M.C.A. girls and helped them throw hard candies and oranges up to the crowded decks, and asked who the men were. "Why don't you know?" was the somewhat scornful reply. "We're the first of the Rainbow Division! Came over on this boat we lifted from the Heinies.... We're on the way to Berlin, and you just watch us! A couple of weeks at those Bosche, and we'll eat 'em alive. Say, where are we now? England or France?"[12]

Even so, despite the relative lack of fighting and low number of casualties, the number of Doughboys arriving in France was finally starting to become significant in the early spring of 1918. During a war in which the opposing sides sometimes counted their daily or weekly casualties in the thousands, the American contribution started to become apparent in March 1918 when almost 85,000 soldiers arrived in France. The next month the number was almost 120,000. It more than doubled in May to 245,000. In June, it was 300,000. The next month, even more would arrive.[13] Some of the most effective propaganda leaflets dropped on the German lines were those that boasted "every day 10,000 American soldiers arrive in France."

2. The Ships and the Ports 37

Almost as important as the soldiers being transported to France were the thousands of horses and mules needed by the combat and logistics units. Here is a rarely-seen view, the stables built on some ships to keep the animals secure during the voyage across the Atlantic (U.S. Army Quartermaster Museum).

A coalition effort. By the signing of the Armistice on 11 November 1918, there were slightly more than two million Doughboys in France. Bringing them there had been a massive coalition effort; British ships carried 48 percent, French ships 2 percent, Italian ships 3 percent and U.S. ships (including the impounded German vessels) had carried 47 percent. The British contribution is notable; they had finally agreed to allow the AEF to set shipping priorities in return for Pershing allowing some of his complete divisions to train in the British sector and later conduct combat operations in conjunction with the British army. It took 13 months to deliver the first half-million Doughboys but only six months to bring the remaining million and a half.[14] Knowing that there remained another two million soldiers in training in the United States awaiting overseas transportation helped drive the Germans to the Armistice table.

Undoubtedly, the use of impounded German ships proved to be a critical element of transporting the U.S. Army and Marine Corps and

On arrival at St. Nazaire, a special ramp was moved into position to allow discharge of the animals on board. Once it was in place, the horses and mules were brought safely down the ramp to the dock. As each animal reached the end of the chute, a soldier waited to lead it to a nearby holding pen. The soldiers in the upper right of the photograph are waiting their turn to act as escorts (U.S. Army Quartermaster Museum).

their equipment to battle. Recognizing the accomplishment, Vice Admiral Albert Gleaves later wrote that it was no exaggeration "the raising, transporting and supplying overseas of this army of two million men will be finally ranked as one of the greatest achievements in the annals of history."[15] That it was accomplished under the direction of an ardent pacifist and using vessels "borrowed" from the enemy makes the achievement that much more remarkable.

As troops arrived in France, they were moved as quickly as possible through the reception camps at the ports and on to their training areas. Pershing and the U.S. Army staff had developed a strategic and tactical concept that centered on a "million-man field army" structure. This force would consist of 30 divisions divided into, and controlled by, five corps with six divisions each. Each corps would also contain a number of corps-owned units such as heavy artillery, long range-signal, aviation and observation balloon units, and engineer specialty units. Within each corps, four divisions were to be combat divisions, one was to be a replacement division to send replacements to the combat divisions, and one was to be a depot division for receiving and training individual replacements as they arrived in France. The section of France set aside for AEF training camps was subdivided into smaller sections, each designed to reset the unit into proper formations and reassemble the divisions for service. By September and October 1918, it became obvious that another force, as deadly as the German army, was going to be playing a part. This new enemy was the second and deadliest wave of the Spanish flu.

Spanish flu and the transports. There had been some warning signs that the disease was making the rounds. At the end of 1917 and early into 1918, a wave of sicknesses had swept through the training camps in the United States. This epidemic, consisting of measles, pneumonia, meningitis and flu, seemed to attack each of the training camps differently. National Army camps Pike, Travis and Funston all reported significant numbers of measles and scarlet fever cases in the divisions training at their sites. In addition to measles, National Guard camps Sevier, Doniphan and Bowie also reported outbreaks of meningitis. Other National Guard camps such as Cody and Beauregard reported large numbers of Doughboys sick with measles followed by pneumonia.[16] In France, the wave passed through all of the armies and, while it was deadly in some cases, most soldiers and civilians recovered fully.

In mid–September, the SS *Kroonland* arrived in Brest, discharging her complement of soldiers, cargo and the newer strain of the virus. The epidemic was quickly again at full steam, this time in the more deadly form. Ultimately, 1,696 soldiers would either die en route to or shortly after arrival at Brest. General Johnson Hagood later wrote: "The *Leviathan* alone arrived with 514 cases of 'flu,' 463 cases of pneumonia, and 68 dead. [General] Harries reported that the men in his camps were dying at the rate of about one every ten minutes."[17] By the Armistice, influenza, measles and pneumonia had killed more American soldiers, sailors and Marines than had the German army. Far too many would be buried in cemeteries located just a short walk from the arrival piers and would never see any more of France than what was visible from their deathbed.

No one was safe from the Spanish flu, even on ships at sea. In this somber photograph, an Army band gathers to participate in the ceremony for the burial at sea of a shipboard flu victim (courtesy Peck Family).

After the Armistice. With the signing of the Armistice, the SOS began to look at shutting down some of the port facilities. In January 1919, Marseilles and Le Havre were restricted to use for troop movements. By February 1919

From the newspaper published on the USS *Agamemnon*, which was printed every day during the voyage to the United States. This issue was preserved by a Mehun Ordnance Depot soldier. It makes for interesting reading for several reasons: the listing of the number and type of passengers (including 162 wives) as well as the number and variety of animal mascots (private collection).

On Board the Agamemnon

Army Officers	811
Navy Officers	2
Marine Officers	4
Couriers and Field Clerks	35
Army Nurses	4
Navy Nurses	10
Army Enlisted Men	1440
Navy Enlisted Men	75
Marines	25
Officers and Enlisted Mens Wives	162
Children	12
Salvation Army	11
Y. M. C. A.	100
Y. W. C. A.	4
Red Cross	1
Civilian Passengers	17
Civilian Employees	18
Crew	650
TOTAL	3381
ANIMALS	
Dogs	18
Cats (1 tail-less)	2
Fox (Chateau-Thiery)	1
TOTAL	21

There are some inhabitants of the Ark that we have no figures on.

the Army closed the door on six ports, including Rouen, La Rochelle and Rochfort. It was determined that Bordeaux and St. Nazaire would continue in use for cargo and troops, but Marseille, Brest and Le Havre would be used to redeploy solders back to the States. La Pallice would only remain open until all the locomotive and rail car parts stored there had been turned over to the French government. As part of the port closing plan, the SOS inspected what was on hand in the ports, arranged for what the Army still needed to be transported elsewhere, and then made arrangements to sell the remainder to France or other European countries.[18] Any supplies and equipment needed by the Third Army for their occupation duty in Germany would be routed through the newly opened U.S. Army port operations in Antwerp and Rotterdam.[19]

In order to speed up the return of the AEF's soldiers to the States even warships were converted to troopships and fitted with hundreds of bunks to accommodate these non–Navy passengers. Many of these ships, particularly the cruisers and battleships, made a number of crossings loaded with homebound AEF soldiers.

However, those port operation changes lie in the future. For the moment, with 10,000 soldiers arriving in France every day in July and August 1918, the size of the AEF and its supporting logistics organization

The crowded loading of soldiers traveling on American warships going back to the East Coast is seen in this photograph from the USS *Seattle*'s fourth voyage. Fortunately, by the time most of the AEF's soldiers were being redeployed homeward, the sailing conditions on the Atlantic were fairly calm, negating some of the negative effects of the overcrowded berthing spaces (courtesy Jeff T. Giambrone).

was growing ever bigger. It is therefore appropriate to take a look now at the transit camps that served as the launching pads for sending soldiers to France and the camps in Europe that were waiting to receive them. These camps, on both sides of the Atlantic, would also play a major role when the time came to bring the soldiers home.

3

Transit Camps and a Marine Brigade

The tail end of winter in Pagny was about as exciting as a
little girl's piano recital.¹

If the movement of the troops to and from France proved to be a much bigger challenge than originally expected, the issues associated with dealing with thousands of troops arriving at same time were overwhelming. Even in modern military operations, the reception, staging and onward movement of military units at each node of a deployment are recognized as complex operations. Adding to that complexity is that often the route and conveyances for troop movements are the same ones needed for moving supplies and equipment. Ports either become congested or they sit idle, awaiting the next arrival of vessels with men and supplies.

It was no different in mid-1918, at the height of the AEF's deployment to Europe, when thousands of men were arriving every day in France or Britain. Camps originally designed for a few thousand men were overwhelmed having to handle many thousands. The transit camps on the East Coast of the United States were packed with men undergoing final inspections and awaiting arrival of a ship to carry them across the Atlantic. The weather and the arrival of Spanish flu which played a part in the problems seen earlier in the ports were also prevalent in the transit camps. Even after some units were loaded on their ship and ready to sail, there were issues. The case of the 89th Division is illustrative. After travelling by train from Camp Funston in June 1918 the division reached the New York/New Jersey port complex where British transport ships were waiting for them. The men boarded quickly and expected to be headed out to sea before long. The next morning revealed that the ships were exactly where they had been the night before. It soon became clear that the delay was caused by the ships' British firemen having gone on strike for higher wages. Faced with the possibility that a long strike might cause the division to spend the war

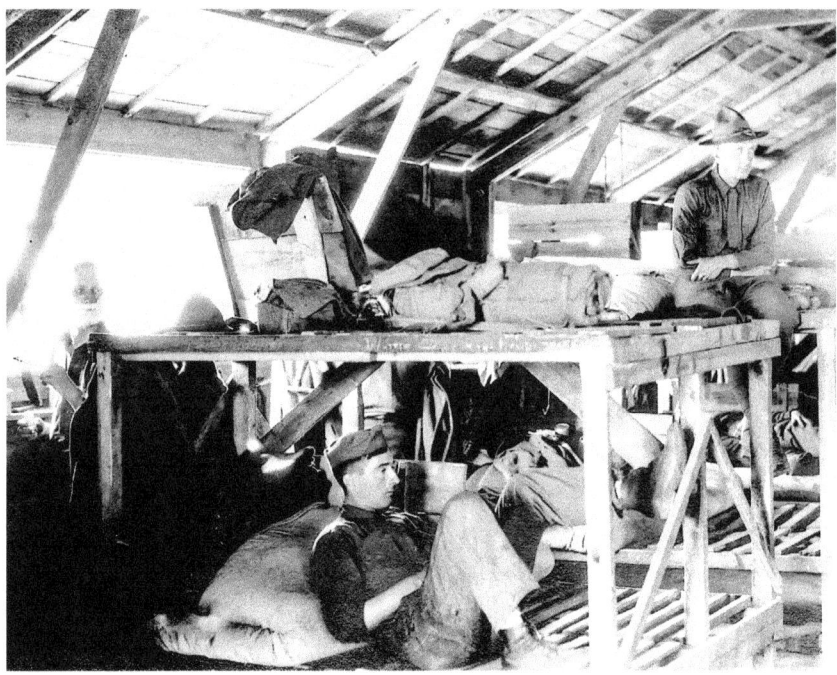

Inside one of the many wooden transit barracks the view was pretty much the same: endless rows of bunk beds filled with the soldiers' personal items and field gear. Any soldier complaining about these accommodations might later reflect on them more kindly when he saw how tightly packed the transport ships and Navy warships bringing him home were (private collection).

in Hoboken harbor, the soldiers of the 89th decided to help. Among them were a number of experienced ship and railroad firemen. They volunteered their services and when sufficient steam was raised, the ships were underway and the 89th Division was finally on the way to France.[2]

Logically, on the eastern seaboard the transit camps were located in close proximity to the major water ports. These camps were built specifically to manage the onward movement of the soldiers and their units through the seaports and onto the transport ships. As time progressed, however, some training was conducted at these sites as well as a final inventory and inspection of the soldiers' equipment prior to embarking for France. In addition to the designated transit camps, other nearby camps such as Camp Upton on Long Island and Camp Lee, near Petersburg, Virginia, also served as temporary transit camps to handle overflow periods. However, the three main camps were:

Camp Merritt. Named in honor of Union Civil War officer Major General Wesley Merritt, the camp was located 15 miles northwest of Jersey

City and set up to support the passage of troops through nearby Hoboken. It consisted of 1,264 buildings and could house and feed 38,000 troops. It could also support 500 prisoners at the camp's detention center. There were six thousand soldiers assigned as the garrison of the camp. Within the camp itself, there were 39 warehouses capable of storing 1,751 train car loads of equipment. Camp Merritt's bakery could produce 22,000 loaves of bread a day. Most importantly, especially for the men returning from France, the camp facilities were capable of delousing 260 men per hour.[3]

Camp Mills. Named in honor of Spanish-American War Medal of Honor recipient Major General Albert L. Mills, the camp was built to support the deployment of the 42nd "Rainbow" Division in September 1917 and the 41st Division in October 1917. After these divisions deployed, the camp was closed. It was reopened in April 1918 to support the massive movement of troops through the port of Hoboken. Originally designed to have only tents for billets, the reopening led to more permanent construction. At peak the camp was capable of handling 40,000 transients at a time and had a permanent garrison of 5,500 soldiers.[4]

Camp Stuart. Named in honor of Confederate Major General J.E.B. Stuart, it was established in August 1917 to support the transit of soldiers through nearby Newport News. The post contained almost 500 buildings and its 296 enlisted and 21 officer barracks were capable of housing 18,000 soldiers at a time.[5]

There were almost 15,000 soldiers working at these three camps to provide last minute equipment issues, manage the transit billets, prepare meals and operate hospitals. The workload never lessened for the soldiers assigned to these camps. Sending soldiers to France right up to the moment of the Armistice, they quickly had to change their focus and prepare to receive the almost immediate redeployment of units returning to the States.

European camps. As hectic and congested as the stateside camps could be, they were no comparison to the camps awaiting the soldiers in France and Britain. One of the earliest arrivals, a Doughboy from Wrightsville, Pennsylvania, wrote of his arrival at St. Nazaire:

> We stayed on the boat one week on account, as I found out later, to put up some barracks for us to stay in. I guess they were put up in a hurry because they looked it. They were built on frozen ground and you should have seen them after we had fires built in them. Just one large mud hole.... We patched up all the holes where the wind could get thru with straw and tar paper, but it was a cold damp hole.[6]

The same soldier also wrote, on a positive note, that he was pleased to be issued a second pair of shoes because that allowed him to have one

A photograph of the barracks at Brest, most likely Camp Pontanezen, taken by a Virginia National Guardsman serving in the 60th Coast Artillery Corps Regiment. The most enduring memory for most soldiers passing through the camp was the ever-present mud (Virginia National Guard).

wet pair to work in during the day and a dry pair for walking around the barracks. He further noted that a "fellow could not have dried those Hob Nailed shoes in a week," so it was best to have one wet and one dry pair. After a two-day and two-night journey in a "40 and 8" French railcar the soldier and his unit, the 301st Supply Company, finally arrived at Is-sur-Tille, the railway and supply complex that would be their home for the next 20 months.

Redeployment operations. With signing of the Armistice, the principal function of the European transit camps now was preparing troops for embarkation and return to the United States as quickly and efficiently as possible. First among these was Camp Pontanezen, located near Brest and soon to become the largest and most famous transit camp in the world. Camp Pontanezen was an interesting facility with a number of stone buildings used for many years by the French army. At first, the only kitchen was in one of the original stone buildings within the walls of the camp. There was no mess hall and the troops were required to eat outside in the open. The kitchen fed about 7,000 men daily and operated around the clock. Other kitchens were added as the camp grew in size. Some of these, and the newly built mess halls, were constructed with dirt floors to expedite completion. Eventually kitchen and dining facilities were added to each of the sections used to hold the transiting units. The new dining facilities were some 300 feet long and capable of feeding 5,000 men in 40 minutes.

3. Transit Camps and a Marine Brigade   47

A Camp Pontanezen pass dated May 1918 allowing Major George Knight (and one other, most likely his driver) to visit the sorting yards or the Depot Quartermaster. Major Knight was a Quartermaster Corps officer in the SOS and would later be the U.S. Army representative on the Inter-Allied Railway Commission during the occupation of the German Rhineland (private collection).

New latrine facilities were added to the camp constantly, and great efforts were made to keep the amount of waste at a minimum. There were very few animals allowed in the camp as most transportation was carried out by motorized vehicles. As a result, the U.S. Army Medical Report stated that from "November, 1918, to July 1, 1919, there were practically no flies at Camp Pontanezen."[7] Given the sanitation issues of the period and the huge number of men transiting the camp on a daily basis, this was truly an impressive accomplishment.

Most of these improvements lay in the future. In October 1918 the camp was capable of providing support for 10,000 men but the arriving number increased some 300 every day. After a hurried conference by the SOS leaders, it was decided to increase the resources for the camp. Quickly "four thousand large tents and thirty trucks" were transferred from the Le Havre Base Section and an engineer regiment was dispatched to install them. They also arranged for a number of soldiers to be assigned to the camp and permission was given to hire local citizens as cooks. The important change, however, was the assignment of Marine Colonel Smedley D. Butler to command the camp.[8]

Smedley Butler and the 5th Marine Brigade. The success of the 4th Marine Brigade as part of the 2nd Division had served the cause of the Marine Corps well. One immediate result was the War Department and Department of the Navy decision to raise another Marine brigade and send it to France. Similar in organizational structure to the 4th Brigade, the 5th Brigade was commanded originally by Brigadier General Eli K. Cole and consisted of the 11th and 13th Regiments of Marines and the 5th Machine Gun Battalion. In contrast to the 4th Brigade, however, the 5th Brigade would never serve together as a brigade and its units would

48 Bullets, Bandages and Beans

Even where there wasn't mud, there was rain as evidenced by this photograph of a transit camp kitchen in France. The soldier on the right looks on skeptically, most likely not convinced that the cook playing with the dog will wash his hands before going back to cooking (private collection).

For many of the homebound Doughboys, a standard joke was that they were against a "Standing Army," especially since they were the ones always standing. Evidence of this is shown here as the men have gathered outside a mess hall for a meal (USMC HD).

never see combat. Shortly after arrival of the 5th Brigade in France, General Cole was transferred to the 41st Division and assumed command of that unit at the St. Aignan camp facility.

The 11th Regiment was immediately split up after arrival in France and its Marines used in a variety of important, non-combat duties. Elements of the 11th served at many of the key SOS camps and facilities throughout France. These included "Brest, Tours, Montierchaume, Havre, Gièvres, Marseilles, Toulon, Miramas, Issoudun, La Pallice, La Rochelle, Mehun" and a number of other sites including a detachment that would serve under the American Peace Commission in Paris.[9] The Marine Corps' reputation for single-minded dedication to duty preceded them and their officers were sought by many organizations for service as post or installation commanders, adjutants and regulating officers.

A Marine Corps noncommissioned officer (NCO) assigned to the 5th Marine Brigade and wearing a 5th Brigade patch. Sergeant Francis Olney Hough was born in upstate New York and lied about his age to join the Marine Corps. After serving in the First World War, Hough also spent time in a National Guard unit and then rejoined the Marines in the Second World War, rising to the rank of lieutenant colonel. After the war, Hough wrote the official histories for some of the Marines' campaigns in the Pacific (courtesy Eric Queen).

The enlisted men were sought for all forms of guard duty at the camps and ports. Other duties assigned to the Marines of the 11th Regiment included: prison officers, POW compound guards, police sergeants, fire marshals, quartermaster property guards and even interpreters.[10]

The 13th Regiment was also quickly broken into small detachments

Two Marines from the 5th Marine Brigade pose for a photograph with a soldier (at left) from the 3rd Division. Denied the opportunity to serve in combat, the Marines of the 5th Brigade made the most of their service in France and contributed to the management of the transit camps and other SOS functions (private collection).

after arrival and served at many of the SOS sites. Among them were Brest, Bordeaux, St. Nazaire, La Rochelle, La Pallice, Beau Desert, Nantes, Montoir and Bessens. Their most famous and notable duty station was Camp Pontanezen where they were responsible for helping build and then manage much of the facility. Colonel Butler, commander of the 13th Regiment, was selected to administer the camp from early October 1918 to late July 1919. Although unhappy at not being given a chance to lead his regiment into battle, Butler accepted the mission of running the "largest embarkation camp in the world."[11] It was a massive undertaking. With the fighting ending only a month after taking command of the camp, Butler had

3. Transit Camps and a Marine Brigade 51

to, in effect, change the direction of a river while standing in midstream. Men recently arrived in France and still in the reception portion of Pontanezen had to be loaded back onto ships and returned to the States. Other units, earmarked by the AEF headquarters for early re-deployment, had to be brought into camp, deloused, inspected, fed, housed, entertained and then embarked onto any available shipping. Butler and his staff worked diligently to put into place an operation that could conduct the many steps required to move the AEF back home. It was a thankless job. In addition to the massive numbers of Doughboys needing passage home, Butler and the other transit camp commanders in France also suffered from another problem which turned out to be an AEF self-inflicted wound. The earliest homebound units had run into a systemic problem; as noted earlier many of the officers relieved from combat units for incompetency had been reassigned to rear echelon billets in the transit camps and port operations. In these positions their lack of initiative or generally poor leadership skills allowed them to hide behind ponderous regulations and orders. This resulted in petty bureaucracy and needless harassment of the home-bound units. Repetitive and unnecessary inspections slowed the troops' movement through the camps. Many officers in the redeploying units hesitated to take on these overly-officious offenders for fear of making the situation even worse for their soldiers. When Colonel George C. Marshall, AEF Chief of Staff, encountered the problem during an inspection tour at some of the ports, he acted quickly to put an end to some of the worst offenses and get the process working as it should.[12]

With his hat cocked back on his head, his hands on his hips and a pocket unbuttoned on his coat, Brigadier General Smedley Butler gives little indication of his reputation as a fiery combat leader. Yet his two Medals of Honor, and his success in managing the huge Camp Pontanezen facility, would certainly mark him as a man who never backed away from a fight (USMC HD).

General Butler's staff car passes under one of the camp gates that has been cleverly constructed out of duckboards and boasts an image of the shoulder patch worn by soldiers assigned there. Note that even in this part of the complex, with cobblestone roads, the Camp Pontanezen gate has been mounted onto wooden platforms to keep it out of the ever-present mud and water (private collection).

Colonel Butler was promoted to brigadier general in October 1918 and took command of the Camp Pontanezen. Prior to his arrival the camp had continued to grow from its original size until it encompassed almost a thousand acres. A Medical Department report noted the

> dimensions of the camp were approximately 1 mile wide by 1 ½ miles long. It lay on a hillside, sloping towards the south [and was] about a mile and half from the harbor ... there were neither good roads, walks, sewers, nor drainage ditches ... and the soil ... formed a deep and tenacious mud.... Other defects were insufficient kitchens, lack of mess halls, inadequate means of sterilizing mess kits, poor latrines, limited bathing and disinfecting facilities, limited means for washing hands....[13]

The report also noted that not only was there an inadequate water supply, the water they did get was polluted. The problem of getting clean water in a combat zone had been foreseen by the Army and in September 1917, the War Department organized the 26th Engineer Regiment (Water Supply) at Camp Dix, New Jersey. Among the members of the 26th was James A. Whitlow, a 23-year-old professional well-driller from Mountainair, New Mexico. Whitlow later wrote:

3. Transit Camps and a Marine Brigade 53

I was sent on a small Detachment of 11 men to Bordeaux to drill a test well for artesian water and good water also. On our arrival there we found a Keystone drilling machine ... to do our work with ... 30 days later we had a good flowing well at 703 ft deep and good water[14]

Whitlow couldn't resist talking shop with his comrades in the 26th. As he told his parents in a letter dated 3 April 1918, that "the driller I am dressing tools for sure wants me to work for him in the oil fields when we get back to US he has a standard rig and said he would give me eight dollars per day to dress tools for him." In spite of the enticing offer, Whitlow promised his parents he was coming home to work on the farm and drill wells there. In December 1918, with the war over and the Armistice signed, he wrote that he was "a little tired of well drilling in France. I am glad I think we are all through with it, guess I'll be good and ready to drill when I get home."[15]

While Whitlow was yearning to go home, the transit camps throughout France were busily adjusting their operations to get the troops home as quickly as possible. With General Butler at the helm, important changes at Pontanezen began to take place. The entire focus was changed to receiving units, not from ships in the harbor, but from the various training areas where they were now concentrated. The changes were obvious by April 1919 when a visitor witnessed the arrival of the 42nd Division at the camp. She wrote that the camp was now a "well-ordered city of tents ... 57 miles of board-walk [duck boards], its corduroy roads, delousing plants, showers and baths and immaculate kitchens."[16]

The camp was divided into sections that could support an entire unit. Within each section were kitchens, medical facilities and recreation huts. Soldiers who arrived sick or who became sick while they were there were transferred to Camp Hospital Number 33. Sterilizing and laundry facilities rid the men of their troublesome cooties and replaced worn-out clothing. The plan was to keep the soldiers of the unit in that section for the duration of their stay at Pontanezen, thereby eliminating the need to move men or equipment between camps and also reduce the spread of any communicable diseases.

On arriving at the camp, the unit was assigned to a previously determined camp section. Commanding officers and their medical staff were given an in-brief and instructions for the camp were explained. They were also told what daily reports were required of them, where to send their sick, and the locations of all support facilities and organizations. Shortly thereafter, the units would receive instruction on when and where to report for medical examinations. The U.S. Army Medical History recorded that

> orders were so issued as to call for 240 men every 10 minutes. The unit reported at a large central building arranged for examination and bathing. This

An important view of Camp Pontanezen showing how the different units' areas were separated by hedges and fences to keep communicable diseases from spreading and maintain unit integrity during the in-processing and inspection phases (NYDMNA).

structure had numbered seats (benches) for 480 men. The men stripped to their undershirts and stood on benches, two rows facing each other. The medical inspector then passed between each two rows examining for venereal disease and vermin.... The men then stepped down from the benches and pulled their undershirts over their heads and the inspector passed along a second time examining for skin diseases, scabies, and body lice. Men found to be diseased or infested with vermin were at once segregated in a special room. The others placed their underwear and socks in bins for sterilization, leaving their outer clothing on the numbered seats. At a given signal, 120 men went to the shower-bath room, where they received a four-minute hot bath. Each man was then given a clean towel, clean socks, and underwear whereupon all men returned to the numbered seats. Here they dressed quickly in their old clothing and then passed out of the building.[17]

It was, by all accounts, an efficient if somewhat impersonal operation. With the large number of men needing to be processed, there simply was no other way.

The other transit camps ran similar operations but none on the scale of Pontanezen. When the 112th Infantry Regiment, 28th Division, received their orders to prepare for returning to the States, they had spent the winter in a camp near Pagny-la-Blanche-Côte. The unit was extremely happy to get the word that they were going home. Along with practicing combat tactics against an imaginary enemy, they had been put to work repairing French roads. One corporal remembered "until this time, we'd mostly considered the French people our friends. After weeks of working on their damned roads, most of us considered them ingrates at best, crooks at worst."[18] After packing their belongings and souvenirs, the 112th set out on foot to the railhead at Maxey-sur-Vaise. There they boarded railcars and moved slowly through the rail system until they reached the Le Mans Transit/Forwarding Camp. On arrival they were unpleasantly surprised to find the "place was a sea of mud which even infiltrated our blankets."[19] From there they finally moved on to the port of St. Nazaire and boarded the USS *Pocahontas*. Unfortunately, their voyage was one of those that encountered rough weather and soon the entire ship smelled of "unwashed men, vomit, and other bodily functions." Sleep proved no relief as the conditions in the berthing compartments were hot and cramped:

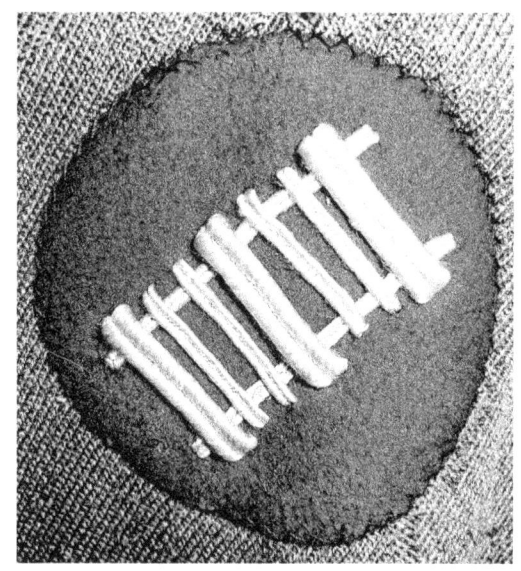

A close look at the official Camp Pontanezen shoulder patch on a captain's uniform; the white lines on a red background symbolize the iconic "duckboards" needed to cross muddy areas in the camp (courtesy Alison Hutton).

> Tiers of chicken-wire bunks were installed.... The heat from the boiler room was hellish; the steady thump of the engines and bilge pumps created a constant source of anxiety. Small wonder that, if a man did manage to fall asleep in such a hell hole, he was likely to awaken, panting in terror, sure that he was back in the Argonne with shells falling around....[20]

Not everyone was in a hurry to process through the transit camps and return home. Max Brakebill, the California National Guardsman, had worked his way from the 40th Division (subsequently converted to the 6th Depot Division) into a job as a military policeman in Paris. His civilian career at a Hollywood movie studio had given him a leg up on his buddies when it came to appreciating music and the arts. While his new unit was being reorganized again for duty back in the city, he wrote his mother:

Dec 15, 1918

My Dearest Mother

Well I'm Back in Bordeaux at Camp De Sange. The camp is about 20 miles from the city. We are only here tho for a short time. It will take about three weeks to organize the new outfit and then we will be [back] in the city [Paris].

We have had quite a bit of rain the last few days but the weather is beautiful today.

This is a very large camp and there are all kinds of war matériel around here. There is four large captive balloons in the air all the time and they look very pretty hanging in the clouds. I heard my [old] regiment (the 144th Field Artillery) leaves for home day after tomorrow. They have been expecting to leave most any time.

President Wilson arrived at Brest this A.M. Wish I could have been there or Paris so I could of seen him and the reception which the allied nations accorded him.[21]

After the Armistice and during his off-time Brakebill managed to make a side trip to Italy and for a while considered remaining in France after his enlistment was up. However, he was in a serious traffic accident during the course of his duties as a policeman and was evacuated to a hospital on the East Coast in June 1919 and then home to California.

From humble beginnings, the AEF succeeded in the mission of building and managing transit camps for the two million soldiers who arrived in France. With the signing of the Armistice, they turned the process around and prepared those same two million men and women for a safe and successful return home. Both efforts required vast amounts of manpower and material and it is a notable measure of their success that while it had taken 17 months to get the AEF's soldiers to France, it took less than half that time to get them home again. The ability of the camps in France to feed, shelter, delouse, inspect and organize the homebound forces, in spite of the typical soldier complaints, was remarkable. Equally remarkable was the ability of the transit camps on the East Coast to turn off the flow of troops to France, demobilize the troops currently in their camps, and then prepare to receive the AEF's victorious veterans while still contending with the problems caused by the flu.

With the shipping problems and transit camps somewhat under

3. Transit Camps and a Marine Brigade

control and improving, our focus now shifts to the complexities involved in creating a viable logistics operation to support the thousands of soldiers pouring into France daily. This support will require reorganization of the units and personnel in the SOS and most importantly, a new leader who will have the drive to make it all work.

4

New Leadership and Support to Combat Divisions

> Wool coats ... last about three months in active service. Hence for every coat on a man's back at the front there had to be a coat in reserve in France, a coat in transit, and a coat in reserve in the United States.[1]

Harbord started at a run and then ran faster. Obtaining a train for his personal use, he planned to see as much of his command as often as he could. The train was equipped with office cars, sleeping compartments and a dining car. To ensure constant communication with his staff at Tours, a box car was attached with a "telephone exchange and telegraph office. During the war in France an official train such as this could connect at any station with the local telephone exchange and the telegraph service."[2] The office cars were wired so they could link to the telephone in the boxcar. Another boxcar was added to carry two vehicles and a loading ramp. Travelling at night on the train, Harbord could visit any site the next morning during working hours simply by unloading his car and driving to the facility. In his first 100 days on the job, he spent 55 nights on the train. It was an operational tempo that he would maintain to the end of the war and after.

After his initial inspection visits in conjunction with Pershing, Harbord reached the conclusion the SOS was organized correctly but it needed to get everything done more quickly. The need for speed was obvious. Although the total tonnage discharged from ships had increased from 16,000 tons a day in June to 21,000 tons a day in July, they actually lost ground. The constant arrival of ever more Doughboys during that same time period meant that the cargo discharge rate per soldier had dropped from 34 pounds a day to 25. To encourage increased effort, Harbord established a competition between the ports to see who, in relation to their size and cargo capacity, could discharge and transport the most tonnage. Recognizing that each port was often used for receiving differing types of

4. New Leadership and Support to Combat Divisions

cargo, Harbord pondered on how to make a fair comparison between the unit that discharged one heavy item, such as a locomotive, against a unit that discharged hundreds of sacks of flour to make the same weight. He finally decided the fairest method was to measure each port against its own previously handled and transported tonnage. This way he could easily measure success by comparing totals and percentages. He also ordered military bands belonging to the units in each base section to go down to the work sites and play while the men were working. Soon all cargo was handled on the docks and off the ships to the tempo of ragtime music. Inter-company competition and inter-squad competition became intense. Each Saturday night the figures were wired to every port in the Services of Supply to be announced from every Bulletin Board and displayed on every moving-picture screen from Le Havre and Brest to Bordeaux and Marseilles.[3]

Calling this competition the "Race to Berlin" added to the enthusiasm of the port workers as well as the promise of the winning unit going home soon after the "Race" was over. Message delivered, Harbord was on the road again, always looking to move men and matériel faster towards the front.[4] Ultimately the "Race" was so successful the amount of cargo being moved increased by 20 percent. Base Section Number 6 and the port of Marseilles won the competition.[5]

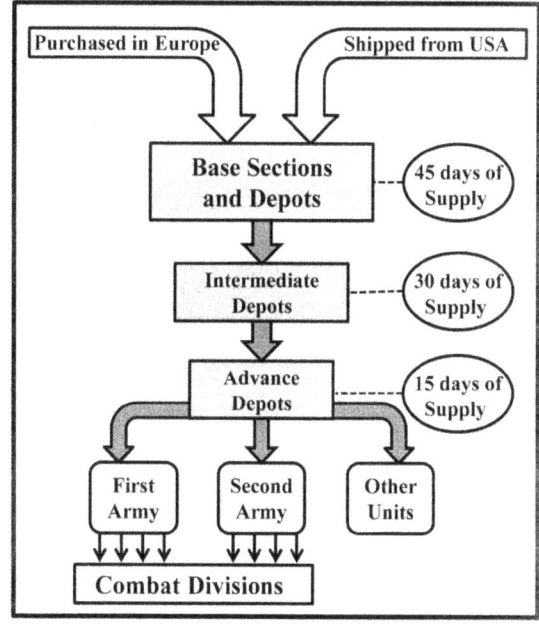

This diagram re-created from General Pershing's Final Report shows how the delivery of supplies by the SOS from the base sections to the front line units was designed to work. The plan takes into account the uneven flow of supplies due to delays or transportation issues by including intermediate staging areas to control the flow. Late in the war, the combined effects of infrastructure problems, manpower shortages, foul weather and the fighting ability of the German army stressed this system to the breaking point (U.S. Army).

Over time, some of the other critically important organizations and functions of the SOS also began to round into shape. Of particular note was the Ordnance Repair Shop located at Atelier de Mehun-sur Yevre, most commonly referred to as "Mehun." At its peak, there were 4,500 soldiers assigned there with the mission to repair or rebuild the guns and field equipment used by the AEF. It was a large facility comprised of eight large shops and five smaller ones and reminded some of a "small industrial city."[6] The facility was divided into six departments with some dedicated to the work of the camp and others to the management and operation of the facilities themselves. A number of the large metal buildings were actually bolted together instead of the usual practice of riveting them. This was done intentionally to allow the building to be torn down quickly and rebuilt elsewhere if needed. Working out of the long, single-story buildings and workshops, Ordnance Corps soldiers could repair every weapon in the AEF, from revolvers to 16-inch naval artillery. The Shops Department of the facility was divided into six working divisions: Artillery Repair, Small Arms and Machine Gun, Woodworking, Optical Repair, Construction and Maintenance, and Electrical. The Artillery Repair division repaired all artillery pieces from 37mm to 340mm in size as well as associated tools and equipment. The Small Arms and Machine Gun Division was responsible for repairing all machine guns, rifles, and pistols. The Woodworking Division made all of the special crates and shipping cases necessary for sending weapons back to the field. The workers in the Optical Division repaired all sighting and fire control devices. The other divisions were responsible for keeping the facilities working and supporting the soldiers repairing the equipment. The Mehun Supply Department made sure that there were sufficient repair parts for the Shops Department and also maintained all required records for the facility. There was also an Inspection Division to verify repairs were made properly and a Transportation Division tasked with receiving inbound equipment and shipping out repaired items.[7]

Among the workforce at Mehun's Small Arms Division were more than 300 Chinese laborers and 100 French women. When the first job announcement was made public, many more women applied than were needed and waiting lists were created. Not only were the French women good workers, they kept the same hours as the soldiers working with them. At other facilities and camps the presence of female workers required construction of separate housing complexes or barracks. For Mehun, this was not a problem since the women were all local residents. Using U.S. Army trucks, the Army small-arms supervisor set up a shuttle to pick the workers up in the morning and return them at night, further reducing the overall cost of housing and feeding them.[8]

4. New Leadership and Support to Combat Divisions 61

Part of the "Race to Berlin" competition set up by General Harbord to improve the speed of cargo discharge and onward movement from the Base Sections and depots, three SOS soldiers pose with a crate filled with canned fruit, destined for movement to the Advance Section and then on to a combat unit (private collection).

Unlike some SOS organizations and facilities, the workload for Mehun did not decrease with the Armistice as the mechanics and repairmen had hoped. Instead of repairing battle damage they now found themselves disassembling and preparing for shipment most of the AEF's artillery. The Army of Occupation's newspaper, the *AMAROC News*, reported that Mehun was receiving as many as 130 [rail]cars of artillery equipment a day. Five Machine shops and two warehouses are being used to repair and store equipment, preparatory to shipment to the States. Heavier guns are dismounted, the barrels, wheels and carriages being crated separately after all parts have been greased and oiled. Rifles are also being oiled and greased before being crated for shipment.[9]

When the war ended, the camp was also a clearing house for ordnance units returning to the States. Using a method that would gain greater credence in the Second World War, the Mehun administration established a points system to determine order of departure for their soldiers. The points were based on an individual soldier's family dependency, length of time spent in France, personal character and awards. As vessels and shipping space became available, the Mehun administration department would rank order the men in the camp by point totals and then a specified number, usually around 600, would be selected. The chosen men would then be organized into an Evacuation Battalion and prepared for departure. The facility ceased operation in mid–June 1919 but still required some 250 soldiers to perform a final cleanup before turning the site over to the French.[10]

The growth and development of the Forestry Service units was also proving to be successful. Following the example of the Canadian army, the U.S. Army had decided to build forestry capability into its Engineer Corps. As the AEF began to deploy to France, the need for this type of unit became even more critical. As recorded in the history of the 20th Engineer Regiment:

> The lines of communication depended on great amounts of lumber and tie; docks, lighterage, storage facilities, shelter, hospitalization, ice-making plants, bakeries, fuel,—and in fact, all of the construction in the Service of Supplies,— were dependent upon lumber; and the Front Lines required it for dugouts, trench construction, entanglements, compounds for prisoners, bridges, and a great variety of other uses.[11]

As a result, the 10th Engineer Regiment, with the first solders ever specifically recruited for lumber operations, was sent to France. It was not enough by far. The War Department received a number of requests for more such units. It was determined in August 1917 that there should be one forestry regimental headquarters with 10 assigned battalions of engineers and nine supporting service battalions for a total of 48,000 soldiers. Although the lumbermen in France never reached that strength, by November 1918 there were more than 20,000 officers and enlisted men serving in the 10th and 20th Engineer Regiments and their many subordinate engineer and service battalions.

The unusually large size of the 20th Engineers made it a great consumer of supplies as well as a great producer of matériel for the AEF. The

4. New Leadership and Support to Combat Divisions   63

20th was one of very few SOS regiments authorized to live in tents. This was because their mission dictated that they would be moving frequently to perform their jobs, and that mission also included a contingency for using the forestry troops as combat units. And unlike most AEF units, the 20th required very specialized equipment for their sawmill and logging operations. Since this equipment was not available in France, it all had to be shipped from America. Among the members of the regiment was Albert Sidney Hucks who had worked as a lumberman and "overhead skidderman" at Alamogordo, New Mexico, before joining the Army. Recognizing the value of his experience, the Army assigned Hucks to Company D, 6th Battalion, of the 20th Engineer Regiment.

With their training completed, the regiment sailed for Europe. Unfortunately 95 of its soldiers were killed when the British-escorted SS *Tuscania* was attacked by German submarine *UB-77* and sank within four hours on 5 February 1918. Hucks remembered: "I never can forget the suffering that our boy[s] had that cold dark night. I'm sure 'no man's land' is far better than 'no man's water.'"[12] Hucks' Company D lost 43 men that night. He and his fellow survivors eventually made it to France in late March, moving to the south to cut lumber. As Hucks recalled:

> Our battalion cut lumber for the British army for about 5 months making a record for itself. In recognition of the valuable services rendered by the 6th Bn, the British decorated our major (F. S. Kellogg) with the Distinguished Service Order.[13]

The regiment cut lumber until April 1919. Hucks returned home and was discharged on 16 June 1919.

The forestry troops exceeded all expectations and provided critical matériel for troops of the AEF throughout France. Although never fully manned to the required level, these engineers produced "190,000,000 board feet of lumber, 3,500,000 [rail road] cross ties, 392,000 cords of fuel wood" and numerous other wood products needed by the Army.[14]

Before Harbord had replaced him, General Kernan had lobbied with the AEF staff and the War Department for more men and increased staffing of the SOS. At one point he and the SOS staff drafted a requirement document for four thousand officers and 100,000 enlisted men to serve in an Army Service Corps (ASC). The ASC was one of the last organizations formed in the AEF, and it was designed to relieve combat troops from being detailed away from their units for duty behind the lines. Originally it was to be composed of the soldiers assigned to the Provost Marshal General's Department, the Post Office, the War Risk Bureau, and various labor organizations. It was later expanded to include the men assigned to the salvage, laundry, and postal units, the Rent, Reclamations, and Claims service, the stevedore regiments, the Graves Registration Service and fire truck and hose companies serving at SOS facilities. The ASC was also used to operate the replacement depots, training centers, soldiers' leave and furlough areas, convalescent camps, and permanent camps in the AEF area of France. The war ended before the ASC achieved full strength. The final total number of men serving in the Army Service Corps was 1,170 officers and 26,000 enlisted men.[15]

Serving in the ASC was Raymond K. Wallis, a 21-year-old automobile mechanic from Elida, New Mexico. Wallis enlisted in the New Mexico National Guard during the Mexican border crisis and served until his mustering out on 30 May 1917. He enlisted in the Army on 9 June 1918 during a call for men to become automobile mechanics in the Army. After completing eight weeks of training at the U.S. Army School of Auto Mechanics at the University of Texas at Austin, Wallis was sent to Camp Joseph E. Johnston, Florida, awaiting overseas assignment. While there, he qualified as a labor foreman and deployed to France with the 3rd Detachment of Labor Foremen. On arrival Wallis was assigned to Administrative Labor Company 188 of the ASC. He was promoted to corporal and assigned as a labor foreman at the Mars-sur-Allier Hospital Center in France. According to Wallis, "the laborers were civilians from nearly every allied and neutral country

Corporal Raymond K. Wallis, from Elida, New Mexico, served in Administrative Labor Company 188 (later 88) of the ASC. Wallis wears an interesting, and unauthorized, unit numerical designation of 88 on his overseas hat (New Mexico Service Records via Ancestry.com).

in Europe, Asia, and Africa." The men did construction work until January 1919. In February, Wallis wrote to his sister that he had been "working a gang of Greek, Spanish and French laborers. There was about 4 or 5 inches of snow on the ground we were digging pits." Soon thereafter, Wallis was sent to the hospital with tonsillitis, and he also contracted diphtheria and then tuberculosis. Wallis returned to the U.S. in April, remaining in the Army as a tubercular patient at Fort Bayard, New Mexico, until 1920. Sadly, Wallis died in Elida on 16 May 1923.[16]

The ASC had proven its worth and some SOS leaders later suggested it be made a permanent Army organization. Based on his experiences in France, Hagood wrote that the ASC "should be the big pool into which the draft boards should dump all skilled labor in order to avoid the devastating raids upon divisions in search of specialists."[17]

Another bright light in SOS operation was the work done by the salvage units. Designed to recover, repair and reuse all types of military equipment, the salvage

Sergeant Charles N. Fisher from Carlyle, Illinois, strikes a serious pose in this French-made studio portrait. Fisher was sent to France in July 1918 as an infantry private in a replacement unit. Promoted to sergeant, he would remain in the Army Service Corps (ASC) in France until October 1919 when he returned home. Note that, although an infantry soldier, he is wearing an ASC collar disk (private collection).

process was pervasive and all encompassing. All members of the AEF were expected to turn in any of their own equipment that had become broken or unusable. They were also required to turn in any unserviceable or abandoned equipment they found. One of the postwar reports stated:

> A system of partial accountability for equipment was established by all divisions of the Army. Division Supply Officers compared issues with receipts [turned-in items] of the Division Salvage Officers to determine whether an organization had turned in a sufficient quantity of old for new equipment and refused to make further issues until the old had been accounted for.[18]

To be successful a salvage operation has to start at the point closest to where the material first appears. This photograph shows one of the 30th Division's salvage dumps located at Montbrehain near Aisne in October 1918. Containing everything from German helmets and American helmets to shovels and mess gear, this dump is being picked over carefully before it is gathered up for shipment to the rear (U.S. Army Quartermaster Museum).

Because of this approach, salvage officers had a vested interest in gathering as much salvageable material as possible to avoid having to explain to their commanders why a unit's supply had been cut off. Many of the Pioneer Infantry and Service Battalions were also employed behind the battle lines as ad hoc salvage units. During the last days of the war and during the march into Germany the 54th Pioneer Infantry Regiment focused much of their efforts on gathering and processing salvage. Another pioneer infantry regiment even referred to itself as the "Salvaging 56th" because of their use in this manner.[19] It was reported that such salvage teams recovered more than $600,000 worth of equipment from the St. Mihiel battlefield.[20]

Even soldiers working in the AEF Base Sections were expected to salvage as much material as possible, recognizing that anything that could be reused meant one less item needing to be transported to France. Some of

4. New Leadership and Support to Combat Divisions 67

French women contracted by the SOS made up the majority of the workforce at American Intermediate Salvage Depot Number 8. In this photograph three of them pose for the camera while wearing their makeshift U.S. work uniforms. By the end of the war there were 5,300 women such as these working at the depot (U.S. Army Quartermaster Museum).

the most commonly salvaged items were overcoats, service coats, trousers and shoes. When it became obvious that the ankle-length overcoat was impractical in the trench, the solution was simple: cut off the heavy wool material below the knee making it a shorter and much more functional coat. The removed wool was then put to use as material for making the new "overseas hats." Likewise, the iconic Montana-peak campaign hats were collected from arriving soldiers and reconfigured to make slippers for hospital patients.

Perhaps typical of these salvage operations was the work done at Intermediate Salvage Depot Number Eight located at St. Pierre-des-Corps near Tours. The Salvage Depot was established in a French building originally intended as a rail car painting facility. The passage of railroad tracks both nearby and through the building was of obvious benefit. Among the first adjustments the AEF engineers made was to replace the wooden and dirt floor with cement. A nearby building served as the facility power plant as well as the laundry and sterilization sections. The facility began

Another indication of the massive effort put forth by the AEF to recover and reuse items and equipment. This photograph, taken in June 1918 at the Intermediate Salvage Depot Number 8 in Pierre-des-Corps, shows a part of the Canvas and Webbing Department at the depot and also gives another indication of the critical role played by French women in the U.S. Army's war effort (U.S. Army Quartermaster Museum).

operation in January 1918 with a total of 17 personnel including officers and seven civilian employees. By September 1918, there were 26 officers, 745 enlisted men, 730 male civilians, and some 5,300 female civilians, making a total of more than 6,800 workers, a population larger than the town of St. Pierre. There were five sterilizing machines, 16 washing machines, 20 shoe repair machines, 80 clothing repair machines, 20 harness repair machines, and a number of rubber boot and raincoat repair machines.[21]

The depot received rail car loads of material from the Advance Section which were delivered directly to the main building where they were separated into categories, i.e., uniforms, shoes, etc. After being sorted, cleaned and repaired, the salvaged items were assembled into rail car lots and shipped to the appropriate SOS issuing facility. The average weekly production was approximately 50 railcar loads. In January 1919 it was reported that there were 2,600,000 pieces of clothing and equipment "worth over $7,250,000, restored in depot shops at St. Pierre-des-Corps."[22] The SOS's salvage operation extended to the kitchens in all of its facilities and was credited with saving almost half a million dollars. Grease and

4. New Leadership and Support to Combat Divisions 69

fat from kitchens were saved and reused; crushed tin cans were sold at 50 to 100 *francs* a ton, while old cotton rags were sold to paper manufacturers. The 47,000 German prisoners of war in the SOS's labor force were also clothed with salvaged uniforms.

Yet, for every success and increased burst of productivity, there were equally significant issues. As he moved through the SOS area of operation, Harbord and his staff continually ran into some systemic problems.

The problem with replacements. One of the more difficult and resource consuming tasks for the SOS was providing trained soldiers as replacements for the combat divisions. Initially the AEF had set up a "replacement camp" at St. Aignan using the 41st Division which had arrived in November 1917. The division was re-designated a month later as the 1st Depot Division, and a cadre from the 41st ran the operation and prepared the arriving soldiers for their next assignment at the front. On arrival at the camp, the individual soldier was inspected and all non-essential stateside-issued equipment (campaign hats, canvas leggings, etc.) withdrawn. He showered, received a haircut and was given a complete new uniform, weapon, ammunition and field gear. His records were examined to determine his next assignment and his war insurance paperwork was brought up to date. He was also given remedial instruction in any basic soldier skills that he had not received previously such as marksmanship. It was noted that

> there were men who had been in the Army four months and had never fired a rifle, had any gas instruction, or marched a mile with a pack; that man of them had spent their time ... learning the customs and courtesies of the service, singing and acquiring a knowledge of court-martial procedure.[23]

The replacement depot usually kept each man about 10 days and did their best to bring him up to speed before sending him on to his assigned unit. However, the circumstances in the summer of 1918, with the German army attacking along all fronts, often led to recently-arrived officers and enlisted men being shoved into groups and sent forward almost directly from the ports or transit camps. These men did not receive any of the replacement camp's remedial training so, in some cases, men who had never fired a rifle were sent to combat units. It showed. The compression of training cycles, both in the States and in France are reflected in the 1918 diary entries of Wayne A. Keith, a soldier assigned to 37th Division:

> April 15 Parkersburg WV. Received my [draft] notice today.
> April 26 I am sure getting myself prepared for the Army. Drank more today than I have downed in a long time.
> April 27 Reported at Courthouse in Akron today.
> April 28 We left Akron for Camp Meade [Maryland] Had one grand time all the way thru.

April 29 Arrived at Camp Meade. Got our bed clothes and assigned to the 316th Inf Co F.

April 30 Got vaccinated and also a shot in the arm. We did some exercises.

May 7 Got the second shot in the arm and also was vaccinated again. My arm is stiff as hell

May 30 Transferred from Camp Meade to Camp Lee [Virginia]. Had a fine time. [Transferred to] the 112th Eng Corps Co D

May 31 Transferred to the Infantry Co G 146th It sure is as hot as I like it here. [Authors' note: the 37th Division, originally comprised of Ohio National Guard units, had trained at Camp Sheridan near Montgomery, Alabama, but part of the division was sent to Camp Lee, Virginia, for additional training en route to their port of embarkation. Private Keith was most likely transferred into the 37th Division's 146th Infantry Regiment on his arrival at Lee.]

June 3 Transferred into the Machine Gun Company of the 146th Infantry. I guess I will stay there a few days now.

June 12 Left Camp Lee for overseas service. We don't know where we are going but we are on our way.

June 13 Arrived in New York and embarked on the USS Leviathan.

June 24 We got off the boat today and marched to [Pontanezen arrival/transit barracks]. Lots of people out to see us.

June 26 Leaving Brest today for I don't know where.

June 27 Ate dinner in Le Mans to-day. Fairly large city. Passed thru Tours this eve.

June 28 Passed thru one town that there were American aviation men in camp. Aeroplanes thick as bees. Passed through Neves.

June 29 Arrived at Beaumont and hike 10 miles with full packs to Nijoie.

July 17 [Went] to a YMCA Meeting. Got a big blister on each heel. Had a hard time getting around but did not miss any drilling. Germany started big drive.

July 18 Signed the payroll. The first one since joining the army. Orders to make full pack in the morning. Turned in overcoats and blankets.

July 19 Took a hike to the trenches and it was some hike.

July 21 The first day we have had off for some time. Had gas masks and helmets issued to us.

July 22 Had another bunch of stuff issued to-day. Got gas [gassed] to-nite, it sure was strong too

July 23 Left Beaumont for the front.

July 30 37th Division Defensive Sector, France. French planes chased enemy planes away. One man of the 146th killed."[24]

In the short 100 days after leaving Akron, Ohio, Wayne Keith changed units four times, trained at two different camps (Camp Meade and Camp Lee), and was in the front lines witnessing aerial combat and reporting combat losses from his regiment. This was certainly not the carefully scheduled, phased training Pershing had planned for his units but it was the reality he faced. Still his expectations were that the SOS would get him the soldiers he needed up front. Private Keith's experience and training were actually better than many of the drafted men who would arrive in autumn 1918. A solution was being developed in the States to turn some divisional training camps on the East Coast into individual soldier training camps so trained men could be rushed to the port on short notice. This would ensure ships were full before heading to France. This plan was not put into effect as the Armistice was signed before the camps were ready to train in this method. In fact, the war would end before the problem of untrained men being sent to combat units was resolved.

The problem with transportation and the Transportation Department. Another equally vexing problem was the matter of transportation and the Transportation Department. At first it appeared that the root problem with transportation was speed at which ships could be unloaded and turned around to head back to the States. It soon became obvious the problem was much bigger. The most efficient way to offload a cargo ship is to remove the cargo and place it directly onto a railcar or bed of a truck. In modern transportation terms this is referred to as "discharging to mode" and serves the dual purpose of emptying the ship while loading the next conveyance at the same time, thereby avoiding the need for local storage space or the need to move something twice. In 1918 French ports, this was seldom possible. With little or no storage/staging space available in the ports, ships which could have been unloaded had to wait for storage space before they could be discharged. Stacking newly arrived material on the piers was no solution as this hindered the unloading of the next ship. Adding to the problem was that many of the experienced port workers and railroad operators were serving in the French army. On the AEF staff there was strong disagreement in how to fix the issue. General Dawes wrote that "the most serious problem of the S.O.S. was transportation. Beside this all other problems sank into insignificance."[25]

Dawes' proposed solution was to place the entire transportation system under military control and create an organization answerable to military authorities. Other equally high-level U.S. leaders believed it would be better to civilianize the entire operation and run it much like a private business. Not surprisingly, many of the participants on both sides of the argument were former shipping or railroad men who had been appointed as officers based on their civilian experience. Dawes was one of these but appeared more prepared than most to think as an Army officer rather than a civilian in uniform. He shared Hagood's belief the underlying problem was the tendency of the businessmen to forget they were now Army officers and no longer in their previous business.[26] Dawes was not shy about making his personal beliefs known to anyone who would listen. Hagood later wrote after an LOC/SOS Redesign Board meeting that Dawes lectured the group by telling them the function of Big Business [is] to offer its services to the military, to do as it was told by the military, to give advice, but to abide by the decisions of the military in case its advice was not taken. He considered it the height of folly to propose any scheme by which a business man, no matter how brilliant, should dictate methods to the military, whether it be methods of conducting combat operations at the front or methods of supplying troops from the rear.[27]

In Dawes, Hagood had found a kindred spirit who encouraged him also to push harder for the solutions to the problems of SOS logistics.

The problem with personnel. Among the problems involved with the Army personnel system, as it pertained to the SOS, was the basic inexperience of so many soldiers at all ranks and levels. Growing from an Army and National Guard which had totaled only 200,000 men before the war into a force of some four million in only 18 months, the entire U.S. Army was learning "on the job." For every untrained or undertrained infantryman arriving in France, there was an equally untrained quartermaster, engineer or signal corps soldier. Making matters worse was the constant shifting of men from one job to another to meet changing priorities. In July 1918 the Provost Marshal reported that the average length of time an officer served in his department was 11 days. Ambitious officers wanted out of the SOS and into combat units, believing that the road to promotion lay in that direction. In many cases they were right as promotions followed the movement of the trench lines. Recognizing this, the leaders of the SOS kept pushing to create a permanent organization that could grow and promote soldiers who excelled in providing logistics support. They recognized that they were up against a strong mindset because "most of the men who come into the war want to fight. They don't want to stay in the S.O.S. They want to go to the front. But everybody cannot go to the front."[28]

Other units in the SOS had their own unique issues. Many of the African American soldiers in the labor battalions or stevedore units had joined the Army for the prospect of fighting the Germans. With the exceptions of the 92nd and 93rd Divisions and the 16 pioneer infantry regiments (the 801st to 816th Pioneer Infantry Regiments), most black soldiers were relegated to SOS and labor battalion duties. Back in the States leaders in the growing Civil Rights movement continually petitioned President Wilson and the War Department to permit African American soldiers to be more involved in the fighting. Conversely, thousands of foreign-born soldiers, many of whom could speak little or no English, were being fed directly into the combat divisions to replace losses in those units. The irony is disheartening. At the height of the Meuse-Argonne offensive in the middle of October, for every African American soldier wishing to go to the front to prove himself in combat, undoubtedly there were a greater number of cold, wet, exhausted, white, Hispanic or Asian infantrymen in the front lines who would have gladly traded places.

The problem with the Advance Section/Divisional Rear boundary. As the supply trains and convoys moved forward from the depots and storage facilities in the Advance Section, they quickly passed through the divisional rear boundaries of the units they were supporting. Arriving at the railheads they discharged their cargo and passed it on to the requesting unit. At this point, all of their actions were now under the control of the combat unit's logisticians. Regrettably there was little or no incentive for the divisional quartermasters to hurriedly turn the trains around and send them back to SOS's control. General Harbord wrote that most officers had no appreciation of how important it was to return the rail cars after they had been emptied. The shortage of rail cars and locomotives soon became so serious that Harbord dispatched an Army colonel with extensive railroad experience to serve as his liaison to the AEF headquarters to solve the problem. In spite of the officer's best efforts, the problem remained. Harbord's despair for resolving it is evident in his later writing where he stated the unwillingness to return the rolling stock "was the greatest single controllable factor in causing the serious [rail] car shortage that existed in the autumn of 1918."[29] Reading these words should give pause to U.S. Army logisticians who were involved in supporting Operation Iraqi Freedom and Operation Enduring Freedom. There the same problem existed for the same reason in both those operations, not with rail cars but with shipping containers. The unwillingness or inability of on-scene logisticians to return the 20- and 40-foot containers to the ocean ports for re-use resulted in a number of Army officers being dispatched to gain control of the containers. Similar to Harbord's era, the results were not very satisfying.

The problem with remount units and horses/mules. One of Harbord's immediate problems on assuming command was that there simply weren't enough draft animals. Of those they had, many were in bad shape through overuse or lack of professional care. Hagood reported that he had seen "2000 horses, standing knee deep in muck in a corral not large enough for 500, with nobody to look out for them except a few infantrymen who, so far as their military experience was concerned, had never seen a horse."[30] For an army with a long a history of cavalry traditions and respect for the military horse, this was inexcusable. Yet, what could be done? Each combat division had a requirement for some 10,000 to 12,000 horses and mules in addition to the thousands needed by the non-divisional field artillery, engineer and logistics units. The remount units were completely overwhelmed trying to keep their own herds alive without having the personnel to support the holding pens in the ports or

Taken in the center of the town of Esnes on 29 September 1918, this traffic jam photograph exemplifies the problems inherent in trying to support a large offensive in an area with few passable roads. Vehicles caught in this snarl were averaging two miles an hour (U.S. Army).

in other staging areas. It was the same with the veterinary units. Clinton Little, a farmer from New Mexico, assigned to Veterinary Hospital #9 in France, wrote:

> Our work on the whole was very interesting, tho some of it was very unpleasant. We handled Horses by the thousands, of all kinds, and varites [varieties]. We had a battle to fight, and that one was the one of Mainge [mange].[31]

Mange and many other animal related problems would not be solved with any degree of certainty until after the war. And in some cases, as will be seen in a later chapter, the solution would please the Germans, upset the French, and turn a profit for the Army.

The problem with women. Always the pragmatist, and serving as the SOS Chief of Staff, Hagood decided to alleviate some of his manpower shortages by engaging "womanpower." The French feminist movement of the period had already proven that peasant women from Brittany could outperform equal numbers of Chinese coolies when employed as stevedores in the ports. He quickly made up his mind after studying the results of that labor test. Borrowing Elise Gunther from the Red Cross to serve as the head of a Female Labor Bureau, Hagood and the SOS were soon employing approximately 12,000 French women.[32]

Dealing with the French authorities concerning female labor laws did prove to be more of a problem at times than was anticipated. The SOS leadership could not understand why they should have to pay a woman for three full days of leave every month and an additional five days if her soldier husband came home on furlough. The Americans also could not understand the rationale for paying a woman with children more than a woman without children. Regardless of these annoyances, the Americans grew to depend on the woman workers and ultimately resolved the differences.[33]

Taking advantage of the availability of another potential labor pool, this time all English-speaking, the Americans reached out to the British army. By July 1918, there were nearly five thousand women from the British Women's Army Auxiliary Corps (WAAC), which evolved into the Queen Mary's Army Auxiliary Corps (QMAAC), working in the SOS. Originally formed in 1916 the WAAC/QMAAC was intended to provide the British army with administrative workers, freeing the men in those jobs to serve in combat units. But even this large number of women wasn't enough. It was estimated that the SOS could have used three or four times as many female workers as they had.[34]

The problem with Russian soldiers. Another source of untapped manpower for the SOS was suggested by the French to Pershing himself; there were Russian soldiers in France that were currently unemployed. In a meeting with Dawes, Pershing intimated that

> it has been a profound secret, but two divisions of Russian troops-about 40,000 men-[serving] on the French [front] line revolted after killing many of their officers. The French have them in barbed-wire enclosures, and are rather at a loss to know what to do with them.[35]

The Russian soldiers had been sent to France in exchange for weapons and ammunition being shipped to Russia. By late 1916 France was running out of soldiers and since Russia had soldiers but not enough rifles and ammunition, it seemed like a good idea to make a swap. It quickly turned into a nightmare when the spirit of revolution sweeping Russia was transmitted to the two brigades in France. Originally, the Russian soldiers had served well but with the failure of the early 1917 French offensives, the same defeatism that threatened to paralyze the French army exploded in the Russian ranks. Soon soldiers' committees were organized and the homesick Russians refused to go back to the trenches. The French high command wanted nothing more to do with the troublesome brigades and stashed them in an out of the way camp. And then it got worse; the soldiers wanted to go home, the French wanted them to go home but the last thing the fragile Russian government wanted was more radicalized soldiers and so they stayed in France. Adding to the problem was that the northern Russia seaports were icebound for several months each year thereby limiting the dates when ships carrying the Russians could sail home. And so they sat. Eventually the French mustered enough loyal Russians and, with the addition of French artillery, stormed the camp which had been fortified by the dissidents. Several thousand of the most radical were sent to camps in Algeria while the nominally more loyal were given the choice of going back to fight or be parceled out in groups to provide farm and factory labor. Most chose the labor option and it was at this point that Pershing received the offer and in turn extended it to Dawes.

General Dawes wisely turned down the offer and moved his discussion with the AEF commander to more comfortable topics such as purchases of much—needed matériel from Spain and Switzerland. Even Johnson Hagood, usually willing to try something new, knew better and never pursued the topic. It was a smart move. A short while later Pershing and Harbord would encounter some of the Russians. With a regiment of engineers inbound from the states, Pershing went to inspect the camp that was reserved for them; there were still a number of Russians living there. He and Harbord were not impressed by them and both Americans were disgusted by their poor discipline and the filthy state of the camp. Harbord even suggested that shooting some of them might solve the discipline problem. The question of employing the homesick Russians in the SOS remained a dead issue.[36]

The problem with coal. During the early days of the German offensive it appeared possible that the Germans might overrun some of the critically important French coalmines. As a precaution, the French miners were carefully gathered and protected by the U.S. Army until the threat passed. The importance of coal was further underscored to the SOS when the mayor of Tours reported that unless the U.S. Army could provide his city with coal, all power, light and water would be cut off to the SOS HQ. Fortunately the SOS was able to find and provide enough coal to the mayor to keep the power plants running. Later, while analyzing the reason behind the shortage, it became clear the problem lay not in the availability of coal but rather in the inability to transport the coal from the ports to the interior sections of France.[37] A similar situation had arisen in the States during the harsh winter of 1917–1918. With a large percentage of the nation's railcars and locomotives being used to move troops from training camps to the ports, the number of trains available to carry coal to the large East Coast cities was reduced. Some city officials went so far as hijacking coal trains passing through their cities to keep the factories working and workers' houses heated.

The problem with the War Department. The attempt to send General Goethals to run the SOS was symptomatic of the disconnect between the Army Chief of Staff General March and General Pershing commanding

4. New Leadership and Support to Combat Divisions 77

the AEF. Their underlying issue was ownership of the AEF. As Army Chief of Staff, March believed he was the sole owner of the entire Army, while Pershing's belief was that that the rest of the Army existed only to support the efforts of his AEF. There was logic to support both sides. Secretary of War Newton Baker split the baby by giving final authority to Pershing for all AEF-related issues and supporting March in all other aspects. Unfortunately, there was enough overlap between the two sides that some friction was inevitable.

One notable place in which the friction between the "stateside" Army and the AEF in France was evident was in the SOS. Harbord later wrote of this problem:

> The military establishment in America was so vast that it was evidently very difficult for [Harbord's AEF supply requisitions] to be transmitted to the grades by whom the supplies actually had to be put on transports. We felt ... our requisitions were not studied.... There [was] a tendency to substitute for the A.E.F. judgement of its own needs, the judgement of someone in Washington. Great activity was being demonstrated but our two movements were not in step.[38]

Harbord further noted that despite all his requests, the AEF was continually short of motor vehicles, machine guns, certain calibers of ammunition, field kitchens, sanitation equipment and construction material. In the end, the Armistice solved some of the shortages but the underlying "us" versus "them" attitude seemed to remain in place until the last of the Doughboys were home from France.

The problem with Allies. One of the biggest problems for Harbord and his staff was the Abbeville Agreement. This agreement, reached in May 1918, had been pushed on the Americans by the British and French and was designed to provide more shipping capacity to the AEF from the British and French merchant fleet. In exchange, those countries would determine what would be shipped in the additional vessels. They wanted infantry and machine gun units and could provide enough ships to bring to France between 120,000 to 150,000 more soldiers each month. Among the units transported by the British ships under the agreement, were the 4th, 27th, 28th, 30th, 33rd, 35th, 77th, 78th, 80th, 82nd and 84th Divisions.

While having more manpower in war is always a good thing, this focus on infantrymen did not fit into Pershing's plan to bring complete divisions to France. Making matters worse, the agreement was only good for May and June, after which time the U.S. would return to its pre-agreement shipping capacity. Under these conditions, the SOS personnel requirements would never be met and the 300,000 soldiers brought to France in Allied ships would have no supporting units. By September the situation had become critical. Hagood wrote:

> Most of the divisions had no 75's and no 155 howitzers and the army and the corps were sadly lacking in long-range artillery.... We did not have the engineer, pioneer, and labor troops to build the roads ... [nor] the ordnance troops to handle the ammunition, the signal corps troops to establish telegraph and telephone lines. We were short of chauffeurs and auto mechanics.... In short, we had the personnel to form ... divisions, but we did not have the personnel to form corps and armies.[39]

Given an impossible situation, the AEF staff decided that the next five divisions to arrive would be broken up and used as labor and replacements. After months of training for combat service, the men were instead to become fillers where most needed. It was an inelegant solution, but the choices were limited.

At the strategic level there was another problem with the Allies. For a number of reasons, the British, French, and Italian leaders believed that the United States was an endless source of manpower. Accordingly, they requested, and received, the deployment of a U.S. infantry regiment to Italy to bolster morale on that front. They requested and received the deployment of railroad units and two infantry regiments to Siberia to support the failing White Russian forces there. They also requested and received the deployment of an infantry regiment and supporting elements to Archangel in Northern Russia, again ostensibly to shore up the White Russians and guard the massive supply depot built there.[40] As a result of these diversions, the equivalent of an entire division was lost to Pershing.

On a more positive note, there were some advantages in cooperating with the other Allied armies. Working with the British supply system proved to be an enlightening experience for some U.S. logisticians. As seen earlier, while American soldiers did not care much for British food rations, the U.S. Army quartermasters did appreciate the basic efficiency of the British army logistics system:

> We found that if we followed instructions, supplies were forthcoming. Not a requisition was sent to the base that was not properly acknowledged, with a statement as to the probability of supply. A wire was always received the day before the [rail] car so that preparations could be made to receive it. Carefully checked lists were always found in the cars, showing exactly what they contained, and shortages almost never occurred.[41]

The problem with the St. Mihiel Offensive. As August turned into September, the AEF was preparing for its first American-led operation, the St. Mihiel Offensive. While there were significant supporting artillery units and air service units from the other Allied armies, all the combat forces going "over the top" would be U.S. Army and Marine Corps. The newly formed First Army was going to attack and reduce the St. Mihiel salient that bulged into the Allied lines. As the combat forces gathered

4. New Leadership and Support to Combat Divisions

Bringing ammunition forward was always a challenge for SOS transporters and quartermasters. The closer they got to where the ammunition was needed, the less equipment there was to move it. In this 15 June 1918 photograph, several quartermaster soldiers unload 155mm shells by hand from a truck near Montreuil-aux-Lions near Aisne (U.S. Army Quartermaster Museum).

for the operation, the staff of the SOS was quickly dismayed to find that, instead of receiving the long-promised men and equipment needed to bolster their operation, they were expected to give up large numbers of their troops to go forward to support the attack. The shortage of corps-level and Army-level logistics units meant that the SOS was harvested for men to become drivers, ammunition handlers, and road builders. It was a vicious circle. In an Army suffering from a shortage of motor vehicles, there were thousands of recently arrived vehicles sitting in port staging areas but incapable of operation as there were no mechanics to put them into service.[42] For draft animals, it was even worse. By this point, the units working in the SOS should have had some 50,000 horses. They had 800.

It was just as bad in all the other SOS staff sections. Harbord sent a letter to Pershing on 13 September stating:

    a. Chief Ordnance Officer reports he has not sufficient personnel to handle requisitions for ammunition.

    b. Chief Engineer Officer reports that construction has been slowed up thirty per cent. Work in quarries has entirely stopped....

c. Chief Motor Transport Service reports that overhaul parks are now operating with one third necessary personnel.... At a time when motor transportation is most needed, it is accumulating in bad condition, with no facilities for being repaired.

d. Chiefs of other supply departments report similar conditions. The situation with reference to railroad transportation is getting worse every day.[43]

And on and on, the list of problems and shortages continued. But Pershing and his Chief of Staff, General James W. McAndrew, would not relent. Having weathered the summer of German offensives, they believed that a strong effort at St. Mihiel right now followed by another, even bigger, offensive might flip the board and perhaps end the war in 1918. Pershing himself was insistent, as Dawes wrote in his daily diary on 18 September 1918: "John [Pershing] is going to strike his maximum blow. He is taking his chances on supply. He believes a reserve is meant to be used in an emergency.... May God be with him and his army during the next month."[44] Breaking the supply and replacement system was a risk Pershing and McAndrew were willing to take. They were

Major General James W. McAndrew, Pershing's chief of staff from May 1918 to May 1919, was a veteran of Indian Campaigns and the Spanish-American War. McAndrew was a firm believer that the war could be brought to a close in 1918 if the AEF diverted all resources to the Meuse-Argonne Offensive (U.S. Army).

4. New Leadership and Support to Combat Divisions 81

Delivery of supplies got harder. When the cold, rainy weather set in during the Meuse-Argonne Offensive, as seen in this October 1918 photograph, delivering ammunition to artillery units became even more difficult, requiring tractors to move the heavy rounds forward (Virginia National Guard).

proven right, but it was exhausted logisticians and untrained infantrymen who paid the price for their bold risk taking.

The problem with the Meuse-Argonne Offensive. All of the problems coming to light during the St. Mihiel Campaign were magnified in the Meuse-Argonne. Beginning on 26 September, the fighting in the Argonne became the almost complete focus of the AEF and the SOS. Newly arriving National Guard divisions such as the 31st, 34th and 38th were skeletonized to provide replacements for units fighting "up in the Argonne." Two National army divisions suffered the same fate. Two more divisions were designated to serve as depot divisions and manpower sources for the SOS, and the 87th was completely broken up to provide labor for the logisticians.

The list below shows the disposition of some AEF divisions that were used for replacements and labor. Depot divisions sent troops as replacements to combat divisions, and some artillery, engineer and support units of the depot divisions were used as corps or Army troops.

31st Division: 7th Depot Division
32nd Division: Personnel temporarily used as labor troops
34th Division: Personnel used as replacements
38th Division: Personnel used as replacements
39th Division: 5th Depot Division

40th Division: 6th Depot Division
41st Division: 1st Depot Division
76th Division: 3rd Depot Division
83rd Division: 2nd Depot Division (one regiment sent to Italy)
84th Division: Personnel used as replacements
85th Division: 4th Depot Division (one regiment and support troops sent to North Russia)
86th Division: Personnel used as replacements
87th Division: Personnel used as labor troops

As painful as the manpower shortages were for the AEF, the problems associated with providing support to the combat units on both sides of the Meuse became even greater. Resupply traffic became snarled on the few passable roads and convoys that should have taken a few hours took an entire day. A 29th Division officer wrote of the difficulties of "feeding 27,000 or more men and 10,000 or more animals even under normal conditions ... under the orders of a corps commanded by a foreign general and composed of different nationalities, speaking a different language and operating over a country which had been a battleground for four years." He also wrote of the difficulties of maintaining an ammunition supply for a division in combat, describing the problems encountered in moving a ton of ammunition from the factory, across the country, through the various Army and corps boundaries and the delivering it forward to the unit, only to be expended in a matter of hours or minutes.[45]

Likewise, another senior quartermaster officer wrote in his after-action report for the Meuse-Argonne about the struggles and ultimate success of one night-long convoy with which he traveled. Moving on nearly impassable muddy roads under constant artillery and gas attack, he endured miles-long traffic jams to deliver the required supplies. He noted that one such supply convoy required 24 hours to make the six-mile round trip. In spite of such heroic efforts, there never seemed to be enough of anything except rain, German machine guns and German artillery.[46] One infantry officer fighting on the east side of the Meuse instructed his men to "hold their fire except in grave emergency because our ammunition was nearly exhausted and [he] did not know when [they] would be supplied from the rear."[47]

It was the same everywhere in the Argonne. With some 1.2 million Doughboys and all of their associated draft animals, vehicles, cannons and aircraft consuming tons of supplies each hour, the struggles of the SOS to maintain them was never-ending. The same officer who wrote earlier about the lack of ammunition also reported that "since we had gone over the top on 10 October ... we had been practically three days without

4. New Leadership and Support to Combat Divisions   83

Taking the word "dump" literally, this ration dump in the 101st Infantry Regiment, 26th Division, area was photographed on 1 November 1918. With the site still under German observation, two Doughboys hurriedly gather rations for their unit from the loaves of bread and cans of apricot jam spread out on tarpaulins (U.S. Army Quartermaster Museum).

food and scarcely no water and very little sleep–and as I learned later, this was just the beginning."[48] It was equally bad over in the 3rd Division's area. One of the Marne Division officers described his unit's designated ration dump as being just that: "a dump." Unable to deliver the unit rations closer to the front, the quartermasters had deposited the bread and canned rations in one central spot and everyone took what they wanted.[49] A sergeant from the 4th Division later recounted having to scoop rainwater out of the ruts in a road to quench his thirst.[50] Yet still the offensive ground on and more U.S. units were sent into battle. Many units continued to fight and advance right up until the morning of 11 November.

Following that age-old Army adage that "you can only understand that which you can count or measure," the statisticians in the Ordnance Corps provided the following information regarding the amount of ammunition that was expended by the AEF: "623,541,085 rifle and machine gun bullets, and more than 3,500,000 shells including shrapnel, high explosive and gas ... [and] 74,000,000 .45 caliber cartridges for

The strain of the Meuse-Argonne Offensive shows clearly in the faces of these engineers from the 22nd Engineer Regiment, a railway construction unit. This photograph, taken in the Argonne just two days after the Armistice, also shows that although the guns have stopped, the rain and the mud have not (U.S. Army Quartermaster Museum).

automatic pistols."[51] It was an amazing accomplishment just moving this much ammunition, not to mention getting most of it to the right place.

Even when the combat units stopped shooting at 11 a.m. on 11 November with the signing of the Armistice, men, machines and animals still required medicine, food and fuel. In fact, in some ways, the strain on the SOS was about to increase.

Undoubtedly there were many other problems that the SOS leaders faced during the last six months of the war but these should serve to provide a sense for what they were up against. The signing of the Armistice automatically solved some problems but created a new tidal wave of other issues because, up to this point, the SOS had operated in an Allied country. Now the SOS was going to support a quarter-million-man Army of Occupation that would be operating in enemy territory.

4. New Leadership and Support to Combat Divisions

Before we look at that effort, it is important now to turn to another massive effort carried out behind the front lines as a key SOS function: the organization and construction of a hospital network in France to serve the AEF.

5

The Hospitals and the Flu

It's the one red rose the soldier knows
It's the work of the Master's hand
'Neath the War's great curse stands a Red Cross nurse
She's the rose of no-man's land[1]

Among the many functions needed behind the front lines was the oversight and support of numerous AEF military hospitals operating in France. Recognizing the potential for large numbers of casualties resulting from the technological advances in machine guns, artillery and gas warfare, the AEF established a massive complex of hospitals and infirmaries to support the Doughboys. In the early days of the deployment of the AEF to France there had been a problem finding places to establish hospitals and infirmaries. As a result, Medical Corps officers scoured the country looking for suitable locations. In some cases schools, hotels and monasteries were pressed into service as hospitals while the engineers were hurriedly constructing more conventional facilities.[2]

Medical care was arranged by echelons so a sick or wounded soldier was treated first by his local medic or unit medical staff and then, if necessary, moved up the organizational structure to the next highest facility. If more care was required, he would then go up to another, higher level organization or facility. Within the combat divisions, the highest level of medical aid was found at the Field Hospital level, a component of the divisional sanitary train. Each divisional sanitary train held "3 field hospitals, motorized; 1 field hospital, animal-drawn; 3 ambulance companies, motorized; 1 ambulance company, animal-drawn; 8 camp infirmaries; 1 medical supply unit; 1 mobile laboratory."[3] Usually one of the divisional field hospitals was tasked to sort patients and to care for the wounded, another one received sick and a third handled soldiers who had been gassed. The fourth hospital was held in reserve or was used to support the operation of one of the others.[4]

At corps and army-level there were more field hospitals and evacuation

5. The Hospitals and the Flu   87

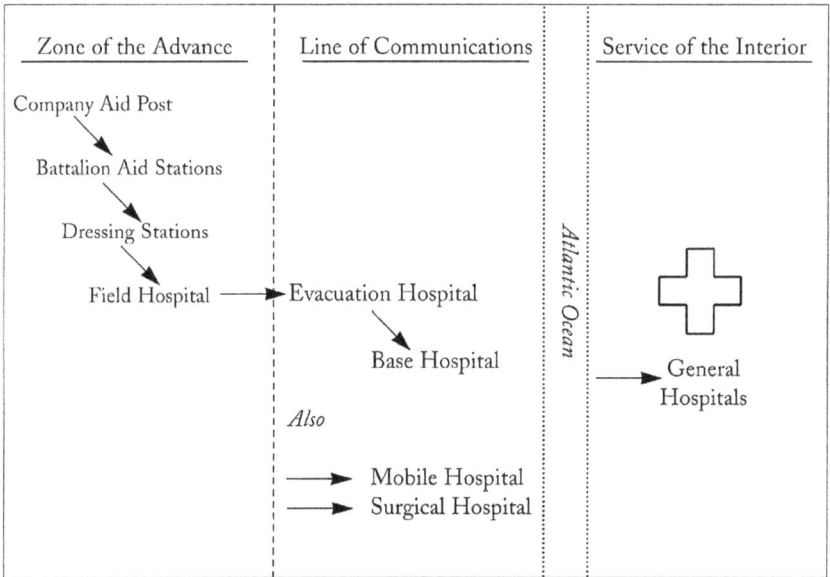

This simple diagram shows the hierarchical structure of medical care for wounded or sick soldiers. Moving from left to right, the injured soldier would receive appropriate care at each level and then either be returned to his unit or evacuated to the next level. Missing from this diagram are the camp hospitals and Red Cross hospitals, both of which functioned in the center section to provide care to specific camps, training areas, schools or localities not covered by other facilities (U.S. Army).

hospitals assigned to the corps or Army-level sanitary trains. The sanitary train of a corps consisted of four field hospitals and four ambulance companies. The ambulance companies were all motorized and were transferred from divisions arriving in France that had been broken up to provide replacements.[5] Each hospital could receive patients from divisional level, providing treatment or passing the soldier on to medical care facilities that were in the SOS. There were also independent mobile and surgical hospitals assigned as needed. The sanitary train at Army-level was even bigger than the corps-level version. It was the same as the divisional train but enhanced with mobile hospitals, mobile surgical units and evacuation hospitals.[6]

In contrast to the combat units, the rear area hospital facilities were base hospitals, camp hospitals, hospital centers, convalescent camps and American Red Cross facilities which also included hospitals and convalescent homes.[7]

Base hospitals. Base hospitals were designed to receive patients from field and evacuation hospitals and any patients from support units

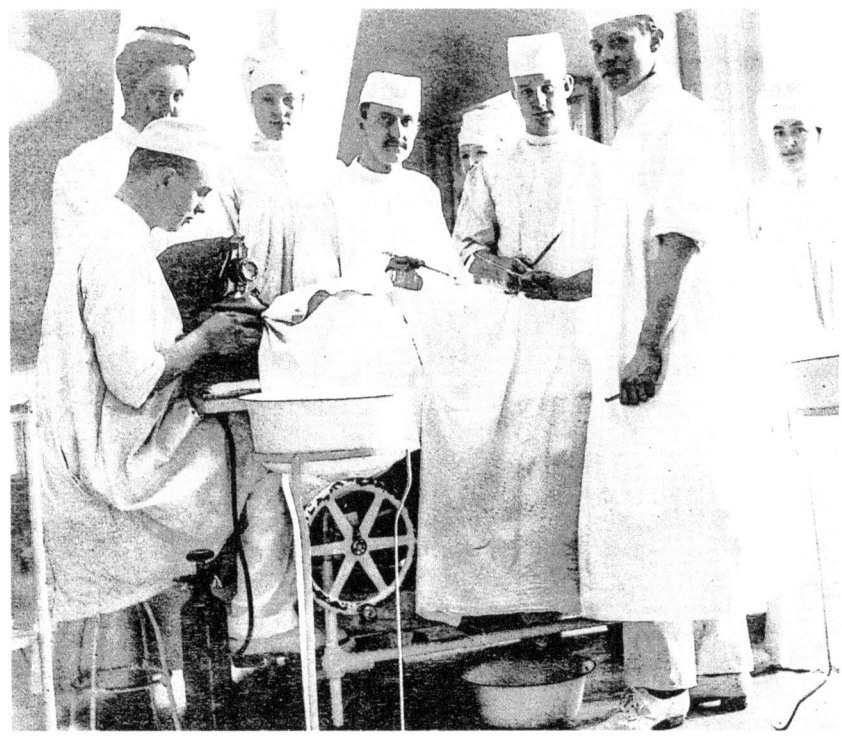

Certainly a rarely-seen view of an operating room staff pausing to take a photograph. Dr. Albert Beck, standing at right front, would later go on to serve in the 42nd Division in the occupation of Germany (private collection).

working in the vicinity. These hospitals were robustly staffed, and the table of organization for them required "35 officers, 100 nurses, 200 enlisted men and a valuable but limited number of civilian employees ... dietitians, technicians, and stenographers."[8] After some study, the Army determined that a base hospital should have the equipment and bed space to care for a thousand patients. It also recognized that some surge capability would be required to expand the number of beds in an emergency.[9] It was intended that these hospitals should be capable of treating most ailments or wounds. They would only evacuate back to the United States those patients who were permanently disabled or whose injuries would require a great deal of recovery time. Army medical care doctrine called for some of these base hospitals to be allocated for each combat division deployed to France. Unfortunately, one of the results of the Abbeville Agreement, discussed earlier, was that infantry and machine gun units received higher priority in the transportation pipeline causing many of the medical units to arrive very late in 1918.

5. The Hospitals and the Flu

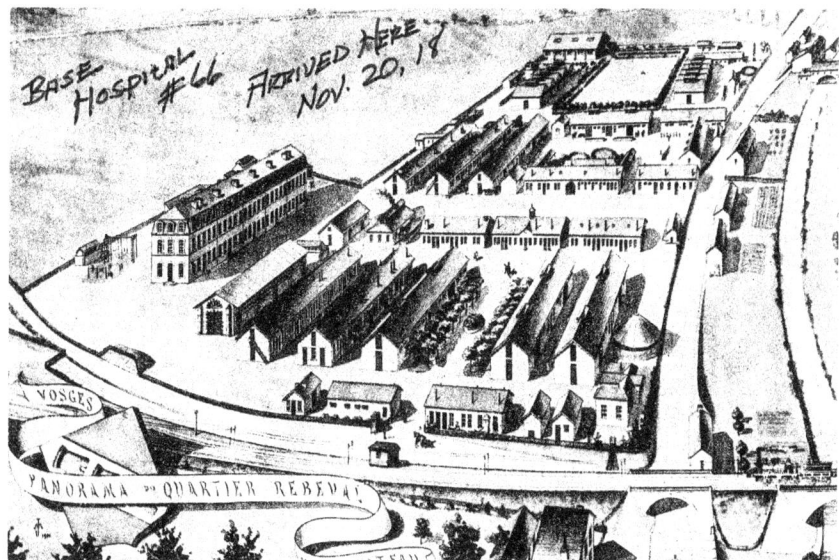

A postcard sent home by an Engineer Corps soldier to show his family what a base hospital looked like. Located in Neufchateau in the Advance Section, Base Hospital Number 66 shut down in December 1918, just a month after the soldier arrived (private collection).

Hospital centers. In the AEF, the constant refrain that "every soldier and piece of equipment must cross 3,000 miles of ocean" ensured the need to pool equipment and personnel was always considered. One of the results was that several "hospital centers" were established to allow the sharing of scarce resources or skills. One of the largest of these was established at Mars-sur-Allier and became known as the Mars Hospital Camp. Assigned to this complex were Base Hospitals Number 14, 35, 48, 62, 68, 107, 110, 123 and 131. Another nearby complex at Mesves included Base Hospitals Number 50, 54, 67, 72, 86, 89 and 108. Other hospital centers were located at Savenay, Bordeaux, Bazoilles, Rimaucourt, Beaune, Allerey, Nantes, Brest and Limoges.

Convalescent camps. On 1 June 1918 the AEF authorized the establishment of convalescent camps to provide care and lodging for soldiers who were recovering from wounds or disease but who needed little or no further medical treatments.[10] These convalescent facilities also served the double purpose of freeing bed space for incoming sick or wounded as well as organizing the recovering soldiers into a central location to prepare them to return to their units. It was noted these facilities would be under the supervision of medical officers but could take advantage of having officers and non-commissioned officers (NCO) from line units who were also recovering to lead the patients in drill and military education.

Camp hospitals. Following the doctrinal approach of treating at the lowest level possible, the AEF established camp hospitals in all training areas and camps. These would handle as many cases as possible to avoid sending men to the base hospitals.[11] With these facilities in place, only those soldiers who were severely sick or hurt, or required other specialized treatment, would be transferred from camp hospitals to higher-level facilities. Based on AEF orders, the camp hospitals were authorized a capacity of 300 beds.[12] Some facilities were much larger, such as Camp Hospital Number 26 with 2,200 beds at the St. Aignan Replacement Depot and Camp Hospital Number 52 at Le Mans with 2,300 beds.[13]

Nurse Harriet Arrington served at U.S. Base Hospital #41 located at St. Denis in the district of Paris. During much of its service, the hospital more closely resembled an evacuation hospital than a base hospital because it received so many patients directly from the front (Library of Virginia).

American Red Cross hospitals. American Red Cross hospitals and convalescent homes were a valuable asset to the AEF. This was particularly true in Paris where the AEF Medical Department was not allowed to establish hospitals until the battle at Château-Thierry. After 1 July 1918, the U.S. Army was able to establish many hospitals in and around Paris and relieve the pressure on the Red Cross facilities. Some Red Cross hospitals were close enough to the front lines to send their ambulances forward to pick up wounded or sick soldiers or Marines. One Red Cross aide noted

5. The Hospitals and the Flu

With all hospital care being provided in echelons, patients too injured or sick to be treated locally would be evacuated to the next level of care. In this photograph taken by a U.S. Army nurse, patients are being carefully loaded onto a hospital train for the journey to the next level of treatment (private collection).

the great politeness of the American soldiers and their willingness to wait patiently for care. She also noted that in the operating rooms, "they would take ether almost as if they liked it, and some really were 'glad of a chance to sleep.'"[14] Although the proximity to the front meant their patients would receive care more quickly, there was an inherent risk. Red Cross Hospital Number 107 was attacked by German aircraft two nights in a row, killing three patients and wounding several others including a nurse. By 11 November 1918 arrangements were underway to ensure there would be 20,000 hospital beds in the Paris area alone. Other notable Red Cross hospitals and convalescent homes for officers, nurses, and men were located at Beauvais, Juilly, Jouy-sur-Marne, Toul, Froidos and Glorieux.

Medical Department replacements. Replacements for the non-divisional medical units were handled entirely through the SOS. A medical casual depot at Blois was planned and almost organized when it was taken over instead as a casual officers' depot. It continued, however, to receive and transfer Medical Department unassigned soldiers until July 1918 when this service was transferred to the 1st Depot Division at St. Aignan. This transfer of mission was made to provide a short course of training in medical field work at the 1st Depot Division site. It was never possible to carry out this plan and provide the training because of the constant shortage of Medical Department enlisted personnel. The shortage necessitated the prompt transfer of all Medical Corps soldiers almost immediately on arrival in France, and the longest stay in the depot was at most two weeks.[15]

Personnel of the AEF Medical Department increased from seven officers and about twice that number of clerks (including two enlisted men) in June 1917, to a maximum of 174,083 soldiers on 11 January 1919. The most important function of the personnel division was to provide enough soldiers to keep activities of the Medical Department up to standard despite a constant shortage of trained personnel, especially of officers and nurses.[16]

The acute needs of the Medical Department for personnel were considerably relieved by the cessation of hostilities, and by the splitting up of two depot and four combat divisions which freed a number of medical personnel for reassignment. On 16 November 1918, a memorandum was written by the AEF to the War Department informing them that no more Medical Department units were required. The AEF did, however, request the additional shipment of 200 medical officers, 125 Dental Corps officers, 41 Veterinary Corps officers and some 2,722 Veterinary Corps enlisted men, 1,500 nurses and 2,000 Medical Corps enlisted men. The reason for requesting such a large number of Veterinary Corps personnel is obvious; the Meuse-Argonne Offensive had been as rough on the AEF's draft animals as it had been on the soldiers.[17]

By 30 November 1918, Medical Department personnel in France totaled 163,841 officers, nurses, and enlisted men, 8.6 percent of the total AEF. This number included the 944 officers, 656 nurses, and 1,314 enlisted men who were serving with the British. The following table of Medical Department personnel shows the totals from 1 June to 30 November 1918. These totals are only close approximations, as reports of arrivals and departures of personnel were often delayed; in some cases, they were never reported at all.

	Officers	*Nurses*	*Enlisted*
1 June 1918	5,198	2,539	30,674
3 August 1918	9,601	4,735	67,140
5 October 1918	14,483	7,522	104,557
30 November 1918	17,487	8,951	137,403
11 January 1919	17,767	9,994	145,815 & 507 civilians[18]

From the slow beginning, the number of facilities, just like the number of personnel, grew rapidly. It was reported that on 11 November 1918

5. The Hospitals and the Flu

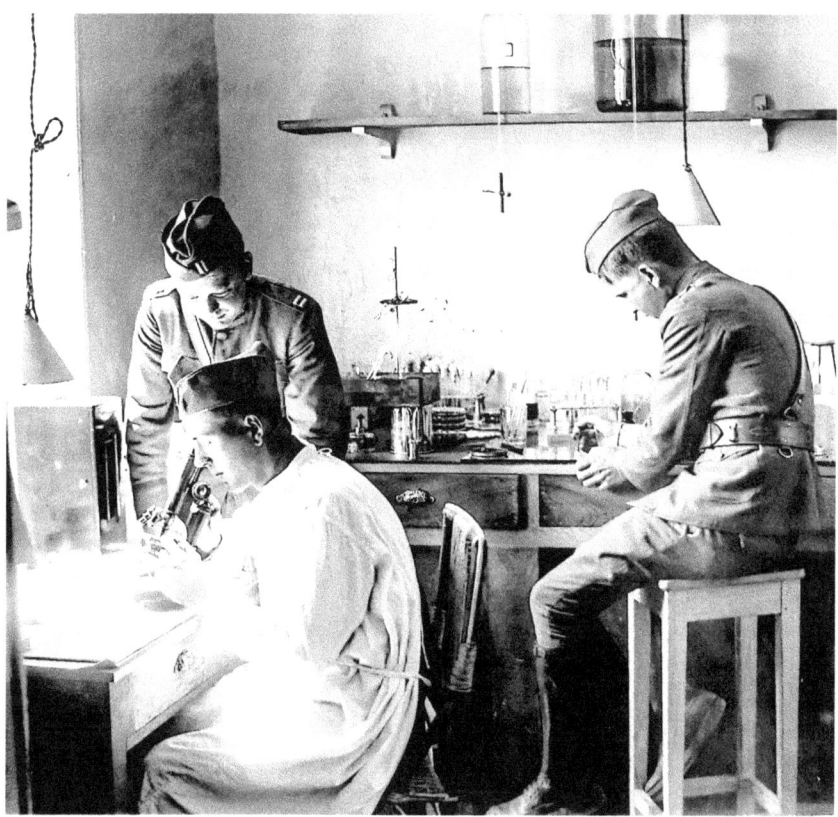

Along with all the base, camp, field and evacuation hospitals in the AEF, there were also a great number of veterinary hospitals. Seen here is part of the laboratory of Veterinary Hospital Number 6, located in Neufchateau, just east of Chaumont. These vets are studying a blood sample from one of their animals to determine what inoculations to give it (U.S. Army Quartermaster Museum).

there were almost 200,000 beds available in AEF facilities with a capability to add 84,000 more should they be needed. There were more than 200 base and camp hospitals, 12 convalescent centers, 21 hospital trains and almost 7,000 ambulances. It is significant that each one of these facilities, large or small, required some measure of dedicated support from the SOS for medical supplies and equipment as well as housing, rations and transportation for the patients and hospital staff. On 7 November 1918, the single busiest day for all the AEF medical facilities, there were 190,564 Doughboys hospitalized, nearly 10 percent of all U.S. soldiers in France.[19]

It was a huge network, starting with the company medic in the front lines, through field hospitals, evacuation hospitals and camp hospitals, all the way back to the seaport facilities and then across the ocean to the

United States. The number of enlisted Medical Corps personnel serving in France was impressive, some 7.26 percent of the AEF. Only the infantry, engineers and field artillery had more enlisted soldiers in France than the Medical Corps. For officers, the percentages were even higher; approximately 18.46 percent of the officers in the AEF were from some part of the Medical Corps and were outnumbered only by the infantry's 23.83 percent.[20]

Because the Chief Surgeon of the AEF was assigned as a staff component of the SOS, all the non-divisional hospitals and centers were under the direct control of the commanding general of the SOS. The only exceptions to SOS control of the medical force in France was in the internal operations of the medical facilities such as discipline of soldiers, professional inspections, requisition of special supplies, establishing guard duty requirements and maintenance of fire-fighting equipment. Most medical facilities were subordinate to the medical head of the facility and the local area commander. It was a good arrangement that suited the need at the time.

This command structure and line of responsibility was further codified in the August 1918 Bulletin Number 29 issued by SOS Chief of Staff Colonel Johnson Hagood on behalf of General Harbord:

AMERICAN EXPEDITIONARY FORCES, HEADQUARTERS, SERVICES OF SUPPLY, France, August 30, 1918.

1. All hospitals, except evacuation and field hospitals, are hereby designated as S.O.S. (Services of Supply) formations. These hospitals are divided into two classes. The first class includes hospital centers and Base or special hospitals disconnected from hospital centers. The second class includes camp or other hospitals serving purely local purposes.

2. Hospitals of the first class have the status of general hospitals and are under the control of the commanding generals of the sections in which they are located only in the matter of discipline, guard, inspection, construction, supply, and fire protection. They are under the direct control of chief surgeon, A.E.F., in all other matters, including general administration, control of personnel, care and evacuation of the sick and wounded, etc.

3. Commanding officers of hospitals of the first class have the responsibility and authority of post commanders in addition to their duty in connection with the general management of the hospitals. They are authorized to appoint disability boards for the service of their hospitals, as provided in section 1, G.O. 41, G.H. Q., A.E.F., 1918. They

are authorized to communicate direct with the American Red Cross convalescent homes and to issue the necessary orders to send cases to such homes, where accommodations are available.

4. They will apply to section commanders for necessary guards. The commander of such guard, if a commissioned officer, will report to the medical officer commanding for instructions as to the character of the guard duty to be performed and he will exercise no control over the sanitary formation. If the guard be [supervised] by a noncommissioned officer, it will be under the immediate control of the medical officer of the day.

5. Hospitals of the second class, including those serving school areas, are under the control of the commanding generals of the sections in which they are located. This control will be exercised through the surgeon on the staff of the section commander.

6. Supplies for hospitals, except medical supplies, and allotments for repairs will be obtained from headquarters of the section in which the hospital is located. Medical supplies will be obtained by requisition on depots in the manner specified from time to time by the chief surgeon.[21]

Treatment of non-combat injuries and diseases. The world in 1917 and 1918 was a dangerous place, even discounting the inherent danger from being killed or wounded in combat. There were three other ways, besides being wounded in action, in which a Doughboy could require hospitalization: work or training accident; venereal disease; or other contagious disease prevalent during the period such as meningitis, mumps, flu and pneumonia. At times, the number of men hurt in aviation and aviation-training accidents outnumbered the men wounded or killed in aerial combat. There was even a hospital set aside near a soldier recreation site to focus mainly on treating injuries caused by bicycle accidents and falls from mountain climbing. The soldiers assigned to the SOS, in particular those of the forestry and railway construction units, were involved in daily work that was also potentially hazardous. Stevedore and longshore units working in the seaports to load or discharge cargo also spent their days in contact with machines, cables, chemicals and tools, all capable of inflicting serious injury or worse.

Without the benefit of the medical advances enjoyed by their sons in the Second World War, many soldiers suffering from gonorrhea or syphilis would undergo painful procedures and regimens in hospital units established specifically for those treatments. Infected soldiers received no sympathy from Pershing either as his tolerance for anything related to venereal disease was well known to be absolutely zero.

PROPHYLACTIC STATIONS

The value of venereal prophylaxis for the prevention of disease has been proven.

STATIONS

For the most central one, see other side.

For Enlisted Men

Other stations are at all Red Cross and Y. M. C. A. Hotels and all barracks where soldiers are quartered.

For Officers Only

At Hotel du Louvre (Red Cross) and Hotel Richmond (Y. M. C. A.)

IF YOU CAN'T FIND ONE, ASK AN M. P.

(OVER)

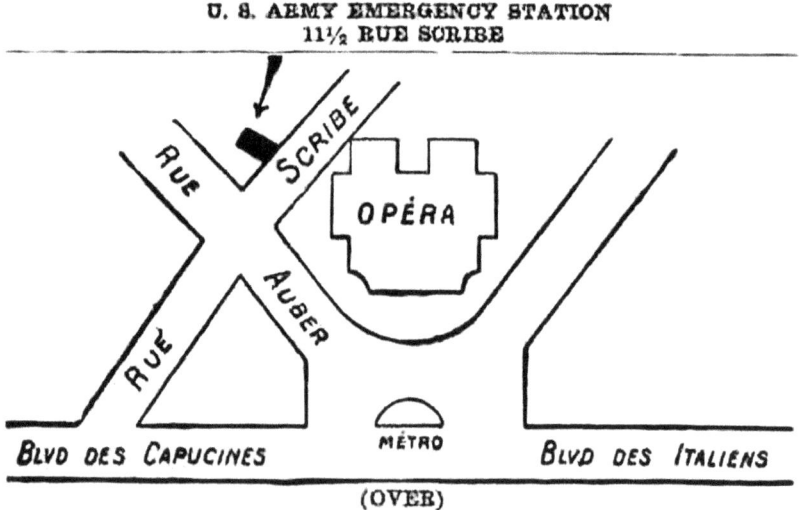

The front and back side of a Prophylactics Station card. These cards were distributed to soldiers on leave in Paris and provided them with directions on where they could find the required services after having sex (private collection).

The third category, contagious non-venereal diseases, was by far the largest. Flu and the associated pneumonia proved as deadly as German gunfire. What made this version of the flu and subsequent pneumonia so deadly for the AEF in comparison to earlier flu epidemics was that it appeared to specifically target healthy young adults. Most previous flu epidemics were deadliest for infants and those over 65; this version took the opposite tack and was particularly deadly for those in the 20 to 35 age group, the exact group populating the Army, Navy and Marine Corps in the United States and France.

In autumn 1918, a new strain of flu hit the East Coast training camps of Devens, Dix, Meade, Humphreys, and Lee and then migrated to Grant, Sherman, Riley, and Pike while moving westward and southward. This version was dramatically more deadly than the version that had arrived earlier in the year. By the end of September, the situation was bad and getting worse. On 24 September 1918, 25 of the stateside training sites across the country reported having flu patients. Just three days later, Army Chief of Staff General Peyton March ordered a delay of the draftee call-ups scheduled for October. It was simply too dangerous to send men to the camps where they might become infected and, conversely, it would be imprudent to send potentially infected men to training sites not yet affected. Sadly, it didn't seem to matter. The flu and pneumonia made their way from camp to camp and soldier to soldier with frightening ease. Extreme measures such as closing the camps to outside visitors and then shutting down the YMCA and Salvation Army huts inside the camps to keep the soldiers from gathering helped somewhat, but still the pandemic raged. Stanley Nasilowski, born in Belsk Bransk, a small town east of Warsaw, and nominally a Russian citizen, was a private in Company K, 1st Pioneer Infantry Regiment. He wrote to a female friend in Chicago that officers

> were treating us like wild animals and slaves. And they [confined] us last Saturday for two weeks ... it will be very bad. Especially with sickness it doesn't matter to die tomorrow or today ... half of us will die by getting sick and infected one to another because every day they put people in the hospital. I think it was cold and flu because they were making people go in the rain ... but if half people die they will learn how to treat people....[22]

Fortunately for Private Nasilowski, he survived the war and then served in the occupation of Germany. He was discharged from the Army as a private first class on 21 July 1919.

As a sign of the seriousness of the spread of the flu, the War Department declared that stamping out the disease in the camps was now considered a "war measure." Given this declaration, home guard and volunteer organizations were now to be organized to provide medical care and support for the training camps. Nothing seemed to work, and the pandemic continued.[23]

In France the situation among AEF units was somewhat better but still not great. Some of the men in the AEF had been exposed to the earlier form of the flu and appeared to possess some immunity to the newer

Influenza Abroad Again. What You Should Do!

ABOVE ALL, DO NOT SPIT!
KEEP AWAY FROM COUGHERS.
If anyone near you coughs or sneezes, move away from him. Don't be afraid of hurting his feelings. He knows that if he coughs without covering his mouth, he is a public menace; and it is a sign of his lack of consideration for others.
KEEP YOUR HANDS CLEAN. Wash your hands thoroughly before eating. Avoid crowded conditions.

When another wave of the Spanish flu passed through Europe again in the spring of 1919, AEF leadership wasted no time in getting the word out to the troops to protect themselves. The admonition against spitting was particularly important as many Europeans noted that the American soldiers tended to chew a lot of gum and spit everywhere (private collection).

strain. Acting Surgeon General Charles Richard, filling in for General Gorgas while he was in France, advised Army Chief of Staff General Peyton March to enforce a week-long quarantine on the soldiers being sent to France as well as reducing the number of troops transported on each ship. March would have none of it, insisting that a careful medical screening before boarding the ships would weed out sick soldiers. Richard stuck to his guns and insisted that such inspections could not guarantee the health or safety of the units going to France. He even went a step further and suggested that all shipments of soldiers be suspended until the epidemic passed. Again, March refused to accept this suggestion, but did issue orders to the ports of embarkation to reduce the number of soldiers on each ship by 10 percent.

As sickness increased in the States, the results landed in France. At the French seaport of Brest, there were 1,817 burials for Doughboys, most of whom had died of influenza aboard ship en route to or shortly after arrival in France in September and October.[24] One such victim was Private William Kruse, a drafted soldier from Alburtis, Pennsylvania. He was inducted into the Army on 15 June 1918 and assigned to the 69th Engineers. He and his unit sailed on the USS *Wilhelmina* on 23 September 1918 from Hoboken. When the *Wilhelmina* arrived in France on 5 October Kruse was dead from influenza and broncho-pneumonia. A few days later, Kruse made the voyage home in the company of a number of other dead soldiers, also on the *Wilhelmina*.

Other French ports reported the same story. It was not just the flu and pneumonia that were killing the Doughboys. Arriving ships reported that meningitis, mumps, measles, scarlet fever, and diphtheria were also taking a toll among their olive drab-clad passengers. It suddenly seemed that a soldier in the front lines in France had a better chance of surviving the war than a soldier training at Camp Grant or on a troopship.

That optimistic notion was a false hope and soon many AEF soldiers were infected. While the variant attacking the AEF in the fall of 1918 was not as deadly as the stateside variant, it was still bad enough to kill many soldiers and civilians. Soldiers being transported from Camp Pike to Europe were later pinpointed as the first group that started the spread of influenza in the receiving camp at Brest. From there the disease made a quick transition to the local population.

By early September 1918, cases of the newer wave of influenza began to arrive in all the French ports. These cases remained fairly few in number until the USS *Kroonland* docked on 12 September. On board were 117 cases of the flu and six of pneumonia. With this arrival, the genie was out of the bottle

Cornelia Elizabeth Thornton was reportedly the first American nurse to die in Britain during the war. Assigned to the U.S. Base Hospital #58 in Portsmouth, she died of disease in September 1918 and her remains were returned to the U.S. in May 1920 with a number of other nurses who died overseas (Library of Virginia).

and the number of sick and dying soldiers rapidly increased; in September and October alone, some 4,187 cases of flu and 913 more of pneumonia were brought ashore from the transport ships. At Base Section Number 5,

> 90 per cent of the pneumonia and 88.7 per cent of the influenza [patients were recently arrived soldiers]. The number of deaths from pneumonia among these troops after landing was 1,217; 497 patients had died of that disease en route, making a total of 1,696 deaths among 218,000 troops transported.[25]

Adding to that total were the methods used to carry the sick soldiers ashore from the transport vessels. While being lowered from the transport ships into smaller boats taking them to the piers, the afflicted soldiers were often exposed to high seas and cold rain. Adding to the problem was the practice of marching the ambulatory sick from the ships to the nearby rest camps. Soon ambulances and medical crews were assigned to follow each column of troops and gather those who collapsed along the route. Finally medical experts and common sense prevailed. Rules were put into place to keep the sickest soldiers on board ship. This was done to avoid endangering them more by moving them ashore through rain and cold weather. Pneumonia patients arriving by ship "were not removed unless they were in the first two or three days of their illness or had passed the crisis at least three days, and were in transportable condition. Eventually it was ordered that no pneumonia patients be transferred from ship to shore unless safely past the crisis."[26]

The flu of late 1918 and early 1919 was no respecter of rank or position. It struck at every level and in every organization in the AEF. The major in charge of the Postal Express Service and supervisor of the Central Post Office was hospitalized for 13 days at Camp Hospital Number 8. William Borland, a U.S. Congressman from Missouri, died of broncho-pneumonia while on a fact-finding tour in France and the U.S. occupation zone in Germany.[27]

Just getting to France during the worst of the flu epidemic was a dangerous experience. The staff of Base Hospital Number 63 had the

These two Advance Section nurses are posing on 17 March 1919 in what appears to be a mobile photography studio with a nicely painted backdrop and folding chair set up on a dirt floor. On the back is a handwritten note: "Honey Bunch. Miss Finch & little black eyed devil, Miss Bartlett" (John Adams-Graf Collection).

During the worst days of the flu epidemic in September and October 1918, some ships arrived with nearly as many sick Doughboys as healthy ones. At St. Nazaire, a sick soldier has been lowered to the pier and is being placed into an ambulance. Later, it was determined that it was better to keep the sickest soldiers on board the ship, as the journey ashore in the cold, rainy weather usually worsened their condition (U.S. Army Quartermaster Museum).

misfortune to sail late in September 1918 and the flu struck them as hard as any other unit. One of the nurses reported:

> I was [in the infirmary] ten days with very little care because there was only one nurse for about twenty girls, all with influenza. You had terrific pain all over your body, especially in your back and head, and you felt as if your head

was going to fall off. The odor was terrible in that ship's infirmary-I never smelt anything like it before or since.[28]

She also recounted that hundreds of the soldiers on the ship had the flu and 80 died. Because the decision was made in this case to bring the dead to France for burial, all the ship's refrigerators were emptied of food and filled with corpses. It was just as bad on other ships. The USS *Olympic* made the crossing and landed in Southampton. By the time the soldiers reached the nearby rest camp there were 1,900 sick soldiers; of these 119 died. Of the 342 nurses on board, more than a third had the flu.[29]

Even those soldiers who survived the ocean voyage were not safe. The African American 808th Pioneer Infantry Regiment, awaiting movement to the front, lost more than 150 soldiers while they were in the Camp Pontanezen transit camp. The flu proved to be an equal opportunity killer. While the 808th was suffering, a similar unit with white soldiers, the 57th Pioneer Infantry Regiment, which had travelled on the *Leviathan*, arrived in Brest. They buried 200 of their fellow soldiers in the Brest cemetery before even leaving the port.[30]

Under different circumstances, the transport trains and ships could have been stopped on the East Coast and the soldiers quarantined until they were healthy. The Meuse-Argonne Offensive, however, was taking place at the same time as the worst of the flu epidemic. The need for replacements for battle casualties in the combat divisions reached a critical point. The SOS had already been stripped of all available manpower and could provide no more men for the front. So the ships continued to sail. In the end, more soldiers would die from the flu and related diseases such as pneumonia than would be killed by German gunfire.

The flu was not the only disease decimating the ranks of the AEF. One Pennsylvania soldier, having survived front line fighting in the Meuse-Argonne, was unpleasantly surprised to find himself hospitalized as he was starting a seven-day leave in Aix-les-Bains. After checking in at the designated leave hotel, he and his comrades were escorted to Hospital Number 45 for a physical exam before they were allowed to visit the casinos and other entertainment sites in the resort town. Sadly, the doctor determined that he had dysentery and ordered him to report to one of the hospital wards. He later wrote of his friends' amazement at the turn of events: "You mean you came all the way across France to the best resort in the whole damned country, got rid o' your lice, and now they're gonna put you in the damned hospital?" It was so. The hospital did release him with one day left on his leave, so he was able to enjoy a few meals and get his picture taken before he had to return to his unit which was preparing for the attack on Metz.[31] For the now dysentery-free Doughboy things took another turn for the worse. Immediately on return to his unit he was diagnosed with a case of mumps. He was dispatched to Hospital Number 27 at Tours. Fortunately for all concerned, the Metz attack never took place as the Armistice was signed.

Another SOS soldier reported that fear of a spinal meningitis epidemic in Tours caused many of the soldiers to be quarantined and restricted to their billets when not at work. In typical soldier fashion, he complained that none of the officers or the assigned female staff were quarantined. Adding to that, he wrote that most of the enlisted men had found ways to sneak out of the camp anyway.[32]

Caring for the wounded. The main purpose for the large hospital network was to care for men wounded in combat. After a slow start, by mid–1918, there were certainly enough of these to keep the hospitals and Medical Corps busy. With more than 200,000 wounded and gassed soldiers in addition to the 53,000 killed or missing, there was plenty for everyone to do.

Two doctors from Base Hospital #32 take a break and pose for a picture. The hospital unit arrived at Contrexeville in the Advance Section in December 1917 and cared for 9,698 patients before it ceased operation in January 1919 (private collection).

Marine Lieutenant Laurence Stallings spent a lot of time in AEF hospitals. Badly wounded at Belleau Wood, the later author of *The Doughboys* and numerous Hollywood movie scripts wrote:

> Someone in Tin Pan Alley had written a song about the Red Cross nurse being the "Rose of No Man's Land" and back home people thought of Red Cross workers as being the sole custodians of the casualties. There were some in France, and devoted; but around-the-clock work was done by the U.S. Army nurse in her unsung thousands.[33]

Stallings also commented sarcastically on a report in the *Stars and Stripes* that the two million Doughboys in France were all served a full Thanksgiving Day dinner. For Stallings and his fellow patients at Hospital Number 65, he wrote their full Thanksgiving dinner consisted of baked potatoes.

Hospital salvage operations. As part of the SOS, the massive U.S. Army hospital network and its associated units were also expected to participate heartily in the recovery of salvageable material. In most hospitals this work was under the purview of a quartermaster officer. Collected for potential reuse or repurposing were fats, burlap, paper, tin cans, bottles, bones, rubber, and wire. Fats collected in the several units were clarified by boiling and straining before shipment; burlap

A portrait brought home by a soldier of a French nurse or Red Cross volunteer named Blanche. She appears to have been one of the many French civilians hired by the U.S. Army Medical Corps to supplement their staffs (private collection).

and paper were baled, and a few carloads of tin cans were shipped to salvage depots. ... Bottles were turned in for reissue or shipment if not needed in the center. Nails, wire, rubber, and bones were shipped to the depots designated. Salvage operations extended far beyond these simpler items, however, for all articles that could be employed to some alternative use or could be renovated were turned in for local repair or cleaned, and shipped to appropriate depots; e. g., instruments, appliances, clothing, ordnance, utensils, etc.[34]

Use of civilian labor. It soon became obvious to all in the AEF and SOS that the staff sizes for the hospitals were insufficient to care for the large number of sick and wounded patients. With most transatlantic shipping space dedicated to infantrymen and machine gunners, the Medical Department was forced to look elsewhere to augment their staffs. Very quickly most hospitals had 50 or so Frenchwomen working in their facilities. By consolidating the recruiting and hiring process into a central employment bureau, they were able to add "interpreters, cooks, waitresses, laundry workers, and scrub women."[35]

Establishment of a Medical Department Depot. In addition to the other supply depots, a medical supply depot was established at Allerey. Primary among its missions was the procurement and stockage of medical specific supplies and the ability to quickly dispatch these supplies as needed to hospitals and medical facilities. Inside the depot, the work force was further divided into a Records Section, a Receiving and Storage Section and an Issuing Section. The first mission of all assigned soldiers at the depot was to inventory the large amount of matériel that had already arrived, and from it build the on-hand listing of medicines and supplies. With that completed, the staff was then able to turn to the constantly arriving supplies. Particularly important were the soldiers in the receiving section who documented the railcar loads of inbound supplies. They then either stored the supplies in the appropriate location or moved them for immediate issue based on need. Early in the depot's operation it was necessary to buy some critically needed medicines from local merchants in order to meet the demand. After the supplies began to arrive in a regular and timely matter, these purchases were seldom necessary. As the depot operation became more formalized and structured, it became the policy to request replenishment of the depot's supplies whenever any item dropped below 10 days' supply on hand.[36]

From examining the operation and maintenance of a huge medical organization with more than 200 sites throughout France, we now turn to the complications of building, managing and running a railroad in a war-weary country where all the rail equipment was as worn out as the people.

6

Working on the Railroad

"Was you ever in France?" [a returning soldier] asked a canteen worker, and when she answered "Yes," "Ain't they backward?" he returned.[1]

Most soldiers of the AEF would tend to agree with the soldier above when it came to the French rail system. For many soldiers, their first experience with that system came as they departed the port or transit camp en route to their unit. The ride of the famous "40 and 8" railcars left much to be desired. What the soldiers didn't appreciate was that the French railroad system was worn out; four years of war had taken a heavy toll on the cars, locomotives, train crews, maintenance crews and even the rails. And now, a growing American Army needed the rail system to move the troops and their massive logistics support from the arrival ports to the front.

Early in the AEF's deployment, its senior leaders had worked on the assumption that the French railroads could handle the transportation requirements for men and cargo. They soon learned differently. It was therefore decided to bring the needed rail equipment across the ocean to serve the AEF. Fortunately, the industrial base in the United States was up to manufacturing and shipping all the rail components that were needed. Also crossing the ocean, in August 1917, was the vice president of the Pennsylvania Railroad, William W. Atterbury. Appointed the Director General for Transportation, Atterbury was commissioned a brigadier general with the mission to make the AEF's railroad operation a success.[2]

Along with the equipment came U.S. Army Engineer Corps railroad units. Atterbury pushed for having commercial railroad men brought over to manage the system as they would back in the States. Later, when the SOS was reorganized, Atterbury was not pleased to find he no longer reported directly to Pershing but instead his organization was now placed in the SOS under the newly created Services of Utilities.

The Service of Utilities. There were four departments in the Service of Utilities:

Under the careful watch of an officer, soldiers offload mail and bakery goods from small-gauge railcars. These smaller-sized cars were extremely useful in delivering supplies and equipment from the Advance Section forward to the logisticians of the combat units (U.S. Army Quartermaster Museum).

    Construction Department: responsible for construction and repair of buildings, wharves, roads and railroads. Its forestry service units were tasked with lumber and railroad tie production.
    Transportation Department: responsible for operating the railways and waterport complexes under American control, ocean transport of troops and matériel, and the unloading of ships at European ports.
    Motor Transportation: responsible for operation of all motor vehicles except those, such as locomotives, operated by other offices.
    Light Railways and Highways: responsible for construction of highways and the construction and operation of smaller gauge railways.

    Remembering well the importance of railroads in the American Civil War and the potential for moving large amounts of cargo and personnel quickly on the rails, the U.S. Army created and fielded a wide variety of

One of the narrow-gauge railroad locomotives sent to France. This engine was built by the Baldwin Locomotive Works of Philadelphia and was one of more than 5,500 locomotives built during the war (U.S. Army Quartermaster Museum).

railroad units. These included standard and narrow gauge railroad track construction, operation and maintenance units, standard and narrow gauge shop units, and standard and narrow gauge maintenance units. In addition to constructing and maintaining railroad lines and manning train crews, stations and offices, the men in these regiments also worked in shops that maintained locomotives and rolling stock. Some, such as the 35th Engineer Regiment, a railway maintenance shop unit, were stationed near ports of entry where they received disassembled locomotives and railway cars straight off the ships, reassembled them, and sent them to their final destinations. Fortunately, many of the soldiers assigned to the 35th had been railroad men in their civilian life and brought their expertise to the job. The 35th arrived in France in January 1918 and was capable of reassembling some 60 railcars a day. Under surge conditions they could even do more. This was soon necessary as the production lines in America were running constantly. As early as August 1917, the Baldwin Locomotive Company in Philadelphia was busily churning out locomotives for the AEF at the rate of about 30 a day. Under contract to produce 680 locomotives and 9,000 freight cars, Baldwin had the first ready to ship only 21 days after the contract was signed. While these locomotives were not as powerful as those usually found on U.S. railways, they were certainly a welcome addition on the French railroads. Each of them, "painted battleship

6. Working on the Railroad 109

gray and [bearing] the letters 'U.S.A.,'" could haul some 60 loaded railcars.[3] Being able to move this many loaded cars was important because each combat division in the AEF required almost 25 carloads of supplies each day. It was impossible to catch up; as the number of divisions grew, so did the requirement for more rail capacity which required more trains. So while the news was good that the AEF was growing into a large fighting force, the growing need for supplies and replacement soldiers to travel via railroad was a continuous struggle. The 19th Engineer Regiment, a standard gauge railroad shop maintenance unit, was stationed at St. Nazaire and reassembled the locomotives that arrived there in "knocked down" condition.[4]

While these units were busy at the port, some of their rail comrades had a much different job. The Division of Light Railways was responsible for operating 600 miles of narrow-gauge railroad track. Most of this work done was close to the front lines, and often under fire, to deliver supplies to the logisticians assigned to combat units.[5] In October 1918 it was estimated that these narrow-gauge rail lines delivered an average of 8,100 tons of supplies a day to the combat units. In some cases the rail cars were pulled forward to advanced positions by draft animals and at times even by soldiers.

A sign of the haste in which many supplies were dispatched to the front: the interior of a box car loaded loosely with four-pound loaves of bread produced by Bakery Company 322 in Dijon in September 1918 (U.S. Army Quartermaster Museum).

From the Rail Regulating Station at St. Pierre-des-Corps on 7 December 1918 comes this image of American soldiers and German POWs unloading rail cars filled with materiel salvaged from the front lines (U.S. Army Quartermaster Museum).

By November 1918 the railway engineers had taken control of several hundred miles of German-laid rail tracks in captured areas and operated on them also.[6]

A quick study of the mission of one of these units, the 21st Engineer Regiment (Light Railway Operation) gives us a further idea of what was expected from them in France:

> [The regiment] would operate over a certain section of the front and that within these limits it would maintain all the existing track, build such new lines as might be necessary, and make all repairs to its engine and car equipment, using for this purpose its own shops, except for the very heavy repair work, which was to be done in a railroad shop in the rear.[7]

Supply distribution/rail delivery concept of operation. At the railheads forward of the advance depots, supply and transportation soldiers from the combat or supported units would receive their supplies. As noted earlier, if combat units were within eight miles of the railhead, their motorized vehicles or horse and mule drawn wagons would receive the supplies. Those units more than eight miles away were supported by having the matériel trans-loaded to smaller-gauge railroad cars or motorized convoys for delivery forward.[8]

6. Working on the Railroad

A railcar load of remount horses destined for the 101st Engineers, 26th Division, are offloaded at Nanteuil-sur-Marne on 14 August 1918. On this date, the 101st Engineers had finished supporting the Aisne-Marne campaign and were receiving badly needed replacements, animals and supplies (U.S. Army Quartermaster Museum).

Working in such close proximity to the front, train crews and track maintenance men were not immune from danger. Private 1st Class Louis G. Griffin, formerly a locomotive fireman in New Mexico, recounted in his own grammatical style his experiences during the final phase of the Meuse-Argonne Offensive:

> Our company [Company E, 21st Engineer Regiment] received orders for one engine and crew also train crew to handle detachment of men to front to follow drive and repair track and roads for the quick handling of suplies of all kinds to reach the front—about day brake we left Cheppy with detachment for the front myself the fireman, about 10 a.m. after detachment had been safely unloaded and scattered and while a most terrific bombardment was going on from each side our engine was hit in the deck of [illegible] with a German 77[mm] high explosive shell killing the engineere [Jess T. Ritchie of Gallup, New Mexico] and wounding me in 7 different places.[9]

Griffin spent the rest of his time in service in France and the United States in hospitals until his discharge on 14 May 1919.

In spite of the importance of the rail operations, the Army's efforts to put the right man in the right job didn't always work. In the case of railway units, one would guess that it would have been comparatively easy to find and assign men with railroad leadership experience to Army railroad units. Indeed, while that often occurred, as seen above, in many cases it did not. Clarence E. Habiger, prior to the war a train dispatcher for the Atchison, Topeka, and Santa Fe Railroad in New Mexico, made this observation about railway unit officers:

Private First Class Louis G. Griffin, 21st Engineer Regiment (Light Railway Operation), was an experienced railroad man from back in the States. He was wounded in the Meuse-Argonne Offensive by German artillery (New Mexico War Service Records via Ancestry.com).

I do not know of any railway organizations that were officer[ed] by all railroad men. There were too many of the officers in railway regiments that knew nothing whatever about railroading, which made it bad for those that did, and worked quite a hardship on the enlisted personnel, so many of them who were only privates, but had had 15 to 25 years of good hard practical railway experience on our best railroads in the United States. There were officers in other organizations that were railroad men that could have been transferred. If their services could not have been spared there, there was plenty of good material in the railway organizations in the ranks that could have been promoted to executive positions and the railroading in France would have been much more successful.[10]

Rear-area troops, especially newly arrived men, were sometimes in awe of combat troops or those perceived to be "veterans." Adolph Abeyta, a machinist from Tucumcari, New Mexico, serving in the 21st Engineer

Regiment (Light Railway Operation), recalled his experiences upon meeting men from the veteran 11th Engineer Regiment (Standard Gauge Railway Construction) shortly after his arrival in France:

> We were much impressed by the stories these veterans told us. When we left for the advance on February 15th [1918] some of us thought that we had our last good night's sleep in France since we knew from the experience of the 11th Engineers that the German aviators would bomb us night and day.[11]

In addition to relating harrowing stories of being bombed, the veterans also took advantage of the newcomers' gullibility. Abeyta continued:

> Incidentally we had acquired quite a number of German souvenirs from them [that is, from the men of the 11th Engineer Regiment], part of which were afterwards, to our discomfort, discovered to be English and French.[12]

Private Adolph Abeyta was a former railroad machinist's helper from New Mexico. Abeyta enlisted in the Army the day before the June 1917 draft registrations were required and sailed to France on the day after Christmas in 1917. He was wounded and gassed, and he did not return home until June of 1919 (New Mexico War Service Records via Ancestry.com.).

American railway units encountered problems even in rear areas, let alone in forward areas under enemy observation or fire. Captain Morris E. Pumphrey, 21st Engineer Regiment (Light Railway), described some problems with prefabricated rail sections:

> For instance, the sectional track was found to have been thrown together and in many cases on one side of a section there would be a twenty-pound rail and the other side a twenty-five pound rail. As fish plates were only available for one type of rail, it was necessary to cast these sections aside. Also the curve sections were composed of two rails of exactly the same length, thus necessitating the sawing off of one end of the inside rail. This small matter trebled the time necessary to lay the track.[13]

The 21st Engineer Regiment operated both in rear areas and closer to the front. They, along with other railway units, had to contend with differing sizes of rails, roadbeds, locomotives, and rolling stock. Conversion from metric to standard measures was a daily routine. After the regiment had built and maintained some lines, the arrival of American locomotives caused some consternation:

> When the first American locomotive made its appearance, the size, height, and width astounded the track men. They realized that their work was cut out for them to prevent derailments. To get sufficient clearance for these locomotives (their width over all was seven feet) it was necessary to change the alignment in some cases and cut down trees in others.[14]

When one considers that this occurred in late spring 1918, just as the need for transportation for the AEF was increasing dramatically, the problem was urgent and demanded much attention and more hard work.

And speaking of hard work; it is important to remember that fuel, supplies and equipment were not the only commodities riding the rails. A significant number of American soldiers and units were carried to their destinations by the railroad. The French railcars proved to be a memorable experience for the American soldiers more accustomed to the larger railcars of the United States. The French cars were about half their size. Most memoirs from the period include mention of the American soldiers' first encounters with the infamous "*hommes 40, cheveaux 8*" boxcars. One NCO wrote of his exasperation with the small rail cars: "I got all my forty artillerymen in the boxcar, Lieutenant. But if you try to put eight of our horses in, somebody's going to get trampled to death."[15] A draftee from Virginia who was familiar with trains, on seeing the French rail cars for the first time, wrote that they

> belonged in a museum for the preservation of antiquities rather than in a busy rail yard. Attached to our cars was a locomotive which had rolled from the factory in 1884 ... [and] which sat too high above the track and had wheels with spokes as spindly as the legs of an ostrich.[16]

It should also be noted that railcars did not return to the rear empty. In an effort to increase the efficiency of rail usage, returning railcars carried a variety of items, including salvaged material. After a battle, divisional salvage squads systematically combed the battlefield for items to salvage. Items that could be immediately re-issued were held near the front; other items were "concentrated in huge piles known as advance dumps. These were for convenience placed adjacent to lines traversed by auto trucks and, if possible, railheads."[17] Workers sorted the salvaged items and sent them to the rear in carload shipments for further sorting, refurbishing, repair and other disposition. To help relieve railway congestion, every effort was made to make up carloads of the same type of salvaged equipment destined for the same depot.

6. Working on the Railroad 115

By the time the Supply Company of the 54th Pioneer Infantry Regiment arrived in France in September 1918, they too were greeted with "three very cold and very tiresome days" travel in the "40 and 8's" from one muddy camp to another, arriving in time to be issued helmets and gas masks just before heading into the Argonne.[18] More disturbing was the trip to the front by another company from the 54th. The men of Company E "were soon relieved of the curiosity as to whether they fell under the title of Hommes or Chevaux" as their train pulled out of Brest filled to capacity. On the third day of their journey, they passed through Versailles and Paris but soon came to a sudden stop. There had been a train collision "in a long tunnel directly ahead, about eighty French civilians and soldiers were killed and some of the men and officers of Company E worked for eight hours extracting dead and wounded from the debris."[19] Moving on at last, they finally reached the railhead at the town of Fleury, some seven miles from the front. After two days of practicing their gas mask drill, they received their first exposure to German aircraft and were soon set to work repairing artillery damaged roads while under enemy shelling. After three days of such labor, they were finally issued their helmets.

The Spanish flu epidemic in the fall of 1918 caused other problems for the railroad men and rail transportation in general. The units of the 29th Division arrived in June and July of 1918. The two infantry brigades and most of the division support units were hurriedly placed in the "40 and 8" railcars and transported from the port to a staging area in preparation for duty at the front. Instead of undergoing a carefully scheduled and measured training regimen, the 29th was sent to a "quiet" sector in Alsace to learn on the job and relieve another unit. Although not even close to being ready for front line combat duty, the 29th took over the sector occupied by the 32nd Division in late July, freeing the 32nd to head north and join the American forces preparing for the St. Mihiel campaign. While the infantrymen of the 29th were getting their baptism of fire in the "quiet" sector (and suffering some 500 casualties), the 54th Field Artillery Brigade of the 29th Division was sent to an artillery training center near Brest after arriving in France. When the rest of the 29th started moving to the Meuse-Argonne, the field artillerymen were scheduled to join them in the offensive. Unfortunately, the flu had so devastated the railroad crews in the Brest area there were no trains available to carry the freshly-trained cannoneers to the front. By the time they caught up to the rest of their division, it was the morning of 11 November 1918 and the war was over.

7

Service Organizations
The Red Cross and the "Seven Sisters"

So all honor to the welfare workers of France—the Red Cross, the Y.M.C.A, the K. of C., the Jewish Welfare Society, the Salvation Army, and all of the smaller brothers. There is glory for them all. It was not the Army that won the war. It was the American people.[1]

General Pershing realized early in his command of the AEF his soldiers were going to be exposed to things in Europe for which their American upbringing had not prepared them. Having seen much of the world during his Army career, he knew that soldiers needed to be kept busy as much as possible in order to avoid misbehavior. During their limited off-time, however, they would need entertainment, preferably wholesome entertainment. The earliest arriving troops in France brought their unit canteens and sports equipment with them. Pershing quickly put an end to this practice because it was an impractical solution and worse, a waste of valuable cargo space.[2] He was also aware of the good work that had been done by the many service organizations in the training camps in the States. The most prevalent organizations, the Young Men's Christian Association (YMCA), the Young Women's Christian Association (YWCA), the Salvation Army, the Jewish Welfare Board, the Knights of Columbus, the War Camp Community Service, and the American Library Association, became known as the "Seven Sisters."[3] Together they were tasked by the War Department with providing social, health and welfare services to soldiers in training camps under the watchful eyes and oversight of the Commission on Training Camp Activities.

It was therefore the logical step for Pershing to allow those same organizations to come to France and perform similar duties. Unhappily, for the YMCA in particular, not all of the publicity it received was good. As will be seen, the YMCA would become known as "that Damned Y" in many soldiers' opinions. For the most part, it was a bad rap that besmirched the reputation of many hardworking and dedicated workers. One insightful Doughboy tried to explain it:

> The main cause of the criticism is the canteen.... The Y took over, at the Army's request, the sale of all U.S. goods formerly handled for soldiers in peacetime by commissaries. The U.S. Army probably realized what a difficult job it would be, so they passed the buck to the Y.[4]

The Red Cross, as an international organization whose nursing and medical care was accepted and respected on both sides of the front lines, already had an established presence in Europe. The other organizations didn't have this advantage and had to build their organizations in France from the ground up. Also adding to their challenges was the obvious fact that they would have to compete for the limited shipping space on the same vessels carrying the troops and supplies of the AEF. Nevertheless, they persevered and by war's end, all had established their "huts" and recreation centers in nearly every AEF camp and facility in France.

The American Red Cross. Due to its unique and international non-combatant status under the Geneva Convention, the Red Cross was the only service organization allowed to operate near the front lines. The Red Cross was also well-equipped for hospital work and caring for sick or wounded soldiers. As a result, they were also assigned to the troop trains to care for soldiers being carried on them. Very quickly, Red Cross hospital trains were seen very close to the front evacuating soldiers from the field hospitals. Red Cross workers were assigned to every base and camp hospital to assist the patients and provide comfort items such chocolates, cigarettes, stationery, toilet articles and other items.

Red Cross workers' activities in promoting recreation were coordinated with hospital chaplains and were under their overall control but more immediately under the direction of the Red Cross worker in charge of the Red Cross hut. In the provision of medical supplies the American Red Cross supplemented the U.S. Army Medical Department and was often able to make large scale purchases from local vendors in France faster than the Army supply system could.

The Young Men's Christian Association (YMCA). Although nominally restricted from serving near the front lines, YMCA workers often traveled close to the fighting to support their troops. Under the supervision of the SOS, the YMCA's 20,000 men and women workers established 33 leave centers which catered to some 300,000 Doughboys before the facilities were closed. In addition to running "the largest system of hotels and restaurants in the world," the YMCA also managed to rent casinos and resort centers throughout France.[5] Many of the travelling French

A small poster showing all seven of the major service organizations engaged in supporting the Army training camps in the States. All but the War Camp Community Service organization also supported the soldiers of the AEF. When the Second World War began, all of the organizations were rolled into the United Service Organizations (USO) to provide better management and oversight of their activities (private collection).

vaudeville acts and the soldier shows and revues put on by the different units were supported financially by the YMCA. Donations to the YMCA by stateside patrons enabled them to provide more than $200,000 worth of musical instruments for use in the YMCA and YWCA huts. They also managed to put on some 70,000 motion picture shows with many of the audiences numbering in the hundreds. By April 1919 there were almost 800 YMCA workers in the recreation centers alone.

Eleanor Roosevelt, the wife of President Theodore Roosevelt's oldest son, Teddy Roosevelt, Jr., was among the leaders of the YMCA's efforts. Mrs. Roosevelt quickly became a force to be reckoned with in France using her considerable influence to recruit YMCA workers and establish rest centers for the troops. She was also very willing to take to task those who failed to meet her rigorous standards. She wrote

> the great majority of women in the Y.M.C.A were conscientious, unselfish ... and ready to work until they dropped, there were always a few who were not content with clean comfortable quarters ... but demanded more. These were usually the shirkers....[6]

The YMCA was also in the forefront of the campaign against venereal disease, providing lectures, pamphlets and prophylactic materials in every one of their huts. One soldier wrote that "the Y.M.C.A. huts put out free

GENERAL PERSHING Cables:

"No other organization since the world began has ever done such great constructive work with the efficiency, dispatch and understanding, often under adverse circumstances, than has been done in France by American Red Cross in the last six months."

This poster bearing General Pershing's image and words gives strong testimony to the important work being done by the Red Cross in France (Library of Congress).

A fascinating photograph of some of the YMCA females assigned to AEF units. Clearly visible are shoulder patches representing the 1st, 2nd and 37th Divisions and the District of Paris. Interestingly enough, the woman second from the left in the front row is displaying three overseas stripes, indicative of 18 months spent in France (Library of Congress).

chocolate and doughnuts once a week. They also have amusements day & night with lots of religion thrown in."[7]

African American men and women also served in the YMCA in France. Although too few in proportion to the number of black soldiers in the AEF, they also were proud to serve. Among the first unusual sights two of them encountered after arriving at the port of Bordeaux was the sight of African American soldiers guarding work details of German prisoners. They noted that "somehow we felt that colored soldiers found it rather refreshing—even enjoyable for a change."[8] In total, there were only 87 black YMCA workers who served in France. Of this number, only a few were females. Expressly forbidden from serving with combat units, a privilege sometimes extended to white female YMCA workers, the black women spent their time in service to the many African American troops of the SOS.⁹

In addition to the facilities in France, the YMCA also opened huts and canteens in Britain, Italy, Russia and the Azores to provide services to the soldiers, sailors and Marines in those locations.¹⁰ When the flu epidemic hit in late 1918, YMCA workers also pitched in to help nurse the sick soldiers as well as their coworkers. With so many dying, sometimes the only attendees at the graveside funerals were the gravediggers, a chaplain and some YMCA workers.¹¹

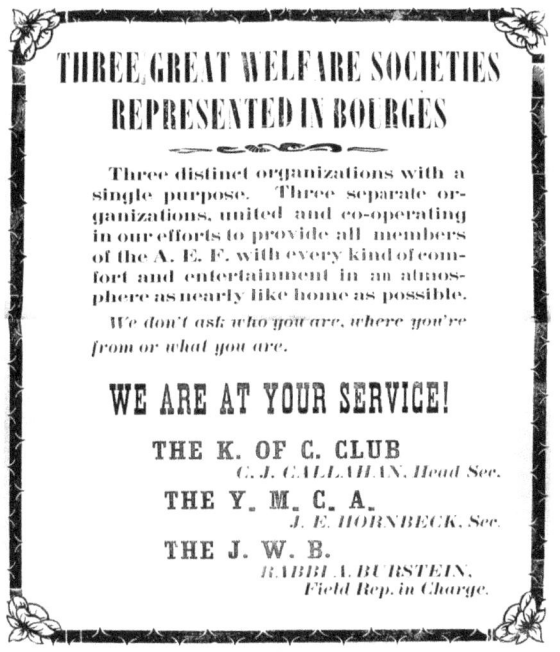

The Central Records Office weekly newspaper, *The CRO*, printed this full-page advertisement letting the soldiers know that the Jewish Welfare Board, the Knights of Columbus and the Young Men's Christian Association are working together on their behalf (private collection).

Though before the war the YMCA was in the forefront of the struggle against smoking, dancing and vaudeville/stage shows, it was forced to accept these as necessary evils in order to serve the soldiers. Ironically, as will be seen, it is because of smoking and cigarettes the YMCA received some of its worst criticism which led to a bad reputation.¹²

The Young Women's Christian Association (YWCA). Although it operated on a much smaller scale than the YMCA, the YWCA played an important role in providing safe and clean lodging for many female workers in France. Like the YMCA, it had a strong pacifistic history, but signed up to support the American effort "over there" as well as at home. Although it had a workforce of only about 350 females, it provided the same services to the many female workers and visitors the Army would have while overseas. In France it was particularly effective in helping the French women working in the SOS ammunition and maintenance depots

Looking very much like a standard YMCA hut with a "Movies and Orchestra" announcement board, two pool tables, and a ping-pong table in the foreground, this is the lobby of the International YMCA hut in Vladivostok, Russia. However, the presence of the British, Italian (House of Savoy), Czech Legion and Japanese flags set this postcard image apart as something different (private collection).

by providing economic lodging and some daycare facilities for their children. The YWCA also maintained a presence with the American forces deployed in Siberia, and some of the workers would even find themselves embroiled in the on-going revolution in that country.

One of the larger YWCA establishments was the Hotel Petrograd in Paris which had 250 rooms and catered to the women of the AEF and other countries who needed lodging. Near the SOS headquarters at Tours, the YWCA established a reception station to assist the "English, Irish, Australian, American, French, Belgian and even Welsh, Spanish, and Italian" women coming to work for the AEF.[13] When the U.S. Third Army moved into Germany to perform occupation duties after the war, the YWCA managed a hotel for the many female nurses, telephone operators and office workers assigned there.

The Salvation Army. The Salvation Army operation was on a much smaller scale than the YMCA and the Red Cross. It was noted for its husband and wife teams who set up recreation huts. Rather than conducting religious services, the Salvation Army workers preferred baking pies and serving coffee for the soldiers. One soldier wrote home that "the Salvation Army, of course, stands out in front, here, in Brest, just as it did

FOUR YEARS IN THE FIGHT
The Women of France
We Owe Them Houses of Cheer

UNITED WAR WORK CAMPAIGN

One of the YWCA's most important missions was to provide safe and clean living conditions for the many American and European females who were working to support the AEF in France. The YWCA even provided some measure of daily child care as well as lodging for French women working in the U.S. supply depots (Library of Congress).

up along the 'Fighting Front.'"[14] In total, there were only some 250 American Salvation Army workers in France, although another 550 men and women from European countries were hired to fill out its workforce supporting the AEF.

The Knights of Columbus (KofC). The KofC provided numerous Catholic-based services and recreation facilities in the training bases in the States. Although their presence was not as great in France, they too were well known and respected for being "soldier-friendly." Early in their deployment to France, the Knights decided against sending female workers to staff their huts and canteens. This was based on their established policy against placing women workers in harm's way. Yet, as Dorothy and Carl Schneider pointed out in their book *Into the Breach*, the Knights hired French women to perform administrative and clerical work in Paris "where they were bombarded and shelled" by the Germans.[15] The KofC also delivered an important service by providing priests to the AEF. One

In a unique addition to the postcard, a soldier has written that these two Salvation Army workers were the "McCallister sisters" and "were with us nearly all the time we were at the front." Although the soldier misspelled their last name, there is little doubt that Alice and Violet, the McAllister sisters, were as well known in the 1st Division for their singing and musical performances near the front lines as they were for their nursing and baking skills (private collection).

7. Service Organizations

An interesting gathering of soldiers, nurses and service organization personnel pose for a group photograph in front of the Knights of Columbus Hall in Lourdes, France. One of the famous U.S. Army Signal Corps "Hello Girls" is in the picture (standing at left) as are several Knights of Columbus representing the 26th Division (standing at right), 37th Division (seated on the ground, far left) and the 84th Division (seated on the ground, third from left) (Charles G. Thomas Collection).

of them, Michael Nivard, was born in Holland and had been an ordained priest working in the United States for almost 20 years when he volunteered for service with the Knights in France. After serving in the front lines as a civilian priest, he was commissioned in July 1918 as a 1st lieutenant and assigned to the 103rd Infantry Regiment as its chaplain.

One of the largest KofC facilities was set up in Antwerp after the war to provide recreation and a taste of home for soldiers working in or transiting the port. As with all of the religious-based organization facilities, every Doughboy, regardless of religious denomination, was welcome in the Knights' huts.

The Jewish Welfare Board (JWB). The Jewish Welfare Board was formed just three days after the United States declared war on Germany on 6 April 1917. Its charter was to provide support to Jewish soldiers in the U.S. military. In this role, the JWB was present in all of the main training camps throughout the United States and with the AEF in France. Although nominally dedicated to serving the men and women of Hebrew faith, its services and facilities were open to all. The JWB was also responsible for recruiting and training rabbis to serve as military chaplains. These chaplains were particularly important in some units, such as the 77th Division, where there were many Jewish soldiers. With the influx into

War Library Bulletin

PUBLISHED BY THE
LIBRARY WAR SERVICE, AMERICAN LIBRARY ASSOCIATION
Headquarters: Library of Congress, Washington, D. C.

| Volume I | MAY, 1919 | No. 9 |

A good indication of the size of the American Library Association's efforts to provide books to the soldiers is seen in this monthly bulletin published by the Library War Service. It contains the details of their efforts to provide books to soldiers and sailors in France and Russia, with the occupation forces in Germany, and even to the sailors and Marines at Guantanamo Bay, Cuba (National Archives).

the Army of many foreign-born soldiers there were many Russian and Polish Jews spread throughout the Army and in need of religious support as much as their Christian comrades.

The American Library Association (ALA). The American Library Association was in existence before the war and played an active role in supporting the soldiers and sailors in the stateside training camps. The ALA established the Library War Service (LWS) to provide books and library services specifically to training camps and to the men and women serving overseas. From donated funds the LWS built 36 camp libraries and distributed several million books and magazines. The Library War Service also provided braille books for soldiers who were blinded. The LWS librarians wore uniforms like those worn by other volunteer groups. Alas, internal politics in the ALA proved prejudicial by not allowing women or African American men to serve in the LWS in the training camps or overseas. In the United States, the field of library science was dominated by women so the restriction against allowing women to serve in the camps or France was controversial. It also hindered the organization's ability to provide as much support as was needed. As a result of this stand, many female librarians left the organization and joined the other service groups that allowed them to serve in France. Ironically, some of the women who left the ALA ended up as librarians in YMCA and YWCA huts. At the end of the war, some of the restrictions were relaxed and women were allowed to serve overseas at LWS sites. By the summer of 1919 a large percentage of the LWS employees in France were females but the ALA had missed its chance to have made a greater impression on the AEF in specific and the nation in general.

Hundreds of public libraries in the United States also supported the LWS activities and were used as collection points for donated books. Although the pre-war ALA had only 3,300 members and an annual budget of $25,000, the LWS eventually raised more than $5 million and collected more than 10,000,000 books for distribution. The ALA was even able to convince General Pershing to allow 50 tons of cargo space monthly for donated books. Nearly every YMCA, KofC, Red Cross facility and base or camp hospital was a distribution point for LWS books.[16]

Despite all of the good works of the Young Men's Christian Association and the Red Cross taking care of the troops in their training camps, there were some detractors of their efforts in France. Among the accusations leveled against the two largest soldier-support organizations were complaints that the workers expected to be treated as Army officers. This was certainly understandable to a degree, since the AEF had decreed on 28 July 1917 that all service organization workers in France were subject to military law and regulations.[17] Yet the sight of YMCA "officers" wearing uniforms and Sam Browne belts acted like a red cape to a bull for many of the Doughboys who believed they already had enough officers to salute.

It also seemed to many soldiers that there were an inordinate number of healthy young men working in service organizations who could have better served their country by wearing a helmet and carrying a rifle. A July 1918 report on the civilian agencies working in France stated that although "the YMCA and Red Cross were doing good work in the leave areas ... they were the most hated organizations in France."[18]

The YMCA, in particular, was vilified for not allowing soldiers to play cards in the recreation huts while insisting on conducting prayer meetings. The most common and loudest complaint, however, was based on the widely-held belief that the YMCA was charging the soldiers for cigarettes that had been donated to the YMCA for distribution. The soldiers were angry at having to pay for what they believed should have been freely given in the first place. Opening the tobacco packages and finding evidence that their purchase had been donated to the AEF for free distribution made their anger that much worse. Yet, like so many things in war time, this was only half of the story. The rumblings were so loud against the YMCA that that the SOS Chief of Staff, Johnson Hagood, felt compelled to set the record straight writing that

> in the confusion of supply it was impossible to keep different lots of tobacco separate. Supplies were turned over to the Y.M.C.A. in bulk at shipside or elsewhere in France.... "Gift tobacco" got mixed with the rest and was sold, not only by the Y.M.C.A., but by the Army.... I myself gave orders that if a soldier bought any tobacco anywhere which upon being opened was disclosed to be a gift, he could go to any Army commissary and have his purchase duplicated free, without returning the original.[19]

Despite Hagood's attempts to defuse this problem, the discontent with the YMCA and Red Cross reached the point that when George Foster Peabody, the American philanthropist and social activist, suggested to Secretary Baker that more service organization workers were needed in France, Baker replied that the real need in France was for "men in khaki and trained nurses not souvenir hunters."[20] These were crushing words from Baker to a man who had previously had been his friend and had found favor with the Secretary of War for supporting equal treatment for African American soldiers.

Regardless of the rights and wrongs of the controversy, there is one indisputable fact. Duty in the service organizations anywhere near the front lines in France could be deadly; nine male and two female YMCA workers were killed as a result of enemy action. Another 167 were listed as wounded, gassed or shell-shocked. Adding to the casualty lists were the 50 male and 21 female YMCA workers who died from accidents or disease.[21] The numbers for the other organizations were comparable. France in 1917 and 1918 was a dangerous place to be, and wearing a Salvation Army uniform, a YMCA uniform or a Red Cross nurse's smock was no protection against artillery fire, aerial bombs or the flu. Although most of the organizations kept a presence in France and Germany until the last Doughboy was home, the Red Cross received notification that their role in the AEF was completed on 10 June 1919. This included the Red Cross volunteers who had been serving with the Central Records Office in Bourges as well as the many nurses and doctors.[22]

A magnified portion of a larger photograph: standing in the center, a typical Army senior NCO is expressing his displeasure at some aspect of a YMCA-given tour of Paris. He may be wondering why the YMCA workers on his left (wearing a campaign hat and District of Paris patch) and on his right (wearing an SOS patch and "Information" armband) were not in Army uniform instead of YMCA uniform. It was a common complaint (Charles G. Thomas Collection).

In retrospect, perhaps one of the greatest services these organizations provided to the AEF was in providing access, although very limited, for the Doughboys to American women. Nearly every memoir of the period contains some poignant moment where the sick, work-exhausted, battle-tired, homesick or wounded soldier recounts a meeting with one of the women of these organizations. Although the men of the service organizations were often mentioned favorably as great providers of sporting equipment, stationery and a rousing group song, it was the few moments spent with the women that resonate. During the occupation of the German Rhineland after the war, Dr. Frank Crane wrote:

> About the best thing I have seen in our army of occupation is the girl. Under the direction of the Y.M.C.A. there are about fifty or sixty girls who are stationed here. Their business is to assist in looking after the clubrooms, reading rooms and canteens. ... They bring with them a breath of normal and wholesome home life, which the men need.[23]

As the 29th Division's history reported:

> While there may be conflicting opinions as to the advisability of having sent woman workers to France ... it will be difficult to find any member of the 29th Division who has anything but words of praise and gratitude to them for the very real help and the many hours of companionship they provided.[24]

8

Biographies

Of all ages and epochs this is the greatest, and the one to which all those of the future will hark back—this, in which, though we played our great part, we yet live heedlessly and with little thought of the future.[1]

Harry Hill Bandholtz (18 December 1864–7 May 1925)

Bandholtz was born in Constantine, Michigan, and graduated from West Point in 1890. He was the 29th of 65 cadets in his class.[2] Commissioned as an infantry officer, Bandholtz served with the 7th Infantry Regiment in the Spanish-American War. He was the Chief of Staff of the New York National Guard Division under General John O'Ryan during the Mexican border campaign in 1916 and 1917. Bandholtz was selected to command the 29th Division's 58th Infantry Brigade in 1918 and led them until September 1918 when he was named the U.S. Army Provost Marshal General, responsible for reorganizing the AEF's military police.

After the war, Bandholtz continued to serve in the AEF and was appointed to the Inter-Allied Military Mission to Hungary in August 1919. In this role, he was responsible for supervising the withdrawal of the Romanian and Serbian armies from Hungary. As the senior Allied officer on the commission, Bandholtz made his biggest contribution in October 1919. Armed only with a riding crop, Bandholtz confronted Romanian soldiers intent on ransacking the Hungarian National Museum in Budapest. Intimidated by Bandholtz blocking their path, the Romanians quickly left and Hungary's treasure was safe.

General Bandholtz also planned the ceremony for the entombment of the Unknown Soldier in Arlington National Cemetery in November 1921. Bandholtz is considered the "Father of the Military Police Corps."[3] There is a full-sized bronze statue of Bandholtz, commissioned in 1936 by a grateful Hungarian government, located near the U.S. Embassy in Budapest.

The formidable-looking statue built in 1936 to honor General Bandholtz's defense of the Hungarian National Museum from plunderers in 1919. Armed only with his riding crop and stern countenance, he put the looters to flight and saved the country's historical treasures (U.S. Embassy in Budapest).

The statue, which had been removed by the Communist regime in 1949, was restored in 1993.

Smedley Darlington Butler (30 July 1881–21 June 1940)

Smedley Butler was born to a Quaker family in West Chester, Pennsylvania. His father served as a congressman during both the Warren G. Harding and Calvin Coolidge administrations. Very athletic as a youth, Butler lied about his age to enlist in the Marine Corps during the Spanish-American War. He soon received a commission as a Marine Corps 2nd lieutenant.[4] While serving in the Philippines in October 1899, he led 300 Marines to take the town of Noveleta from Filipino rebels. Next up was the Boxer Rebellion and Butler fought in the Battle of Tientsin on 13 July 1900.

The following years saw Butler active in the Caribbean and Central America in the so-called Banana Wars. From there he returned to the Philippines for a more placid tour of duty until illness forced him back to the States to recuperate and worked a short stint as a coal mine manager. Returning to the Corps, Butler served in Nicaragua from 1909 to 1912. In 1914, Butler and a Navy officer slipped into Mexico to spy on the Mexican army. During the fighting at the Mexican port city of Vera Cruz in 1914, Butler received the first of two Medals of Honor he would

Brigadier General Smedley D. Butler, veteran of many battles and recipient of two Medals of Honor. In this photograph, most likely taken in France while he was in command of Camp Pontanezen, Butler is wearing the shoulder patch of the 5th Marine Brigade (USMC HD).

receive for valor in combat. By 1915, Butler was in Haiti and campaigning against the native bandit-like *Cacos*. Butler earned his second Medal of Honor on 17 November 1915 for capturing a native stronghold.[5]

Butler was given command of the 13th Regiment of Marines in the 5th Brigade and deployed with them to France. Most of the Marines of the 5th Brigade were dispersed in small detachments for service in the SOS. Butler, now a brigadier general, was placed in charge of Camp Pontanezen in October 1918; the large transit camp near the port of Brest in Base Section Number 5. The problems with the camp's antiquated facilities and generally muddy environment were well-known and Butler took on the mission of fixing them. The famous "duckboards" of the camp, emplaced by Butler and his men, soon came symbolize the camp in everyone's mind. Butler became commander of the 5th Brigade in April 1919 but also remained Camp Pontanezen commander until July 1919.[6]

With the return of the AEF to the States, Butler also made his way home and soon found himself selected to be the Director of Public Safety in Philadelphia in 1924 and 1925. As director, he took an active role in reducing police corruption and enforcing Prohibition. Returning to the Corps again, he was assigned as commander of the Marine forces in China from 1927 to 1929. He was promoted to major general and at age 48, he was the youngest major general in the Marine Corps. Although strongly supported by some to become the Commandant of the Marine Corps, Butler had made too many enemies and was not selected. He retired from active

A unique image of the original duckboard "personally carried" by Smedley Butler from the port of Brest to begin the network of wooden walkways. These duckboards and the sea of mud they covered came to represent Camp Pontanezen in the minds of most Doughboys passing through (USMC HD).

duty on 1 October 1931 with 33 years of service. He later became an outspoken critic of the U.S. policies in Central America and supported the Bonus Marchers in their attempt to receive a war bonus for their World War I service. In 1940, he suffered from a gastrointestinal problem and died in the Philadelphia Naval Hospital.[7] Always a controversial or polarizing character in the Marine Corps, no one ever questioned his personal bravery or his willingness to lead his troops from the front. He remains one of only two Marines to earn Medals of Honor for two separate actions.

Charles Gates Dawes (27 August 1865–23 April 1951)

Dawes was a multi-faceted man with strong willpower and an equally strong drive to excel. He was born in Marietta, Ohio, the son of Civil War General Rufus Dawes who had commanded the 6th Wisconsin Infantry Regiment. Dawes studied law and was admitted to the bar in Nebraska, practicing from 1887 to 1894. During this period he met John J. Pershing and the two became close friends.

Dawes was a self-taught musician and in 1912 composed *Melody in A Major*, which in 1951 with added song lyrics became a pop music hit under its new name: "It's All in the Game." When the First World War broke out, Dawes received an officer's commission in the Corps of Engineers and deployed to France with the 17th Engineer Regiment, a standard gauge railway construction unit formed in Atlanta, Georgia.[8]

When Pershing discovered that Dawes was in France, he immediately transferred him to the AEF Headquarters staff and then placed him

Charles Dawes (right), seen here serving as the 30th vice president of the United States, poses with President Calvin Coolidge. This picture is undated but most likely was taken in 1925 or 1926 (Library of Congress).

in charge of the General Purchasing Board for the AEF. Dawes also represented the AEF on the Military Board of Allied Supply where he pushed the other countries to pool their supply and vehicle resources for greater efficiency. Promoted to brigadier general in October 1918, Dawes was privy to many of the AEF's strategic plans through his personal relationship with Pershing, Harbord and other senior leaders. After the Armistice, he was responsible for disposing of the AEF's assets and property not being returned to the States.

Dawes resigned from the Army in 1919 but was called upon to explain the AEF's and SOS's purchases in front of a U.S. Senate committee in 1921. The heated debate and Dawes' colorful language made him a favorite of the newspapers.[9] He was appointed to the Allied Reparations Commission in 1923 and worked to make the demands on Germany's weak economy less stringent. He received a shared Nobel Peace Prize for these efforts. In 1924 Dawes joined Calvin Coolidge on the Republican ticket as the vice-presidential candidate and together they easily won the November election. However, Dawes' relationship with Coolidge remained rocky. After the four-year term was up, Dawes was selected to be the Ambassador to the United Kingdom where he served from 1929 to 1932. He retired from public life in 1932 and returned to the banking business. He died in 1951 at the age of 85.

Johnson Hagood (16 June 1873–22 December 1948)

Hagood (pronounced "Hag-wood") was born in Orangeburg, South Carolina. He graduated from West Point 23rd out of 73 cadets in 1896.[10] He was commissioned an artillery 2nd lieutenant, serving in Rhode Island, Connecticut, and South Carolina before returning to West Point as an instructor in the Department of Philosophy. He served on the Army General Staff and was selected to serve as Aide de Camp to Major General J. Franklin Bell from 1908 to 1910. He served in the Philippines from 1913 to 1915. Hagood arrived in France on 11 September 1917 and helped organize the Advance Section Line of Communications (LOC) for the AEF. Hagood was one of the driving forces behind the revamping and reorganization of the AEF's supply system and served as chief of staff for the Services of Supply.[11]

Hagood participated in the Meuse-Argonne offensive in October 1918 and was selected to command the 66th Field Artillery Brigade during the occupation of the German Rhineland. He returned to the United States in May 1919 and was assigned to command the 30th Brigade of the Coast Artillery Corps and Camp Eustis, Virginia. He commanded the Philippine

Division from 1927 to 1929 and then the Third Army from 1933 to 1936. As could be expected from such an outstanding Army leader,

> his administration and leadership were characterized with brilliance, bluntness, and a great impatience for unnecessary routine and red tape. He was famous for his annual report to the Secretary of War which consisted of one line, "Nothing to report."[12]

Always outspoken, Hagood ran afoul of President Franklin Roosevelt's New Deal by criticizing some of the financial aspects of its policies. As a result he was relieved of his command. By the time the smoke had cleared, Hagood had been reinstated to another command but he requested retirement instead. Hagood was a prolific writer with a very sardonic and humorous writing style. His books *The Services of Supply* and *Caissons Go Rolling Along* make very entertaining reading.

A formal portrait of Johnson Hagood as a Major General. Hagood later commanded the Philippine Division from 1927 to 1929 and the U.S. Third Army in the mid–1930s (Library of Congress).

James Guthrie Harbord (21 March 1866– 20 August 1947)

Harbord was born in Bloomington, Illinois, and attended Kansas State University, graduating with a master's degree in 1895. He enlisted in the Army in 1889 and worked his way through the ranks until commissioned as a lieutenant in the 5th Cavalry. Serving in a number of cavalry units, he was assigned to the Philippine Constabulary from 1903 to 1914. Pershing selected Harbord to be chief of staff for the AEF in May 1917, a position he held for a year until he was assigned to command the

Marine Brigade in the 2nd Division just in time for Belleau Wood. By July 1918, Harbord commanded the entire 2nd Division and led them through the fighting in the Soissons offensive. At this point Pershing selected him to command the Services of Supply for the AEF. Unhappy with the decision, but with characteristic drive, Harbord threw himself into the work of turning the SOS into an effective organization. After the war was over, he was once again assigned to be Chief of Staff of the AEF. Harbord later commanded the 2nd Division again but now composed only of Army soldiers at Fort Sam Houston, Texas.[13] He is buried in Arlington National Cemetery.

Francis Joseph Kernan (19 October 1859– 3 February 1945)

Considered by many to be one of the ablest generals in the U.S. Army, James Harbord proved his worth both as the AEF's Chief of Staff and as a combat leader during the German Summer Offensives. As the Commander of the Services of Supply, he faced a rigorous test of his ability to manage the 600,000-man logistics force (Library of Congress).

Kernan was born in Jacksonville, Florida. He graduated from West Point eighteenth out of a class of 53 cadets in 1881 and was commissioned as an infantry 2nd lieutenant.[14] His first assignment was to the 21st Infantry Regiment. Kernan later served on the staff of General Arthur MacArthur in the Philippines in 1898 and as General MacArthur's aide from 1900 to 1903. During his time on the Army General Staff, Kernan was considered "one of the keenest and best men the General Staff ever had."[15] He was serving as the Commander of the 8th Infantry Brigade stationed in El Paso, Texas, when the U.S. declared war in April 1917. He was selected to command the 31st Division undergoing training at Camp Wheeler. By late 1917, Kernan had been relieved from commanding the 31st and was sent to France for a new

The simple headstone in Arlington National Cemetery for Major General Kernan, the original commander of the Services of Supply. Kernan served in the Army for 41 of his 86 years (courtesy Alison Hutton).

assignment. The new job was a tough one: organizing and commanding the Lines of Communication which in turn became the Services of Supply.[16] War Department politics led to Pershing replacing Kernan with General Harbord.

After the war, Kernan returned one last time to the Philippines, this time as the Commander of the Department of the Philippines. He retired from the Army in 1922 after 41 years of service. He is buried in Arlington National Cemetery. Kernan had four children, a daughter and three sons. Two of them became medical doctors and the other two became Army officers.[17]

Brehon Burke Somervell (9 May 1892– 13 February 1955)

Somervell was born in Little Rock, Arkansas, and attended the United States Military Academy, graduating near the top of his class in 1914.[18] He was commissioned in the Army Corps of Engineers and served under Pershing during the 1916 Punitive Expedition against Pancho Villa. In July 1917, Somervell deployed to France with the 15th Engineers, a railway construction regiment, the first such unit to join the AEF. The 15th Engineers built ammo dumps as well as depots and regulating stations for the SOS. Somervell quickly became known as a demanding officer who drove his units hard but always got the job done. This reputation for singlemindedness followed him throughout his career. He was reassigned to the 89th Division and stayed with them for the duration of the war and into the occupation. When the 89th returned to the States, Somervell remained with American Forces in Germany as the Assistant Chief of Staff,

After serving in the SOS in the AEF and then as the Chief of Staff for logistics in the U.S. Army of Occupation in Germany, Brehon Somervell was the obvious choice to command the Army Service Forces in World War II (U.S. Army).

G-4, in charge of supply. While in Coblenz, he met Anna Purnell who was serving as a YMCA volunteer. The two were married in August 1919 and had three children together, all daughters.

Returning to the States, Somervell rose steadily through the ranks. As the Depression deepened, he was appointed head of the Works Project Administration in New York City and was responsible for the construction of LaGuardia Airport. Appointed to lead the Construction Division of the Quartermaster Corps in 1941, Somervell took charge of the construction of the camps being built to house the draftees who were now pouring into the Army. He was responsible for building the Pentagon, one of the most recognizable buildings in the world. He also commanded the Army Service Forces, the World War II worldwide equivalent of the SOS. In his 1955 obituary, the *Washington Post* called him "one of the ablest officers the United States Army has produced." The Army's Combined Arms Support Command (CASCOM) Headquarters building at Fort Lee, Virginia, was named for him and when the new Army Logistics University was finished, the campus was dedicated in his honor.[19]

9

Unique Events and the Problem with Prisons

I seen all I wanted to see of France.[1]

It's probably safe to say that every military force has had unexpected or unusual episodes that fail to fit the mold of the rigidly disciplined ethos most people expect. This is due to the human nature of these forces that, when viewed as large formations appear to be similar in every way, yet in fact are uniquely individual. This chapter presents some stories of the Services of Supply people, places and events that do break the mold. While some may be hard to believe, it is that anomaly or absurdity that makes them so interesting. Equally thought-provoking is the story of the AEF prison system, run by Doughboys, for Doughboys. It is quite possibly the most distasteful aspect of the AEF in France we have ever come across—and that's really saying something in a chapter that includes discussion on the systemic racism in the U.S. Army of the period.

The True First AEF Fatalities

It is widely held the first American soldiers killed in action in France during World War I were Corporal James Gresham and Privates Thomas Enright and Merle Hay, members of Company F, 16th Infantry Regiment, 1st Division. They were caught in a trench raid in the early morning hours of 3 November 1917. These men were indeed the first *infantrymen* killed in action, but the first American soldiers to be killed in action in France were Lt. William Fitzsimmons and Privates Rudolph Rubino, Jr., Oscar C. Tugo and Leslie G. Woods, members of Base Hospital 5 who were killed during a German air raid on the hospital at Dennes-Camiers on 4 September 1917, two months before the 1st Division soldiers were killed.

Major Roger I. Lee, a surgeon assigned to Base Hospital 5, provided an eyewitness account of the raid. It is worth quoting in its entirety as it provides a detailed description of these first fatalities and shows the danger which even those behind the lines occasionally confronted. Lee had been away from the hospital and had returned at 10:30 p.m. on 4 September 1917. According to Lee:

> Shortly after our arrival the lights flashed. Just before we heard two reports from Etaples (no casualties). Then search lights played the sky. Then the hum of the aeroplane. Then a report near No. 18 and then hissing and reports, four in all, and sparks and whistling in our midst followed by groans and shrieks. Of course no lights. Rushing about in the dark we found FitzSimmons blown to bits and charred, [Pvt. Charles D.] Whidden, Smith and McGuire wounded. Hurry call, all sent to the operating room. ... Result, five hits in the hospital, all in a line, two just behind the latrine, killing FitzSimmons, wounding McGuire, Smith, and Whidden. The latrine saved the others and the tents not sheltered by the latrine were peppered. FitzSimmons' tent perforated 20 or 30 times. ... The officers' tents of No. 22 peppered but no casualties. One remarkable thing was that Sergt. [Frederick F.] Steffins' tent was riddled but he in bed was untouched. Two direct hits on [tent] C.5, one direct hit on the reception tent killing Woods and Rubino, and scattering and making holes in the laboratory. Tugo also killed. [Pvt. Aubrey S.] McLeod had an injured foot which had

As noted on the bottom, Private Oscar C. Tugo's portrait was "taken somewhere in France." Tugo was among the very first American soldiers to be killed in action (courtesy Center for the History of Medicine: OnView).

Indicative of the manpower shortage in the SOS, this unique photograph of Doughboys and their German POW laborers was taken inside a supply warehouse. They are apparently under the supervision of the U.S. officer (front row, third from left) wearing a "Sam Browne" belt (private collection).

to be amputated. One [British] patient in C.6 lost an eye and has perforated wound of chest.... One hell of a night.[2]

In addition to the four men killed, there were 33 others wounded at the hospital in this raid. FitzSimmons, Rubino, Tugo and Woods were buried with full military honors two days later.

The Problem with POWs

One idea that did not always work as planned was the employment of German prisoners of war (POWs) as laborers. While some Allied facilities grew to depend on POW labor, there were problems. Hagood noted that among the prisoners were a good number of soldiers who "spoke English and had been to the States. These soon got on easy terms with American recruit sentinels and gave it out to the others that the Americans were 'easy-marks.'"[3] Taking advantage of the perception that Americans were soft or easy going, some prisoners even went as far as going on strike in March 1918 and had to be forced back to work by French soldiers. A U.S. officer told Hagood that among the prisoners in one work group was a young man who had been a clerk in his Baltimore grocery store.[4] Though it was apparent that the German POWs preferred working for the U.S. Army than the French or British, that feeling was not always mutual. The average soldier serving in the AEF would concede that the Germans were pretty good fighters. However, that said, there remained a belief among many of them that the Germans were barbarians of the worst sort, and no act was too foul for them to commit. Max Brakebill, the 40th Division artilleryman from California who was transferred to the SOS to serve as a military policeman, wrote home after an encounter with German prisoners:

> There are lots of Dutch [German] prisoners here in a prison camp. I hate those savages. The US feeds em too good. They are surely loyal to the Kaiser and the "fake" fatherland. I went down to draw our rations yesterday and we were getting these very large Bermuda onions. I asked a German if he had such large onions in Germany and he replied "No not so large but much better etc." I told him he was wrong. One also said that the Elgin watches were no good. Said that German made watches were the best. They are only ignorant. Suppose they have had that stuff instilled in their heads so long that it is impossible for them to think otherwise.[5]

In a similar vein, Robert Koehn, a soldier from Elyria, Ohio, wrote his mother, "The only way is to wipe them in good shape an learn the Kaiser a lesson that he cant lick the hole world." By mid–1918, Koehn did not think very highly of the French either, as he explained to his mother "don't like these French girls very much an it is an awfull Smell to this country[,] don't see how the people stand it."[6]

The General Purchasing Board

General Pershing was able to secure the services of a number of professional businessmen to assist in acquisition, production and distribution of badly needed resources. Everything the Army needed was reviewed and where possible procured from local sources then turned over to the SOS for distribution and management. This included such items as lumber, medicine, fresh vegetables, boots and draft animals. The key to the operation was the selection of Charles Dawes to run the General Purchasing Board. At the time, Dawes was serving as a lieutenant colonel in a Railway Engineer unit. On assignment to the Board, his first mission was to establish his hands-on style of leadership. Although the board was nominally under the oversight of the SOS, it was a fairly independent entity and while bound by very few restrictions it was responsible "for all of the purchasing departments of [the AEF], including also the Red Cross and the Army Y.M.C.A."[7] Dawes later wrote, Pershing gave him

> practically unlimited discretion and authority to go ahead and devise a system of coordination and purchases; …to use any method which may seem wise … to secure supplies for the army in Europe which … will relieve our American transports in their enormous burden."[8]

9. Unique Events and the Problem with Prisons

As the St. Mihiel and Meuse-Argonne offensives proceeded, the requirement for supplies of all types grew even larger. This photograph was taken at one of the large supply points near a railhead and designated for vehicle tires. Of note here are the many varied uniforms, rubber boots, coats and hats of the soldiers and their POW coworkers (private collection).

Dawes, a lawyer and close friend of General Pershing for several years, thus had authority much greater than his rank would indicate. With his staff and the Purchasing Board members, Dawes scoured Europe for supplies for the AEF. He reported,

> The British have provided us 100,000 suits of uniform clothing and we have on order from them, 100,000 coats and 200,000 pairs of trousers, which have not yet been delivered. We have also requested them to supply us with other articles of clothing as follows: 3,000,000 pairs of regulation ankle-type boots; 3,000,000 pairs woolen drawers; 1,500,000 woolen vests; 1,500,000 pairs woolen leggings; 6,000,000 pairs heavy weight woolen stockings; 6,000,000 pairs light weight woolen stockings; 1,800,000 pairs of tartan drab mixture No. 5 trousers; 1,440,000 tunics, same material as trousers; No. 5, 60,000 yards cloth for manufacture of caps; 1,500,000 olive-drab flannel shirts....[9]

He also wrote:

> We have purchased in France 1,007 pairs of rubber boots, exhausting the market ... have purchased in England 800,000 pairs of woolen puttees, of which 200,000 have been delivered. We ... have purchased 540,128 woolen gloves and gauntlets in France, all have been delivered and are mostly worn out.
> We have purchased 100,000 pairs of field shoes from the British and have borrowed 100,000 pairs from the French. Request has been made on England for 800,000 pairs Rumanian shoes, but confirmation has not been received.
> We have purchased 200,000 uniform blankets from Spain, of which about

45,000 have been delivered. Five hundred thousand blankets were purchased in England; all have been delivered.[10]

Among the many other missions Dawes undertook, the procurement of labor to support the SOS and the AEF was a top priority. He later wrote that "Pershing has placed upon me the responsibility of procuring labor for the work of the A.E.F., which will require in the aggregate of 100,000 men, 50,000 of whom are needed now."[11] To a great degree, Dawes was successful in this effort. In April 1918 he received confirmation from the War Department that they would send him 400 officers (captains and lieutenants) and three thousand NCOs to manage the labor force he was contracting.[12] By the end of August he was able to report that he had more than 45,000 workers contracted to support the AEF, including 8,000 German POWs and nearly 7,000 British ladies of the Woman's Army Auxiliary Corps (WAAC, later QMAAC). He also noted that despite the restrictions by Spain, Italy, and Portugal against him recruiting laborers, his workforce consisted of "Spanish, Italian, Chinese, Indo-Chinese, Portuguese, French, Senegalese, Cabyles [more commonly Kabyles or North African Berbers], Moroccans, Tunisians."[13]

The Garden Service

One of the most important duties of the Quartermaster Corps (QMC) is provision of food for the troops. Soldiers fight harder and work better when they are fed. They are more productive when they are healthy, and a big part of being healthy is eating healthy food. The QMC recognized the need to provide soldiers a well-rounded diet with a key ingredient being fresh vegetables. Of course, it would be better to obtain vegetables fresh in France rather than shipping processed or frozen vegetables to France from the United States. French vegetable production had declined since the beginning of the war. The supply of fertilizer ingredients, normally imported from Germany, had been cut off; almost half the French male farm workers had been mobilized, and the government had requisitioned many farm draft animals. In addition, factories that previously had produced farm implements had turned their production to weapons and munitions.[14] This meant there were large tracts of farmland currently not in use. It made sense to use this land, with the help of "unoccupied troops and men unfitted for strictly military service" to ease the general food shortage.[15] In addition, the British and French armies had operated gardens behind the lines, producing vegetables to augment their soldiers' rations. Many of these now-abandoned gardens were in areas that were allocated to the Americans. Using these gardens would prevent previous work from going to waste and gave the AEF a head start on their own gardening program. On 25 February 1918, after detailed study and analysis, General Headquarters, AEF, issued General Order No. 34 establishing the Garden Service as part of the Quartermaster Corps. Thus, some soldiers became gardeners. As the official QMC report suggests: "never before, while operating in the field against an enemy had the Army been called upon to engage in the systematic cultivation of truck gardens on the scale required in the A.E.F. This was truly an innovation in warfare in a foreign country."[16]

Garden activities extended beyond simple planting, weeding and harvesting. The Garden Service Technical Headquarters at Versailles handled the procurement and distribution of seeds, seedlings and farm tools. With the assistance of the French, the Garden Service in 1918 distributed 15,000 cabbage and onion seeds and seedlings to its many small gardens. The initial workforce at Versailles consisted of "150 men, physically disqualified for combat duty."[17] The soldier-gardeners had to contend with poor soil and a severe drought. They studied French agricultural methods and experimented with dry-farming methods. The soldiers were aided in their agricultural efforts by a group of American women who arrived in France in June 1918 to assist in general rehabilitation efforts for devastated areas of France. Their employment alongside the soldiers was deemed successful:

> The devotion displayed by the American women to the work in hand, coupled with the spirit which they aroused in the men as fellow workers, was invaluable in the development of morale, always so vitally essential to the ultimate success of a new enterprise.[18]

A brief survey of the records of some of the Garden Service men confirms that many served in combat units before their transfer to the Garden Service. Some men, such as John H. Matterness of North Lebanon, Pennsylvania, were very well traveled. Drafted in September 1917, Matterness was, at various times, assigned to the 154th Depot Brigade, the 316th Infantry Regiment, the 864th Aero Squadron, the 221st Aero Squadron, the 344th Field Artillery Regiment, and Camp Hospital #29 before being assigned to Garden Service Company #4 in December 1918.[19]

It is likely some men were assigned to the Garden Service much later in their service period. Many, no doubt, were previously wounded soldiers. As an added benefit resulting from the cultivation of crops, "healthful exercise in the fields, natural environment, and careful medical attention accelerated the recuperation of men employed on Garden Service work."[20]

Most of the Garden Service men returned home in detachments from February through July 1919 after having performed an unusual and thankless job behind the lines. They earned no medals for bravery in the garden, no accolades for producing the most cucumbers, and no wound chevrons for pitchfork blisters. But there's no doubt those soldiers who were able to enjoy some fresh vegetables appreciated the gardeners' efforts.

Pershing Sees Everything (April 1918)

In his published diary about his experiences in the war, Charles Dawes freely admitted that his attention to detail when it came to military protocol was somewhat lacking. While recounting the ability of his friend, General Pershing, to be able to focus on both great and small details concurrently, Dawes wrote that his "own somewhat pronounced indifference to certain military conventions, born as often as not of ignorance as of intention,—though not always,—is a matter at times of some embarrassment to [General Pershing]." As evidence, Dawes recounted an episode where Pershing and General Harbord were standing on the other side of a road saying goodbye to French Field Marshal Foch. Dawes noticed that, despite the crowd of officers around him and the distant gunfire, Pershing was staring directly across the road at him. Dawes began to review the recent events and wondered if he had made a mistake or failed in some manner but could not bring any particular action to mind. He noticed Pershing talking to Harbord who then walked across the street to where Dawes was standing. Harbord stood in front of Dawes and buttoned up his overcoat for him, saying, "This is a hell of a job for the Chief of Staff—but the General made me do it."[21]

Coffee Blenders Detachments?

The French *Poilu* had his *pinard*, the British Tommy had his tea, and the Doughboy had his coffee. To supply American soldiers with this staple, the QMC opted to procure coffee locally. This had the obvious advantage of saving precious space on transports. So voracious was the AEF's appetite for coffee that the QMC "bought 16,000,000 pounds of coffee, practically the entire European supply at that time [that is, prior to autumn, 1918]."[22] This European coffee was green; to roast this coffee, the QMC established Coffee Roasting Plant No. 1 at Corbeil-Essonnes, near Paris. During the height of its operation, it "was the largest coffee roasting and grinding plant in Europe, with an initial capacity of 500,000 rations a day which had been increased to a million and a half rations a day when the Armistice was signed."[23] In addition to the plant at Corbeil-Essonnes, the QMC constructed plants at Bordeaux and Le Havre. To construct these plants, the QMC studied the latest developments in the processes and machinery involved in roasting and grinding coffee.

American soldiers were needed to run these plants, and the War Department was quick to find them. There were two Coffee Blenders detachments dispatched to France. The first, Coffee Blenders Detachment, QMC, sailed from Hoboken, New Jersey, aboard the USS *Great Northern* on 31 August 1918. This detachment consisted of one sergeant first class, one corporal, three privates first class, and 34 privates. The second detachment, incongruously called the First Coffee Blenders Detachment, sailed from New York Harbor aboard the *Empress of Britain* on 13 November 1918. This detachment consisted of one officer, 15 sergeants, and 63 privates.[24] Other men were transferred into the detachment in France.

Some of the men in the Coffee Blenders Detachment had prior coffee roasting or wholesale experience. Private (later sergeant) Walter W. Biedermann was the manager of Biederman Brothers Wholesale Tea and Coffee in Chicago; Private (later sergeant) Frank H. Goldhardt was a coffee broker for Sprague and Rhodes of New York; and 1st Lieutenant Frank L. Cheek was among the managers of the Cheek-Neal Coffee Company in Nashville, Tennessee. At least seven other men also had previous coffee experience.[25] The SOS also employed French civilians to work in the plants and warehouses.

The system followed at Corbeil-Essonnes was like the systems followed at the other plants. "The Essonnes plant consisted of storage rooms for green coffee and testing, roasting, grinding, packing, and power rooms."[26] The coffee was roasted and ground and then placed in "an air and waterproof interlining of paper" and then in double bags of burlap and cotton.[27] Coffee left the plant in waterproof 50-pound packages. From the packing rooms, the coffee was loaded aboard trucks or wagons for transport to the railhead. Each railcar bore a load of about 20,000 pounds of coffee. The coffee then made its way through supply channels until some of it reached the front lines.

Fortunately for the Doughboys, the Army recognized the importance of good coffee:

> The testing of the coffee was an important step in the process, for our soldier is particular about the quality of his coffee, more so than the soldier of any other army. With the establishment of these new coffee-roasting plants his taste was studied with fine discrimination.... So the job of the coffee tester under this system was one of responsibility. Officers and men were chosen for this duty who had long experience in it in the United States.[28]

So What Do You Do with Cavalry in a Trench War?

Many of the senior AEF officers were former cavalrymen, so it is no surprise that among the units they requested for service in France were cavalry regiments. During the Mexican Border campaign, the cavalry had proven their worth but the war in France was a different animal altogether. Unfortunately for the soldiers and officers of the cavalry, there was little or no use for them in the front lines. So what does an army do with such men? It assigns them to other duties. For a period of time some elements of the 2nd, 3rd, 6th, and 15th Cavalry were assigned to the SOS.[29] Similar to the 5th Marine Brigade, the men assigned to these units were used for everything from serving as escort detachments for senior officers to mail guards and provost marshal's patrols. A number of the troopers and officers of the 3rd Cavalry Regiment were assigned to staff and support jobs in the SOS Headquarters at Tours while the rest of their comrades were assigned to work in the remount squadrons.[30] This was certainly not what they had envisioned but, like many in the SOS, they made the best of their revised missions.

In this French-made portrait, a trooper from E Troop, 3rd Cavalry Regiment, has chosen to pose while wearing his helmet. Serving in a war of trenches, U.S. cavalry units found themselves employed as military police, escorts and honor guards (private collection).

Harbord Fixes a Broken Staff (July 1918)

For his personal staff, Harbord brought many of the soldiers and Marines who had worked for him during his command of the 2nd

Division. What he had no control over, or at least not right away, was the SOS staff he inherited from General Kernan. After just a few hours on the job, he realized that most of the officers were competent at their job, but he faced a different problem. He "was at once struck by the fact that the officers of the various departments of the staff seemed to see little of each other and were conducting business largely by correspondence even when in the same building."[31]

Without hesitation, Harbord set out to change that. He established a series of luncheons on alternating Sundays and invited all department heads to attend. If they were elsewhere, they were required to send their deputies. He made sure the cooks laid on a good meal and served good wine. Very quickly, the luncheons became popular events, and Harbord noticed that many issues or problems that had in the past taken days and excessive written correspondence to resolve were now solved during the course of the meals. He also made sure that any senior officers visiting on the days of the gatherings were also invited so they could personally meet his staff.

There Are Many Ways to Die in a War Zone

The world of the early 20th century was a dangerous place. Even after the Armistice had been signed, France, in particular, was a hazardous place where many soldiers died. While the remnants of the Spanish flu were still adding to its deadly toll, other soldiers were killed simply for being in the wrong place at the wrong time. In one notable May 1919 incident, Lieutenant Hugo Fales, the American officer in charge of the Carnot Motor Transport Park, was working at his desk when an explosive artillery shell was being tested nearby by some French soldiers. The shell exploded prematurely and a "piece about the size of the palm of a hand" blew through the wooden wall of the building where the lieutenant was working and into his buttock. Fales was quickly placed in a car and driven to the local infirmary which further evacuated him to Camp Hospital Number 68. His men commented on his coolness and demeanor, saying that "as he lay upon the stretcher before the operation, the lieutenant quietly smoked a cigarette." The doctors at the hospital removed the shell fragment but the officer died shortly thereafter.[32] Ironically, Fales, from Belding, Michigan, had served in the front lines as a member of the French Ambulance Service before he enlisted in the U.S. Army. Another SOS soldier, this time an NCO, Sergeant Ulmont Crumley, was killed in Tours on 9 May 1919 when he attempted to board a trolley car. The New Kensington, Pennsylvania, native assigned to the Delousing and Bath Unit

Number 2 was killed when he lost his grip and slipped between the cars. The footboard of the second car hit him in the head and he died on the scene. Crumley's father later received his son's Pennsylvania war service compensation of $200.[33]

Even experienced soldiers were not safe. The 9th Infantry Regiment Newspaper, *The 9th Infantry "Cootie,"* reported in April 1919 that 1st Sergeant Frank Styert, formerly of Company F, had "died suddenly of acute indigestion." It further reported that "Sergeant Styert was an old army man having entered the Service at the beginning of the Spanish American War."[34] Styert had been in the 9th Infantry Regiment for 13 years and served in the Cuban campaign, the Philippine insurrection as well as at Château-Thierry and the Soissons offensive.

Private George Kennard, a soldier from the Educational Department of the Central Records Office, avoided being killed but came awfully close. He was on leave and bicycling with another soldier in the mountains near Menton, France. As they were descending one hill, Kennard's bicycle skidded and he was sent flying over the side of a cliff, fracturing his skull and breaking his shoulder. It was reported that for a while "he was out of his mind, talked at random, and failed to recognize even his closest friends."[35] Fortunately, Kennard recovered from his injuries and later was able to return to work.

Racism in the U.S. Army and the Services of Supply

It is estimated that some 160,000 men, almost a third of the soldiers assigned to the SOS, were African Americans.[36] A review of First World War manuscripts quickly reveals the confusing aspects of race relations in the U.S. military at that time. The AEF was truly an integrated force— unless you were an African American or dark-skinned immigrant from an African or Caribbean country. Even a cursory glance at the unit rosters of many units shows the strong presence of Hispanic, Asian, Eurasian and Native Americans in the ranks. There was no shortage of Jewish, Greek Orthodox, Russian Orthodox, House of David, and even Muslim soldiers serving in the same units of the U.S. Army. In May 1917, a regiment known as the Porto Rico Provisional Regiment of Infantry was deployed to the Panama Canal Zone to protect the waterway passage between the Atlantic and the Pacific oceans. During the war, more than 13,000 soldiers, mostly from Puerto Rico, were trained at the U.S. Army base of Las Casas.[37]

It was only African American soldiers who were excluded from most Army and Marine combat units. This meant, with the exceptions of the two combat divisions (the 92nd and 93rd), the pre-war "Colored" regiments (9th and 10th Cavalry Regiments, and 24th and 25th Infantry Regiments), and 16 pioneer infantry regiments, black soldiers were effectively restricted to serving in segregated Army support units.

Depending on which aspect of unit accomplishment or specific quote is used, two of the more famous SOS leaders, Harbord and Hagood, appear to be either the strongest supporters of black troops or their biggest critics. On one hand, Harbord is reviled for insisting on keeping the black SOS soldiers segregated from their white counterparts and from the French population but is praised for attempting to get the Army to approve a special award for "black [men] from the Southern swamps who put in many a thirty-six hour stretch at a backbreaking job."[38] Harbord was also perceptive enough to notice that black stevedores in the ports did not appear receptive to, or even slightly inspired by, General Pershing's personal appeal to them to work harder and faster unloading ships. Pershing had made a point of telling the SOS soldiers that good workers would be given a chance to go to the front lines and fight. And since the black and white stevedores were the critical element of increasing the flow of supplies, Harbord knew he needed a different approach. Among his ideas was the "Race to Berlin," described earlier as means to invite competition between the ports in unloading and transporting cargo. He took that competition to the obvious conclusion and wrote: "We commercialized homesickness perhaps for the first time in the history of armies."[39] If being offered a chance

A Doughboy assigned to a butchery company, Angelo Zammuto was born in Aragona, Italy, and was working in a meat market in Rockford, Illinois, when he was inducted into the Army. In this French-made portrait from the Paravisini Studio in Marseilles, Zammuto affects a very confident pose and has added an officer's quartermaster device to his hat (private collection).

to fight did not inspire the stevedores, the opportunity to be the first stevedore unit to return home after the war certainly did. Less than two months after the competition started, the Armistice was signed. Harbord was a man of his word, and appreciative of the large jump in productivity; the winning unit received passage on one of the first Stateside-bound vessels.

Johnson Hagood, the SOS Chief of Staff, evidenced similar pragmatism. While he complained that during visits to the worksites he often found

> ninety percent of the negro hands resting. In the warehouses and on the wharves gangs of several hundred negroes would be sitting down waiting for some job that was not quite ready for them, and in one warehouse I noticed fifteen or twenty lying around asleep.[40]

In spite of the bad impression he received from these sights, Hagood was smart enough to realize that the men were not being properly led. This realization matched completely the claim of many of the supporters of the black soldiers: by limiting the ranks to which they could aspire, there was no incentive for the black soldiers to work harder or show leadership.

Other U.S. Army leaders were not so favorably inclined. General William W. Atterbury, although at first a supporter of African American troops, became discouraged by what appeared to be a general unwillingness to work. He wrote that a

> number of these negroes are so lazy that they perform very little work.... Fining them and putting them in the guardhouse is very little punishment to them, and to be dishonorably discharged and sent home is just what they desire.[41]

In response to claims like this, Pershing's inspector general, Colonel H.K. Taylor, believed the entire Army manpower system was at fault because the black soldiers "had been recruited in haste, sent abroad with little training and there put to work without any further training or discipline."[42] It was a no-win situation for everyone. An army so starved for manpower that thousands of POWs had to be employed could little afford to divert NCOs from their jobs to provide better training or supervision for the soldiers in the service battalions, white or black. And because the men in these units needed exactly that training and supervision, the results were predictable. Fortunately for the war effort, Harbord was given the freedom to use such tactics as the "Race to Berlin" to provide suitable motivation for the soldiers.

Ultimately, the men assigned to the labor battalions, particularly the African American units, did get the dirty end of the stick. The daily work of being a stevedore was physically demanding and thankless. A worse job still, battlefield recovery of bodies was not only disheartening, it was also potentially dangerous because unexploded bombs, shells and grenades littered the battlefields. Gathering weeks-old corpses was distasteful and certainly not what most had expected to do when they enlisted or were drafted into the Army. Their living conditions were also so poor the YMCA sent "black women workers to the area, hoping that they would be able to improve the men's morale."[43]

Given the state of race relations in the United States during this period, none of these insights comes as much of a surprise. What is surprising, given the circumstances and the less than equal working conditions, was the willingness of many of these men to work as diligently as they did. And while it is true that most combat soldiers in the AEF tended to look down on the soldiers, white or black, of the SOS, it was these same SOS soldiers who worked long hours, sometimes under fire, to get the necessary food, ammunition and fuel delivered forward to the very men who mocked them.

Precision Instrument Repairmen in the SOS: An Occupational Analysis

During wartime, things break. Weapons, equipment, vehicles and engines all wear out or are damaged in combat at an alarming rate. Since it is neither economical nor wise to simply discard any items that could be repaired, there existed a vast army of men whose sole responsibility was to make such repairs. In large repair depots in the United States, in the rear areas of France, and in smaller repair and salvage units closer to the front, these men toiled in unheralded, if not completely unappreciated, anonymity.

Many of the jobs performed by men behind the lines required no special skills, or skills easily learned on the job. Other duties required special skills that were not easily or quickly learned. For these duties, military authorities had to glean qualified men from the draft pools. From the moment of draft registration (when men were required to state their occupation) through induction and classification (where men were again examined and questioned about their occupational skills) the Army collected data on their soldiers. The idea was, of course, to put the right man in the right job. How successful was the Army in using their available manpower efficiently? To get an idea, we can examine five detachments of men with specialized skill who sailed together to or from France in 1918 and 1919. They are identified, per the title of their detachment, as having a specific, skilled military duty in the SOS. The detachments and their composition are as follows.[44]

Surgical Instrument and Typewriter Repair Unit. One officer and 79 enlisted men sailed aboard transport Number 506 on 23 January 1918, from Hoboken, New Jersey, to France. Surgical instruments in 1918 were basically small steel hand tools such as saws, knives, scalpels, scissors, hemostats, clamps, etc. Only a skilled worker could repair, sharpen or fabricate these tools. Typewriters were mechanical devices comprised of hundreds of small parts; they required skill to maintain and repair. Many of the men in this detachment had occupations related precisely to surgical instrument and typewriter repair. Twenty-four men could be identified as doing some form of typewriter repair or assembly (mechanic, inspector, repairman, aligner, foreman, etc.). This variety reflected the duties in a typical typewriter factory or repair shop. The typewriter repairmen had worked for such companies as Royal, Remington and Underwood. Eight men were surgical instrument makers or sellers; related occupations included machinist, bolt maker, polisher/buffer, knife finisher/maker, tool gauge maker, dental supply clerk, mechanic, "mechanical dentist," optician and a worker in orthopedic appliances. Other men were caught in the draft and assigned as needed with previous occupations of candy maker, liquor dealer, tobacco salesman and carpet weaver. Most of these men were destined to be assigned to the Medical Department Repair Shop No. 1 (MDRS 1) at Neuilly, France. The commander of MDRS 1, Captain Henry M. Pilling, owned a surgical instrument manufacturing business in Pennsylvania.

A family member of Sergeant Edward G. Schmid, previously a surgical and dental instrument maker at Penn Surgical and Dental Instrument Company in Philadelphia, Pennsylvania, wrote that Schmid was assigned initially to his place of civilian employment: "He was detailed at the Penn Surgical Instrument Co. plant at 8th and Jefferson Sts, Phila., he being a good mechanic, as the above mentioned firm held government contracts."[45] While in France, Schmid "did various kinds of work for the medical corps, mostly repair work on instruments."[46]

Corporal Edward H. Scheutz also described some of his duties overseas:

> I was on detached service with the French in [their] large Medical Repair Shop at one of there large Forts 2 miles outside of Paris. Length of service with the French 9 months from there transferred to my own company. My line of work with the French = Otomobile [automobile] repair work, and with our company—testing [and] instructing on sterilizer camions [trucks], Laundry Outfit, and Setting of heating plant for mobile Hosp. operating room.[47]

It appears that Scheutz, at least, worked with French troops for a time, and some of his duty included working on sterilizer and laundry vehicles and equipment.

9. Unique Events and the Problem with Prisons 157

As a reflection of their valuable skills and the performance of their duty, most of the men were promoted to NCO rank sometime during the war. Sergeant Clifford W. Powers, a typewriter mechanic at the Royal Typewriter Company in Hartford, Connecticut, reflected on his wartime service by writing that it "is a very fine training for any young man even if it is disagreeable at times. I have had an experience that I would not give up for anything. I am glad that I did what little I could do in this great war."[48]

Sergeant Clifford Powers, a typewriter assembler for the Royal Typewriter Company, from Hartford, Connecticut. Although serving as a typewriter repairman, Powers was a member of the Medical Department Repair Shop No. 1, as reflected in his Medical Corps collar disk (Connecticut Service Records via Ancestry.com).

Detachment of Camera Repairmen. Fourteen men sailed from New York to France aboard the *Ulysses* on 16 August 1918. Most of the men in this detachment worked at civilian jobs that well fitted them for camera repair. Three men worked as assembler, repairman and shutter maker for the Eastman Kodak Company in New York. Related jobs included cameraman, motion picture industry worker, polisher and watchmaker/jeweler. Some of the men were eventually assigned to the U.S. Air Service in various roles including work in one of the photographic sections involved with the nascent aerial photography field. Other men were assigned to Signal Corps photographic units.

Optical Repair School, Ordnance. One officer and 12 enlisted men sailed from New York to France, on 20 October 1918. It's not known exactly what type of work these men were engaged in, but since they were in the Ordnance Corps, they probably repaired optical instruments such as binoculars, telescopes, range finders, and other such items rather than eyeglasses or microscopes. The occupations for the 12 enlisted men are broken down as follows: nine were jewelers/watchmakers, one was an optometrist, one was a shoemaker and one was a typewriter repairman. The nine men listed as jewelers/watchmakers included men identified as working in or operating a jewelry store; at least three of them worked at the Elgin National Watch Company. Watchmakers and jewelers would possess the knowledge and skills involved with the repair of micromechanical devices. The men who worked in the Elgin factory could have been associated with any one of several "watchmaking" activities, from the basic assembly, timing, and adjusting of watches, up to the complete repair of watches. The other three were a shoemaker, typewriter repairman and an optometrist; each of these would be familiar with small mechanical devices and skilled in the use of small tools.

The importance of skilled labor in the Army is reflected in the fact that, of the 12 enlisted men, six men achieved the rank of sergeant, ordnance sergeant, or sergeant first class; two men reached the rank of corporal; three men were privates first class while one man remained a private. All the men appear to have been assigned to various Ordnance Corps repair shops or depots.

Detachment of Surgical Instrument Repair Unit, Sanitary Corps. Nine men sailed aboard the *Empress of Britain* on 13 November 1918 from New York to France. The first thing to notice about this detachment is that it was heading from the United States to France at a time when tens of thousands of troops were preparing to head in the opposite direction. In fact, many men began their trip to the former war zone after the Armistice, including some replacement troops joining the U.S. Third Army as part of the occupying force. Other troops left the United States immediately after the Armistice, and most of them were in medical-related units. This detachment was among that number. The civilian occupations of seven of these men were as follows: chemist, dredging, farm implement salesman, machinist, stenographer, switchboard man and tester. It was impossible to determine the occupation of two of the men. All these men served in MDRS 1. Most of the men would have possessed skills useful in the repair of surgical instruments. Most of these men returned to the U.S. aboard the *Prinz Friedrich Wilhelm* on 14 July 1919 after serving overseas for about eight months.

Headquarters, Band Instrument and Typewriter Repair Detachment. One officer and 32 enlisted men sailed aboard the USS *Louisville* from Brest, France, to Hoboken, New Jersey, on 28 June 1919. Most of these returning soldiers had been assigned to various Quartermaster Mechanical Repair Shops and Medical Repair Depots. As the detachments already described, most of the men had civilian occupations somewhat related to their military duties. Nine men worked as typewriter mechanics, aligners or assemblers, mostly in Royal and Underwood typewriter factories. Other occupations related to precision repair duties include cobbler/shoemaker, tailor, watchcase engraver, embroiderer, jeweler and machinist. Other occupations were laborer, cook, clerk, milliner and iron salesman.

Many of these precision instrument repairmen had served in one of six Quartermaster Mechanical Repair Shops, numbered from 301 through 306. The duties of mechanical repair shops must have been diverse; some of them no doubt handled the repair of automotive, or larger, engines, while others must have handled smaller, more delicate machines.

When we consider these men, it is apparent that the War Department, working under dire necessity for speed, was successful in assigning qualified, experienced men to these unheralded, yet important, positions.[49] Even when an exact fit was impossible, some of the men, such as shoemakers or tailors, would at least be familiar with small machinery and the use of small hand tools. The men performed what could be considered thankless and mundane duties in relative safety and comfort. Perhaps many men felt as Corporal Herbert W. Morrow did. Morrow, an aligner with the Royal Typewriter Company in Hartford, wrote: "I wished to get into the service as soon as possible. Money couldn't buy my experience."[50]

A Quartermaster Officer Sets the Record Straight (17 January 1919)

The mid–January issue of the *Stars & Stripes* published a pertinent letter entitled simply "S.O.S." and written by "Q.M.Officer." The quartermaster officer wrote about the recent experience of being in the presence of a group of aviators who sang "Mother, Pull Down Your Service Flag, Your Son's in the S.O.S.," the popular song meant to mock the soldiers of the SOS for their safe and cushy jobs. When the quartermaster officer asked the air service officers how much action that had seen, their reply was that they had arrived in October and made no flights over the front before the fighting ended.

At this point the letter-writing quartermaster reveals to the reader that until 29 October 1918, he had been a line officer in the 3rd Division with significant combat time. He had only recently transferred to the Quartermaster Corps as a promotion. He also reveals that he had seen quartermaster soldiers in action providing food and supplies to the infantrymen of the division and that many of them became casualties from this duty. As he had seen both sides of the coin, it was his opinion that those officers that make the most fun of the SOS "were combatant officers who never saw front line service."[51]

Pershing's "First Fifty" Meet the Boss (4 March 1919)

Among the soldiers to be reviewed at Tours by General Pershing were women from the first 50 U.S. military females assigned to the SOS. Given two days' warning before the visit, the SOS units in Tours received instruction from their commanders on the importance of being properly uniformed for the review. Having just passed the six month requirement to earn their first overseas stripe, the women from the Quartermaster Corps made sure the golden chevrons were properly affixed to their left sleeves.

Just prior to the arrival of the AEF Commander, all of the designated units assembled. In the formation were 35 of the women of the Quartermaster Corps, the men assigned to the headquarters signal and ordnance units and a large number of the British WAACs. As was so often the case for Pershing's visits to the AEF, the French weather refused to cooperate and the soldiers waited in a driving rain for their commander to appear. He didn't disappoint. Despite the elements, Pershing climbed up on a table and spoke to the large formation, saying:

> Now that the time has come for demobilization I felt that I must visit you and express to you for myself and in the name of the American Expeditionary Forces and the entire American people, the gratitude we feel for the great service you have rendered toward bringing the war to a successful issue.

Pershing promised them as quick a return to the United States as possible but reminded them that "a few of you will remain here some time." At these words, an enlisted soldier in the farthest outer rank let out a loud and clearly audible groan. As the laughter subsided, Pershing looked at one of the nearby quartermaster female soldiers and said, "I did not mean that to be a joke." He then continued to speak:

> You justly may be proud that you are a part of the greatest Army of modern times and you will carry home with you and keep with you always, a feeling of deep thankfulness that because of your work the war was more quickly won.[52]

Aware of the large number of female soldiers in the formation, Pershing also spoke of the great service and sacrifice performed by women in the Army. He closed by saying, "Much will be expected of you and you will be able to give much through close contact and intimate acquaintance with the true American manhood as service over here has brought it out." As he dismounted from the table to return to his waiting automobile, several women offered their hands to assist him. Ever the gentleman, Pershing gave them each a firm handshake and then, with a rare smile, said, "Well, this is nice."

The Quartermaster Corps women were not the only American females in the SOS. In September of 1918 another 50 women, this time from the Ordnance Corps, were sent to France to serve as stenographers. The request for this group originated from General J.H. Rice, head of the Engineering Department of the Ordnance Corps. Shipping out to France with little notice, the women were not issued uniforms and initially performed their jobs in civilian clothes, making them "the only feminine soldiers in France not in uniform."[53] Eventually they equipped themselves with Ordnance Corps armbands and purchased outfits similar to the uniforms worn by nurses to give themselves a standardized and military look.

The Supply Operation at Gièvres Impresses the AEF Commander (August 1918)

General Pershing was a notoriously hard man to please and certainly earned his reputation as a stickler for details. During a visit to the enormous supply and storage depot at Gièvres with General Harbord, Pershing admitted his admiration for the work being done. Both he and Harbord later mentioned the episode when

> a telegram was received [at Gièvres] one morning at 8:15 ordering exactly 4,596 tons of supplies ... 1,250,000 cans of tomatoes; 1,000,000 pounds of sugar; 600,000 cans of corned beef; 750,000 pounds of canned hash; and 150,000 pound of dried beans. By 6:15 that evening, this demand had been filled and 457 freight cars were loaded with it and on their way to the advance depot at Is-sur-Tille.[54]

It was an astonishing performance and one that, no doubt, could not be replicated today in any of the U.S. military components.

An SOS Sergeant Major Speaks His Mind on Alcohol

One of the hot topics for debate in the AEF after the war ended was the impending enactment of prohibition laws in the United States. While most of the Doughboys had enjoyed easy access to alcoholic drinks in France, some, known as "Drys," believed the world would be a better place without the curse of alcohol. One of these stalwarts was an SOS NCO who wrote to the Central Records Office newspaper *The CRO* in response to a letter that defended beer drinking as a lesser evil than consuming whiskey, rum or other strong liquors. Sergeant Major Fischer wrote that he felt an obligation to "defend the manhood of this army by replying to the article." The sergeant major went on to write that beer … is the curse of all mankind. It is the root of all evil. What good has it ever done? You will say, in fact the only thing you can say is that it satisfies a thirst. Does it? It gives you a craving for more. Water will satisfy the thirst, costs less, is a great medicine and has not the evil effect beer has.

By this point Fischer was really warming to his subject and declared, "Beer, that has filled the penitentiaries; Beer, that has destroyed nations; Beer, that has wrecked homes; Beer, that has undermined health; Beer, that has spoiled wealth; Beer, that has ruined young girls." The sergeant major continued in this vein for a number of more sentences before he switched over to giving examples of "dry" cities that have improved since they enacted their own prohibition laws. These cities included Seattle, Boise, and the automobile capital of the world, Detroit. According to Fischer, all of these cities had a marked improvement in productivity and decrease in crime due to their forsaking alcohol. Finally, he tied his argument together with a statement that "German Propaganda is no worse than the liquor curse." In conclusion, he wrote he had no doubt that most of the men of the AEF believed as he did and if a vote were taken "the drys would win by so great a majority that the opponents would be ashamed to have the vote counted."[55]

Based on his strong feelings, it's probably a good thing that the sergeant major was not assigned to the Third Army for the occupation of Germany. While restricted from drinking hard liquor, the Doughboys of that force quickly learned to enjoy the fine beers and wines produced in the Rhineland. By the fall of 1919, most of the combat divisions had left Germany to be replaced by the American Forces in Germany (AFG). One of the inducements for re-enlisting for AFG service was the easy availability of alcoholic beverages; drinks that were now denied to their stateside comrades by the Prohibition Act.

The Forestry Service Takes Care of Its Own

Knowing that the end of the war would lead to rapid demobilization and with so many of the nation's lumber and forestry workers drafted and serving in France, the American Forestry Association decided to get in front of the problem. The Association, located in Washington, D.C., set up a fund with $52,000 to help demobilized soldiers find suitable jobs. To begin the process, the Forestry Section of the SOS was provided with blank job application forms to hand out to forestry unit members. After completion, the forms were endorsed by the unit commander as to each man's abilities and returned to the Forestry Association.

On return to the United States, the men selected from the applications would be placed with appropriate companies throughout the country. Any

9. Unique Events and the Problem with Prisons 163

of the funds left over after all the men had been placed would be donated to organizations helping to provide comfort to seriously wounded soldiers.[56]

End of War = Start of New Regulations (December 1918)

At the end of the 20th century, one of the commonly heard sayings in the U.S. military was "War may be hell, but peace is a real bitch." The implication, of course, is that during wartime and combat operations, many peacetime regulations and restrictions are relaxed. There is less emphasis on haircuts or uniform standards and even some misbehavior tolerated or forgiven. With the return of peace, also comes the return of rules and regulations. It was equally true for the Doughboys in the AEF.

Among the more interesting documents of the period was a memorandum dated 16 December 1918 and published in the District of Paris with instructions that it should be "furnished to all male members of the American E.F. now in or arriving in Paris." The memorandum stated that the local Provost Marshal and undercover policemen would report all ranks and civilians who appeared to be frequenting places where there were "prostitutes and women of questionable character." It further stated that any officers thus found would be subject to court-martial and that all others would be subject to disciplinary action. The final paragraph states that "orders have been issued to take summary action against all officers, other ranks, and militarized civilians who fail to salute or to return salutes, who are not in proper uniform and who present a slovenly appearance."[57]

Another indication on the postwar crack down on uniforms and individual appearance was reported in the 21 February 1919 issue of the *Stars & Stripes*. According to the paper, because the soldiers had been decorating their uniforms with "gaudy" and "unlawful riot of color" patches, the stateside port and transit camp staffs could not determine to which units some of the soldiers belonged. Therefore, it was decreed that all soldiers would remove their unit shoulder patches on arrival in the States.[58] One week later, this order was rescinded. All soldiers were allowed to keep their unit shoulder patches unless they were staying on active duty and reporting to a Regular Army unit stationed in the States.[59]

Prisoner of War Escort Duty

One of the most dangerous assignments in the post–Armistice SOS was the duty of escorting the German and Austrian POWs back to their homeland. Making the duty doubly interesting was that only those prisoners who had been born in the areas now occupied by the Allies in the German Rhineland were allowed back there. Those German soldiers who had family in the Allied occupation zones but had not been born there were out of luck. They and all the others were be taken via train to central locations in unoccupied Germany and turned over to the German officials.

In addition to the German POWs, there were a number of Russian soldiers also needing to be escorted across the expanse of unoccupied Germany to the Russian border for release. With unoccupied Germany undergoing a violent struggle between left-wing Bolsheviks and right-wing Nationalists, the business of escorting these prisoners was fraught with danger and unforeseen occurrences.

Another escort mission was drawn by the 114th and 115th Infantry Regiments of the 29th Division. During the war, a large number of Polish citizens had joined the French army, and by war's end,

Assigned to the 319th Butchery Company, Corporal Adam H. Krebs was from New York City and remained in France until September 1919. One question arises from this photograph: why would a soldier in a butchery company be armed with a .45 automatic pistol? The answer may lie in his temporary assignment to a POW escort detachment which required firearms (private collection).

were serving in a fighting force known as "Haller's Army." With Poland's emergence as an independent nation, it was time to transport these troops home and it was doubly important to get them there quickly. Poland was viewed as the eastern barricade needed to prevent the spread of Bolshevism from Russia and was in desperate need of soldiers. The National Guardsmen of the 29th Division served as escorts for some of the trains carrying the Polish soldiers through occupied and unoccupied Germany and into Poland to ensure a safe and nonviolent passage.

In related duty, Lieutenant Colonel C.R.W. Morison of the 115th Infantry Regiment led a detachment of more than a hundred soldiers into Germany to serve as commandant and staff of a Russian POW camp. Here, too, the fear of the Bolshevik army was great, and it was believed that repatriated Russian POWs would immediately join their Red comrades in an attack on Western Europe. This fear led the Allies and the Germans to agree that the Russian camps had to be maintained at least for the foreseeable future until something could be figured out as to what to do with unwanted prisoners. American soldiers from the Third Army, headquartered in Coblenz, also participated in both missions and found them equally challenging and equally dangerous.[60]

The Worst Possible Duty

Of all the difficult jobs performed by the soldiers in the SOS, by far the worst was the requirement to "find, record, and rebury the dead."[61] The tools and equipment available to the soldiers to perform this "graves registration" work were primitive. To the soldiers of the service battalions ordered to do the job, it could also be dangerous. Not only were many of the dead potentially hazardous to handle because of their exposure to mustard and other forms of gas, the areas in which they lay could be filled with mines or unexploded artillery shells. A telltale sign of the institutional racism of the period was assignment of African American labor units for the vast majority of this work.

Bad Advice

Almost every military unit has what are known as "barracks lawyers" who specialize in giving bad advice to those soldiers foolish enough to take it. For some reason, this practice was raised to an art in 1919 and, surprisingly, even published in a Doughboy newspaper. When the 29 March 1919 edition of *The CRO* was published, there was an article about the return

African American soldiers prepare a burial trench at Fere-en-Tardenois in December 1918 for bodies recovered from their earlier, hasty burial sites on the battlefield. Work such as this continued for a long period after the war as bodies were constantly being uncovered (U.S. Army Quartermaster Museum).

to Bourges of two personnel specialists, Sergeant John McKean and Private Frederick Thuee, after three months of occupation duty in Germany. And what advice did the soldiers have for any of their comrades who might go to Germany on work or as a tourist? Simple. "Take plenty of soap and chocolate. If these cannot serve one personally, they can reap a harvest in [Reichs] marks in exchange for them." With the military police in the Third Army still vigorously enforcing "no fraternization" rules which forbade even speaking to a German citizen except in the line of duty, telling your friends to bring lots of black market material to trade for money certainly ranks high on the top 10 of bad advice.[62]

Even the June edition of *The Messkit*, another Doughboy periodical, perpetuated the bad advice by republishing a poem from the 4th Division's periodical *The Skirmisher* which was titled "Third Army Currency." It had such verses as "A little piece of washing soap, No coin is good that you possess, but show them soap and they'll say Yes. Soap! Soap! Soap! ... Fill your pockets full of soap, Then you are fixed with every Hun. And you can have just gobs of fun."

Doughboys Face a Different Kind of Fire (February 1919)

Service in the military, by the very nature of the work, is inherently dangerous. Even when not actively participating in combat operations, soldiers train and work under strenuous conditions and are often exposed to many things, mechanical, chemical or psychological, that can hurt them. This point was driven home in mid–February 1919 when a fire broke out in the Motor Transportation Corps compound near the Bourges train station. The cause was quite simple. A soldier in the barracks shared by the 448th Motor Repair Unit, the 540th Truck Company, the 350th Motor Repair Unit and the local military police detachment was attempting to rekindle a fire using kerosene. The flames jumped from the fireplace to a nearby tarpaper-covered partition and the entire end of the barracks was quickly on fire. Men who had been sleeping in their bunks awoke to find their exit from the blaze was blocked and were forced to leap from the windows. One soldier was able to rescue the personnel records for the troops living in the building by passing them out a ground floor window. Unfortunately, some men lost all of their uniforms, equipment and war souvenirs except for whatever they could grab on their way out of the building.

The fire spread quickly from the barracks to a nearby repair parts storeroom. Along with a number of spare parts destroyed, more than 100 tires in the facility also caught fire and added to the blaze. The Bourges City Fire Department responded quickly to the alarm. Although, as the soldiers noted, they made an impressive sight in their polished brass helmets, they did little to fight the 30-foot flames because of significant problems with their hoses. The U.S. Army Fire Department from the Central Records Office also appeared on the scene and with their chemical dispersing trucks put an end to the blaze just as it was reaching the area where the compound's gasoline storage was located.[63]

When the fire was brought under control, the good news was that only one man, Mess Sergeant William Rosensweig, had been seriously injured and a few others were slightly injured. It was estimated that the fire had caused more than $50,000 worth of damage in destroying the barracks, supply room and the officer's mess. The fire was particularly disheartening to the soldiers from the 350th Motor Repair Unit as they had driven all the way from Italy, arriving just the day before the fire, and lost all of their personal belongings. It was also noted that work began the following day to replace the lost buildings.[64]

Doughboys to the Rescue (June 1919)

When a bakery in Bourges, operated by a recently demobilized French soldier, caught fire, it quickly got out of control. The fire started on the lower floor of building and worked its way up the stairwell until it engulfed the second floor. Soon there was "fire shooting from every door and window."[65] Although local citizens and the town's antiquated fire pump attempted to fight the blaze, it remained out of control and threatened other nearby buildings. Fortunately, just when it appeared the fire would spread, the U.S. Army's fire department from the camp at Bourges arrived on the scene and used its chemical pumping engines to quickly douse the flames.

Heroism in the SOS

As discussed earlier, many of the men serving in the SOS wanted to serve in combat units but were not given the chance. Nevertheless, as the 31 January 1919 edition of the *Stars & Stripes* reported, heroism comes in many forms. General Order Number 4, Published by the Headquarters of the SOS recognized 21 SOS soldiers for their acts of bravery. Of the 21, seven were serving in or near the front lines and the remainder were further back in the support zones.

Among those to show their bravery in a combat environment were Sergeant Thomas A. Henderson, Private 1st Class Eugene Hufield, Private 1st Class John J. Campbell, and Private Robert Nesbitt. These four soldiers were cited for their rescue of some 80 railcars of government property from a fire caused by German bombing. It was noted that they did this while the attack was still taking place. Another combat-related act was carried out by Captain Wilford A. Fair of the Medical Corps who was killed in action while attempting to rescue another American officer. Another SOS soldier, Private Lee R. Ellis, was killed in action delivering ammunition to a machine gun crew while under attack by Bolsheviks in Russia.

Equally brave was 1st Lieutenant Harold Forsay who rescued the pilot of a burning aircraft after it crashed in England in April 1918. A 15th Engineer Regiment NCO, Sergeant 1st Class Thomas Martin, demonstrated his courage by throwing himself against a pile of wooden rails that were slipping and would have crushed several soldiers. At least three of the soldiers mentioned were commended for saving others from drowning, including Private F.E. Carlton of the 23rd Engineer Regiment who dove fully clothed into the water at Savoie to save a French child. Another soldier, Private

Charles E. Richardson from Motor Truck Company 328, stopped a runaway horse before it trampled two children.

Perhaps the two most unusual tales of bravery involved Sergeant Louis Weisberg, a Chemical Warfare NCO, and Captain J.C. Kennedy of the Transportation Service. Weisberg was recognized for developing an antidote to mustard gas after repeated exposure in the laboratory and Kennedy was recognized for his role in stopping a riot among Chinese laborers in the port of Brest. Unfortunately, the details of those stories are lost but both would certainly be worthy of hearing.[66]

An Unusual Racial Episode in the SOS

As we have seen, the AEF in France was an integrated force—almost. There were Asians, Hispanics, Native Americans, Middle Easterners, South Americans and Europeans from every country serving in combat units of the AEF. The only groups excluded were African Americans and black African or Caribbean immigrants. As a result, there were a great number of African Americans serving in the SOS, primarily in engineer and labor battalion units.

General Dawes would record in his diary an unusual episode involving one of these soldiers that took place while Dawes was serving in the 17th Engineer Regiment at the port of St. Nazaire in August 1917. As he reported:

> Last night there was considerable trouble between our [Army] men and the adjoining Marines. A Marine policeman in St. Nazaire very much intoxicated was found beating a negro. One of our Southern privates interfered to stop it, and the drunken policeman drew his revolver and attempted to shoot the private. Thereupon the private, who—accidentally, according to him, happened to have a bottle of champagne in his hand, delivered the same with telling effect across the head of the policeman knocking him out.[67]

According to Dawes, the private then recovered the Marine's pistol, returned to camp and reported to Dawes. In the meantime, other Marines became enraged by this beating of their comrade took it upon themselves to seek out members of Dawe's 17th Engineer Regiment and arrested 18 of them, placing them in the St. Nazaire guardhouse. After a short investigation the 18 were released and the Marine officer in charge issued an apology to the Army. Rather than seeing this solely as a racial incident, Dawes believed "this is what will happen around camps where liquor is sold." Dawes did, however, understand the significance that a white Southern soldier had "intervened to protect a poor colored man from a severe and undeserved beating."[68] That factor alone made it a noteworthy incident.

Female Vigilantes in Paris (1919)

Perhaps one of the more unusual stories to appear in an SOS newspaper had the title "Yankee Girls are Policing Wicked Paris." According to the report, an unknown organization of young American females were patrolling the streets of Paris and intervening when they saw soldiers engaged in conversation or negotiation with Parisian ladies of the evening. Approaching the man, the young woman would let him know he was "in bad company" and ask him, "Does your mother know you're out of line?" Usually this was enough to make the soldier change his mind, or at least go to another neighborhood. The vigilantes were particularly active on the *Boulevard des Italiens* and the *Rue de la Paix*.

When asked if this was part of their mission, both the YMCA and Red Cross representatives denied any part in the activity. Even the Paris AEF Provost Marshal said the vigilantes were not on his unit roster. The origin of these "Intrepid Volunteers" remains a mystery and so perhaps this is merely a Doughboy "urban legend."[69]

Trouble in Ice Plant Company 301 (1919)

After the Armistice, most American soldiers wanted to come home as soon as possible. Many resented the resumption of training, drills and inspections the AEF leaders reintroduced after the firing stopped. Likewise, most soldiers appreciated the emphasis on sporting events, entertainment and the opportunity for schooling the AEF wisely instituted to keep the soldiers occupied. But not all men were satisfied. Consider the case of Ice Plant Company 301. Their dissatisfaction with numerous delays in returning to the United States, and their disgust at the treatment of the Company in general, prompted a public letter of complaint from someone identifying himself as Private H.D. Clements, purportedly a member of the company. Because some 60 men of the Company hailed from York, Pennsylvania, Clements wrote to the city editor of the *York Dispatch*. In the letter, Clements cites rumors for sailing dates for the return of the Company that failed to materialize. Among other items, Clements claimed:

> That the unit is detained from sailing because of a case of sour grapes between the company and camp officers. That several times the company was slated to return but each time the date for embarkation for the states was canceled.
>
> That from the very first day until this very hour we have received treatment that would be severe to a German.

9. Unique Events and the Problem with Prisons   171

> That we have toiled during the construction of the ice plant in a manner we can hardly imagine another body of laborers would work, even at the point of the bayonet.
>
> That we have been subjected to numerous mistreatments that lead us to believe that there is a personal feeling of contempt against our organization by the higher officials of the camp.[70]

Clements raised other issues such as harsh punishment, including coal hauling, for minor infractions, the confiscation of the men's trousers for use by POWs, the confiscation of soldiers' extra sweaters, and poor treatment while on convoy duty.

The letter was swift to draw comment. First, James M. Holohan, formerly a private 1st class assigned to the 97th Aero Squadron, wrote to the newspaper to say:

> I was stationed not far from the Ice Plant unit and was familiar with the kind of work which was and is being done by the men, and I know that their work was no more severe than that performed by other branches of the service and far less dangerous and severe than that done by the fighters in the front line trenches.
>
> It is undoubtedly true that the Ice Plant men are doing a great work, full of great hardship, but there is no reason for these complaints. The letter makes it appear that these fellows are undergoing undue suffering, when in reality, it is not nearly so bad as others are doing. The boys in the trenches, doing the real work, have gone frequently for days without food or rest. Their hardships are very real and we all know only too much of them. In comparison, the Ice Plant boys have it soft, and I know what I'm talking about when I make this statement.[71]

But even this was not enough. First Lieutenant Frederick Downs, who had served in Ice Plant Company 301, wrote to Thomas Shipley, general manager of the York Manufacturing Company (where many of the ice plant soldiers worked before and again after the war), to refute the complaints. Among other things, Downs wrote:

> In the first place, let me say that there is no such person in the company as Private H.D. Clements, so whoever was responsible for the article was not willing to sign his own name, and shoulder the responsibility of his own charge.... There has been no one discriminated against, as any treatment they have received has been exactly the same as that which all the other organizations in this depot have received. It is true in my opinion, that the rules and regulations of this depot are, without exception, the most severe and strict of any camp in France, and are especially trying, now that all the excitement of the war is over, but the boys, while all anxious to go home, are at present on convoy duty, seeing France and parts of Germany, and as a whole, have a wonderful experience and a good time. Hence, to me the article seems to be the opinion of an individual member who is more homesick than the others, and does not represent the general feeling of the company.... To me the boys are the best group of fellows assembled in one company in France....[72]

Then, in an effort to protect his own, much like the proverbial mama bear, Downs went on to criticize Private Holohan's comments regarding Ice Plant Company 301:

> His statement that he knows what he is talking about when he says that ice plant company boys have it "soft" because he performed duties similar to the quartermaster corps, and hence knows, sounds as though the most strenuous thing he did was to push a pencil or use the "hunt and pick" system on a typewriter in some warm office from 9 a. m. until 3 p. m., instead of manual labor around an enormous refrigerating plant. In any event he showed a lack of "horse sense" in his remarks.[73]

The truth of this matter may never be known. Much of the original complaint voiced by "Clements" can be typical griping common to soldiers everywhere, but some of what he cites would be cause for at least an investigation. Also unknown is the degree to which all members of the Company would have agreed to the claims in Clements' letter of complaint. Surely Lieutenant Downs painted a rather rosy picture of the men's attitude if, as he stated, "the rules and regulations of this depot are, without exception, the most severe and strict of any camp in France." All told, the men eventually returned to the United States and got back to living their usual lives.

The Stevedores Get Some Respect and Appreciation

One of the hardest jobs in the SOS fell to the Army's black and white stevedore units. Unloading ships is dangerous work and the conditions in the French ports in 1918 made it even more a challenge. Fortunately, a noted American poet, Ella Wheeler Wilcox, had seen them at their thankless jobs and wrote a poem in their honor. Wilcox had gathered a measure of fame with her poem "Solitude" which featured the lines:

> Laugh, and the world laughs with you;
> Weep, and you weep alone.

Her work "The Stevedores," in honor of the stevedores, had no such memorable lines but did point out their difficult labors:

> We are the Army Stevedores, lusty and virile and strong;
> We are given the hardest work of the war and the hours are long;
> We handle the heavy boxes and shovel the dirty coal
> While the soldiers and sailors work in the light,
> We burrow below like a mole.
> But somebody has to do this work, or the soldiers could not fight;
> And whatever work is given a man, is good if he does it right.[74]

The poem continues in that vein and ends with the phrase "We are the Army Stevedores; give us our due!" The point was made; the stevedores had a rough job. When Ella Wheeler Wilcox recited her poem to them at their camp in France, they applauded loudly and knew that she appreciated their efforts and gave them their due.

The Problem with Prisons

Obviously in any military force the size of the AEF there were bound to be some men who were habitual troublemakers as well as some actual criminals. There were, however, a greater number of soldiers who got into trouble either accidentally or from alcohol-inspired antics. One of the soldiers in the latter category was Private John Dombrowsky of the 2nd Motor Mechanic Regiment of the Army Air Service. In September 1918, a board of officers was convened in the District of Paris to investigate charges from his company commander that Dombrowsky had acted in an unmilitary manner, had refused to perform kitchen police (KP) duty in the company kitchen and had been found under the influence of alcohol on several occasions. After reviewing his record and finding that he had an eighth-grade education, with no record of criminal offences prior to enlistment and no court-martials previously, but had been "drunk four or five times since arrival in France," the board decided discharging him from the U.S. Army was not warranted. The finding of the board instead recommended that Dombrowsky be transferred from his Air Service unit to duty with a combat unit as "he would be more amenable to military discipline in a line Organization than in the present Organization, which is purely technical."[75] Dombrowsky's sentence may seem somewhat harsh but in some ways he was lucky. Other men in similar situations or having overstayed their leave were remanded to U.S. Army prisons in France that were, by most accounts, just this side of hell.

After the war, a series of congressional hearings were held to look into the charges of brutality in the AEF confinement facilities and prisons. Among the most notorious of the Army facilities was the Chelles Detention Farm, most commonly called Farm Number 2 and located near Paris. Although commanded by U.S. Army Colonel T.Q. Donaldson, it was under the daily supervision of Lieutenant Frank H. "Hardboiled" Smith and Sergeant Clarence E. Ball. Smith had originally been a member of the 40th Division but when that unit arrived in France, it was converted to a Depot Division. As a result, Smith ended up becoming a prison officer.

While not officially sanctioned by the commanding officer of the prison facility, the prisoners were told that "the purpose of this prison is to break a man's spirit and until this is done there is no chance for clemency."[76] Though Smith would later deny the charges of brutality, Sergeant Ball testified that "Smith's orders were to 'educate the men,' and that these orders were carried out by striking the men in the face in Smith's presence."[77] There were also claims that money the soldiers had at the time of their confinement often disappeared. Former prisoners testified that the guards working for Smith would greet the new prisoners with a question: "You're hardboiled, aren't you?" If the prisoner answered "Yes," the guards would strike him and say that they would take the hardboiled out of him. If the prisoner answered "No," the guards would hit him and tell him that they would make him hardboiled.[78] You couldn't win at Farm Number 2. One former sergeant testified that he had seen soldiers from Farm Number 2 on work detail in Paris eating out of garbage cans because they were starving at the farm. Showing that no crime was too heinous for Smith and his cronies, it was claimed they stole the photographs of prisoners' wives and sweethearts, and even took one man's crucifix.

After the war when Smith was brought to trial for his actions, he admitted that conditions were "pretty fierce" but he treated all prisoners alike, whether they were guilty of felonies or simple offenses such as being absent without leave. In his own defense Smith expressed his belief that Farm Number 2 was a "pleasure resort" in comparison to similar facilities at the SOS camps in St. Sulpice and Gièvres. He backed up this statement by recounting the beating he had been given at St. Sulpice after his own arrest for abusing prisoners and stealing their property. Both Smith and Ball were transported back to the States aboard the USS *Von Steuben* along with a number of other prisoners. Smith was eventually found guilty and sentenced to three years in prison, later reduced to 18 months in the military prison at Fort Jay on Governors Island in New York harbor. Ball received a six month sentence, also to Fort Jay. Two other guards at the farm were dishonorably discharged from the Army. Reminiscent of events at the St. Sulpice stockade, as soon as Smith was delivered to Fort Jay, the other convicts exacted their measure of revenge for his brutality towards them in France. They beat him so savagely that he ended up in the hospital. Meanwhile, the trials and congressional hearings continued.

In December 1919 came testimony about an officer reportedly even more brutal than "Hardboiled" Smith. Captain Karl W. Detzer, a former Fort Wayne, Indiana, newspaperman and commander of the 308th Military Police Company, was charged with 28 counts of abusing prisoners through violent beatings and conduct unbecoming an officer while managing the confinement facility at Le Mans. The initial testimony against Detzer and his NCOs was damning and reached the point that Secretary of War Newton Baker was compelled to institute a special investigation.

9. Unique Events and the Problem with Prisons   175

Witness after witness came forward to describe how Detzer and his staff beat the prisoners and deprived them of sleep until they signed confessions of their crimes. Other punishment included

> [standing] at attention for thirty-six hours ... withholding food and water from prisoners until they acknowledge their "guilt"; and pulling prisoners to their feet by their hair. It is alleged that Detzer compelled Private Marcello Gonzales of the 10th Machine Gun Battalion to swallow a live cigarette he was smoking in violation of orders.[79]

Other men testified that they had seen the captain personally beat 30 or 40 prisoners and that Detzer had punched one prisoner so hard he broke his fist. Eventually the testimony against Detzer ended and he was sent to the Fort Jay military prison. On arrival it was noted that Detzer was greeted "with boos and catcalls" from men who had been his prisoners in France.[80]

Before the investigation ended, other witnesses also came forward to testify about what they had seen. One former soldier claimed he became afflicted with epilepsy as a result of his military service and swore that he had personally seen 12 men hanged at Is-sur-Tille during the period January to June 1919. Another claimed that he had witnessed "Hardboiled" Smith hang a North Carolina National Guardsman named Benny King after stealing his money. He also claimed that he and other men had been sent into combat without gas masks as punishment. It got worse. Another witness, this time a newspaper reporter from Atlanta, came forward to testify that 21 prisoners had been hanged at Gièvres and had a photograph showing what appeared to be a gallows with several men hanging. He claimed the photograph had been given to him by a guard whose name he couldn't remember. The picture was quickly proven to be fake and actually was a picture of several soldiers clowning around ("skylarking" was the period term) and pretending to be hanged.

More witnesses testified to crimes committed in France by American officers, but they could not remember the names of their commanders. One former soldier accused a Virginia National Guard officer of the 116th Infantry Regiment of murdering two men in the front lines but no one ever found proof to validate these claims. Another man claimed to have seen two men hanged at the SOS depot at Is-sur-Tille. This claim was refuted immediately by the officer who had been the Provost Marshal for the area from 1918 to early 1919. He testified that

> I had thirty-four towns in my area and in all the time I was in Is-Sur-Tille there were no convictions of serious crimes whatever and absolutely no executions.... Had there been any prosecutions of a serious nature I would have known of them, as they would have gone through my hands.[81]

So whom should we believe? In February 1920, all of the charges against Captain Detzer were dropped as either false or unsubstantiated, including the story of the soldier forced to eat a lit cigarette; he later testified that he was made to stub out the cigarette with his boot.[82] Detzer was freed and returned to active duty, remaining in the Army long enough to also serve during the Second World War. The number of increasingly unbelievable witnesses who testified before the congressional committee also slowly dropped away. Of all of the claims and counterclaims, the only ones that appeared to stick were those against "Hardboiled" Smith and his sergeant, both of whom served out their sentences at Fort Jay. If Detzer was innocent of all the charges, we can be pretty sure that Smith wasn't. Undoubtedly, the conditions at Farm Number 2 and the smaller Parisian facility known as "Petit Rouge," or "the Bastille" by the soldiers incarcerated there, were harsh and many soldiers were treated brutally for minor infractions. Why so many men came forward with fake stories of hangings and other bad behavior is a question that remains unanswered. Also remaining unanswered is the question why men such as "Hardboiled" Smith and his guards felt the need to treat their fellow soldiers so viciously for such minor offenses. Smith's name came up again in more congressional investigative testimony in 1923 but by then Smith was thought to have left the country and joined the Mexican army. It can only be hoped that he was not placed in charge of a Mexican military prison.

10

The Central Records Office and the Postal Express Service

> The mail man of the 1st Division retorted that if the 42nd Division didn't like the way they were getting their mail, they could come get it for themselves.[1]

Among the least well-known organizations in the SOS, and perhaps greatly underappreciated, was the Central Records Office (CRO). Originally assigned to the AEF Headquarters and therefore not truly a component of the SOS until later, most soldiers believed it to be an SOS organization. In fact, because of its key administrative function of tracking unit strengths, mail delivery and close ties to the deployment process it probably always should have been.[2] The Army's original plan had been for a small group of trained soldier-clerks to maintain an index card for each soldier in the AEF with enough information to locate where the soldier was assigned. The bulk of the statistical and tracking work was to be carried out by the soldier's unit. The rapid and almost constant movement of soldiers between locations and units after arrival in France quickly made this impractical. Even with only some 77,000 Doughboys in France by the end of 1917, matching the soldiers to units and keeping accurate mailing addresses proved impossible and the number of arriving soldiers continued to grow exponentially.

The Master Card Division. In January 1918, a message was sent to units already in France seeking administrative experts and men with typing skills. The 30 soldiers who volunteered formed the Statistical Division of the General Headquarters in Chaumont. There were five officers and 25 NCOs in that first group, mostly from the 1st, 26th and 42nd Divisions. With this new establishment came a different approach to maintaining records for the soldiers of the AEF.

The Statistical Division created a "Master Locator Card" for each arriving soldier with his name, unit, service number, rank, home address

The shoulder patch for soldiers assigned to the Central Records Office (CRO) in Bourges. Many of the soldiers assigned to the CRO were detailed out of units broken up to provide replacements for other units and had to learn the complex skills of maintaining service records for the two million Doughboys serving in France (courtesy Alison Hutton).

An unidentified member of Queen Mary's Army Auxiliary Corps poses for a photograph after arriving in France. These ladies' organizational skills, attention to detail and ability to read and speak English made them a vital part of the Central Records Office Staff (private collection).

and next of kin, date of birth and enlistment date. There was also room on the card to reflect changes in unit of assignment, current mailing address, hospitalization, temporary transfers for schooling, return to the States, capture or death. These cards were then arranged alphabetically in the unit of assignment. A locator card, smaller in size and containing updated information, was added later to better track the soldiers as their status changed. It was estimated that each soldier underwent a status change or mailing address change of some sort at least 15 times while serving in France. With the AEF growing to more than two million Doughboys in France, the work effort required to update the cards was enormous and required an equally large workspace. This facilitated a move to more spacious offices in Bourges.

By July 1918, the staff of the Master Card Division and its associated Locator Card Section had grown to 560 soldiers and an additional 400 British women from the WAAC/QMAAC. As noted earlier, these female soldiers were requested in great numbers by the American Army to work in the SOS and to bring order to the massive administrative record keeping of the CRO. The Locator Card section was composed of 147 soldiers and 238 WAACs supervised by Maude Biggs,

10. The Central Records Office and the Postal Express Service 179

The manpower shortage in the Central Records Office was as critical as in the other organizations of the SOS, and because of the nature of the administrative work, being able to speak and read English was a requirement. In this unique photograph, some of the CRO women are standing in formation with their American soldier counterparts as they await the arrival of General Pershing to inspect them (private collection).

an Englishwoman whose rank was the equivalent of an Army captain.

In November 1918, with the signing of the Armistice, the workload on the CRO increased again. Now, in addition to the extremely delicate work of properly informing next of kin of the death or hospitalization of their soldiers, the Master Card Division began tracking the departure of soldiers from France back to the United States. The month of April 1919 proved to be the busiest month of their existence. The record for returns for a one-week period was reached on 22 April when 108,795 soldiers were shipped out in just seven days. By the end of the April 898,978 soldiers had been returned to the States. This left under a million still in France and another 275,000 in the Third Army occupying the German Rhineland.[3] As the summer departures continued, the AEF in France rapidly shrank and soon would be gone. To maintain continuity, another CRO was set up in Antwerp, Belgium, to service the soldiers of the Third Army.

Marines in the Central Records Office. Among the many skills exhibited by the Marines assigned to the 5th Brigade, some that received little notice were administrative skills which provided support to the CRO. There were at least 10 Marines (three NCOs and seven privates) assigned to the CRO. One of them, Corporal Robert G. Henley, had also displayed significant artistic talent in creating line drawings and cartoons.

An unusual job for a U.S. Marine in France: Robert G. Kenly was a cartoon illustrator for *The CRO*. Seen here is a picture showing the delights of living in a crowded barracks. Note that Kenly has managed to insert the Marine Corps "Eagle, Globe and Anchor" symbol on the bottom left of his drawing (private collection).

His work was beginning to make regular appearances in *The CRO*, and he had just been transferred officially to the staff of that newspaper when orders appeared at Bourges directing that all assigned Marines be transferred to St. Nazaire for transportation to the States. As a result, Henley and his fellow Marines, Corporals Frank G. Noonan and John O. Zipperer, and Privates Carl F. Debner, Arthur Hughes, Clifton P. Naylor, Joseph A. Presswood, Clarence L. Ritzen, Felix J. Stevens and Emmanuel M. Wilkinson, had to pack and depart quickly. From Bourges they reported into the Casual Company at St. Aignan awaiting final movement to the ship. By July most of them were back in the States and discharged.[4]

During an April 1919 visit by New York Congressman Charles Caldwell to the CRO in Bourges, the question on every soldier's mind was when they would be going home. Congressman Caldwell, mainly noted for attending an extremely low number of roll call votes in the U.S. Congress, spoke like a politician and told the soldiers what they wanted to hear—namely, they would be going home in about a month and a half. It was a popular answer, and everyone was happy. After the Congressman departed, Colonel David L. Stone, the Bourges camp commander, was asked to confirm the statement. Colonel Stone told the soldiers, "The Congressman doesn't know what he is talking about." He also told the soldiers that they would go home when the work there was complete, and not before.[5]

The Postal Express Service (PES). Among the very few enjoyable moments in a soldier's time away from home is when he receives mail. One of the great U.S. military traditions, reaching back to the First World War and continuing today, is the right of soldiers in war zone to send letters home for free. As a result, World War I soldiers were prodigious writers and, in return, received mountains of mail back from family members in the States. Not surprisingly, the Doughboys wrote often to their hometown friends and family members who also were serving overseas.

By early 1918 it became apparent that there were difficulties associated with a civilian-run post office operating within a military theater. United States civilian postal employees could not easily work with French military postal authorities; they first had to go through U.S. military channels to coordinate with French military and postal agencies. The transportation shortage within the theater resulted in delays and liaison with U.S. Army postal agents proved difficult. Most importantly, frequent transfer of personnel, formation of new units and troop movements caused great difficulty in establishing the correct address for any given man or unit. Because of these difficulties, the Army and the Post Office agreed to a restructuring of responsibilities for military mail.[6]

The agreement reached between the War Department and the Post Office Department in May 1918 outlined a division of responsibilities between the two departments. The Post Office Department was responsible for the delivery of bundles of mail to military authorities at the ports of embarkation in the United States. From there, the Army took control of soldiers' mail. The duties of the AEF's mail personnel were to receive, sort and distribute mail after it had arrived in France. They were also authorized to collect outbound mail for transportation to higher level sorting and distributing facilities. The AEF delivered mail moving from Europe to the United States to Post Office personnel at base ports in Europe; from that point, the Post Office Department was responsible for delivery of mail to its intended recipient in the United States. As an outgrowth of this agreement, the AEF established the Military Postal Express Service

(MPES) on 9 May 1918. This new service, under the Adjutant General's Department, was headed by Lieutenant Colonel Thorndyke D. Howe of the Massachusetts National Guard. Each division and corps in the AEF was authorized to establish a Postal Express section consisting of one officer, six NCOs and 20 privates to distribute the inbound mail to subordinate units within their organizations. The MPES was responsible for mail from the base ports until delivery to mail orderlies at railheads; from that point on, individual unit postal detachments took responsibility for their mail. In August 1918, the MPES was renamed the Postal Express Service, United States Army (PES), and its authorized strength fixed at 215 officers and 1885 enlisted men. The actual transfer of mail from civilian to military responsibility took place in June 1918; 10 civilian agents were commissioned in the National Army and other civilian clerks were transferred, as civilians, to the Quartermaster Corps. This small group was augmented by the transfer of men already in Europe and by the arrival of two 300-man detachments from the United States. Many of these men had prior civilian post office experience.

In the AEF's early days, however, nothing was this well organized, and Hagood wrote:

> One of the absurdities with which we possessed ourselves at the outbreak of the war was that the United States Postal Service should go to France to handle the mail.... Another absurdity was that the Post Office department not only allowed but encouraged the people at home to fill the mails with useless junk that could not possibly do any good....[7]

He wrote that he had personally seen a box delivered to a soldier that had once contained a bunch of bananas. Other such foolishness included a weekly shipment of freshly baked bread to an officer by his wife, most of which took six months to reach him. Well-intentioned people would place stamps on magazines and place them in the mail under the impression that they would be delivered to soldiers in France. Hagood wrote that "what actually happened to them was that they were brought out of the holds of ships in wheelbarrows, carted off in trucks and destroyed."[8]

PES organization. There were three types of PES post offices: base post offices, fixed (or area) post offices and the Central Post Office (CPO). The base post offices operated at base ports and handled mail to and from the United States; they also handled mail service for units located within the base area. Fixed or area post offices were located throughout France and served the postal needs of troops permanently based within the communication zone. The Central Post Office was the largest in the whole system. Its mission was to provide inter–AEF mail service and to re-distribute undeliverable mail. In September 1918 the CPO moved to Bourges in order

10. The Central Records Office and the Postal Express Service 183

Four very young-looking soldiers assigned to the Postal Express Service and wearing the appropriate armbands pose together in this French-made photograph. It is interesting to note that the soldier standing on the left has three wound stripes on his right sleeve, certainly a unique appearance for a soldier in the Postal Service and most likely indicative of a transfer from a combat unit (John Adams-Graf Collection).

to be close to the Central Records Office and to use their locator cards for help with re-directing mail.

At the height of its operation, the CPO re-directed as many as 352,000 letters per day. The CPO worked closely with the CRO to obtain locator cards to correct discrepancies and get the mail to its intended recipient. The causes of all this undeliverable mail were many and included inefficient and inexperienced unit and area mail orderlies, improperly addressed mail, the rapid movement of casualties from hospital to hospital and the system of replacements.[9]

Another issue with outbound mail was the requirement to censor it at the unit level. In some cases, this was impossible due to letters written in foreign languages, of which the censoring officer would have no proficiency. The *Stars & Stripes* reported, while describing the mail censoring process, the soldiers wrote "in forty-six different languages. Out of 600 such letters ... the chances are but half will be written in Italian followed in order of their numerousness by those inscribed in Polish, French and Scandinavian." The article further noted that the postal staff handled on a regular basis letters written in "twenty-five European languages, many tongues and dialects of the Balkan States and a scattering few in Yiddish, Chinese, Japanese, Hindu, Tahitian, Hawaiian, Persian and Greek, to say nothing of a number of Philippine dialects."[10]

Mailing a letter. The steps for getting a letter from its writer to the soldier in France were daunting:

1. The Post Office receives the letter and delivers it to a pier in the New York City harbor complex.
2. A quartermaster assigned to the port loads it (and others) aboard a ship.
3. The ship sails to France.
4. An army stevedore or transportation unit soldier unloads it from the ship and places it in an Army Motor Transport Corps vehicle.
5. The vehicle delivers it to a Post Office unit for sorting.
6. The postal unit sorts it, adds it to a unit pile, and hands it back to a Motor Transport Corps vehicle driver.
7. The vehicle delivers it to a railway station for shipping.
8. The railroad delivers it to a rail station and turns it over to a Motor Transport driver.
9. The driver delivers it to the local military post office department.
10. The post office department sorts it into unit stacks and gives a unit's stack to a driver for delivery.

10. The Central Records Office and the Postal Express Service 185

    11. The driver takes it to the unit headquarters and hands it off to a HQ staff member who sorts it into company-level piles.
    12. A mail orderly picks up the mail for his company and returns to his unit.
    13. The mail is then handed to the soldiers. If one is no longer with the unit, the letter is sent back for re-addressing.[11]

Between 1 July 1917 and 30 June 1918 this process was repeated 35,000,000 times to deliver mail to the AEF soldiers in France. After June 1918 the numbers increased exponentially with arrival of large numbers of soldiers each day in France. Adding to the workload and confusion was that many mail shipments came addressed simply to the *l'armée américaine*.[12]

In June 1918 the Director of the PES was given authority to also take over the Motor Dispatch Service and the Courier Service, both of which had been previously commanded by the AEF Headquarters. The Courier Service had originally been a part of the Ordnance Corps before its transfer to the AEF Headquarters and then to the PES. As an organization, the Courier Service was very small and comprised only some 150 officers and enlisted soldiers. Nevertheless, it was an extremely important organization and after the war made scheduled courier runs to distances as far away as Constantinople, Bucharest, Odessa, Belgrade, and Berlin. Most of the trips were made by either automobile or motorcycle and sidecar.

In September, the image of a greyhound was designated as the authorized collar symbol for officers of the PES. A greyhound and two lightning flashes were designated for enlisted collar disks. Even with their new symbol and a clearly defined place in the SOS organization, the hardworking soldiers of the newly formed Postal Express Service continued to bear much of the blame from irate Doughboys convinced their mail was being held up somewhere by somebody.

By October 1918 the PES had been organized with four sub-divisions: Administration, Inspection, and two Operating Divisions (one in charge of post offices and one concerned with transportation). The Administration Division handled all administrative issues of the PES. The Inspection Division investigated all irregularities associated with the mail, including complaints and the custody of loose items found in the mail. The division handled thousands of complaints:

> Most were concerning lost mail, numerous were about lost articles, of which there were many; for in practically every shipment of mail from the States, due to improper wrapping, numerous articles were found loose in the pouches. It is of interest to note that these articles included almost every conceivable article for masculine use or adornment: safety razors, watches, rings, knives,

cigarettes, fountain pens by the thousands, cameras, money and Liberty bonds.[13]

One wonders how many of these items found their way to their rightful owners and how many ended up in someone else's pocket.

Many, if not most, soldiers sent money home for their own savings or for the use of their family. The safest and most convenient way to do this was through the medium of postal money orders. Because Army postal clerks were not bonded or trained to handle money orders or the sale of stamps, the U.S. Post Office supplied civilian clerks to serve this

The working relationship between the U.S. soldiers assigned to the Central Records Office and the British Queen Mary's Army Auxiliary Corps was quite cordial. The personal relationships proved to be equally so and a number of soldiers married their British co-workers. This cartoon from *The CRO* newspaper points this out as the American soldier arrives home with his "souvenir" wife (private collection).

10. The Central Records Office and the Postal Express Service

important function. While stamps were not needed for soldiers' personal letters, they were required for packages, and the souvenir-hungry Doughboys sent home plenty of packages. For example, "15,000 pouches of German Helmets and other souvenirs were dispatched to the United States in the month of January 1919."[14] The civilian clerks functioned at many unit post offices from Army down to division level. "At the period of maximum operations 120 money order stations were maintained by 140 civilian postal agents."[15]

As can be imagined, the amount of mail handled by the MPES and PES was staggering. During the month of December 1918, 40,450,000 letters and 15,545 sacks of packages were sent from members of the AEF to the United States. Inter-AEF mail amounted to 12,000,000 pieces; mail from the U.S. to the AEF consisted of about 46,000,000 letters and 15,300,000 parcels and prints. "The grand total of all pieces of all classes of mail handled during December 1918 was 123,363,730 pieces."[16]

In common with many of the soldiers who toiled behind the lines in anonymity, the soldiers of the PES bore their assigned duty with as much grace as possible. In a letter to his mother in Oroville, California, Private Neil Duensing said:

> I am as usual doing my little bit away back here in the S.O.S. and that is the only way that I can keep my conscience clear, since the boys up at the front are doing their big bit so well. We see the French boys everywhere and no doubt but that many of us envy all their decorations, shoulder cords and Croix de Guerre. They all seem so happy and cheerful as they go down the cobbled streets with admiring little French mademoiselles upon their arms.[17]

As in many other areas of the SOS, the end of the fighting did not mean the end of the work for the CRO or the PES. Right up to the moment the last AEF soldier departed France in 1919 and the last Army of Occupation soldier departed Germany in 1923 to return to the States, the need to maintain visibility of troop locations and deliver mail remained. Eventually, it did all have to end; the vast apparatus of the SOS had to be shut down and records closed out. It's time now to go see how all that happened.

11

Closing the Accounts

Postwar SOS Operations and the U.S. Third Army

The First Army, A.E.F., congratulates the Service of Supply on its share in the great American success. Without your energy and push back of us our efforts would not have succeeded. You share with us the glory of our deeds.[1]

With these strong words General Hunter Liggett thanked the men of the SOS for their hard work during the Meuse-Argonne Offensive. He also wrote the SOS "never failed us. Food, ammunition, clothing, medical attendance, and other supplies always were at hand. Our confidence in your efforts was well repaid."[2]

It would be understandable if some of the weary Doughboys would have liked to rest on these hard-won laurels, but it was not to be. One of the truck drivers in the Argonne later wrote that "the 35 days from October 8, 1918 to November 11, 1918 were the most nerve wracking days of my life ... we just celebrated the Armistice. I didn't know what the word armistice meant but I sure liked it."[3] By the time the armistice ended the hostilities some 29 AEF divisions were either in combat or moving toward the front lines. And, as noted earlier, although the shooting stopped, the soldiers still required food, their animals required care and fodder, and their weapons and vehicles required maintenance. While many people in France were celebrating the end of the fighting, the AEF and SOS staffs at Chaumont and Tours were not among them. They were still running full blast as they had to prepare the movement order and support plans required to dispatch an occupation force to the German Rhineland. The terms of the Armistice required the British, Belgian, French and U.S. armies to occupy that part of Germany for an indeterminate period.

For a while it appeared that almost every division in the AEF was being considered for occupation duty. Rumors flew and soldiers of the AEF spent the days following the Armistice debating whether their unit would make the march into Germany. On 14 November 1918, it became obvious which units were to be part of the occupation when many units still serving in or near the Meuse-Argonne battle area received orders to hand over their best draft animals to one of the selected divisions. Colonel George Marshall, knowing that the Meuse-Argonne campaign had severely damaged the health of the horses and mules of every combat division, decided the divisions selected for occupation duty should have the best equipment and healthiest pack animals available. The non-occupation force divisions were therefore directed to turn over their fittest animals to units that would be marching to Germany. Each U.S. Army division had, on average, 10,000 draft animals to transport assigned equipment. Therefore, the need was clear for healthy animals to carry to Germany the equipment of the newly created Third Army.

In addition to serving as the occupation force, the Third Army and its Allied comrades would serve as buffer between Germany and the battered countries of Belgium and France. The occupation zones stretched in horizontal layers from north to south: Belgium, Britain, United States, and France. These four zones also served as administrative centers for receiving and inspecting war reparations material that Germany was required to provide to the victorious Allies. The movement of the Third Army's 250,000 Doughboys into potentially hostile territory caused a wave of new problems for the SOS because these units had to be quickly brought to full complement of soldiers, unit equipment and vehicles. Two more divisions would move to Luxembourg to protect the logistics pipeline running from France to Germany and administer that country until its complicated political situation could be sorted out.

Sustaining the Third Army in Germany. The initial plan for logistics support to the Third Army called for moving supplies and equipment by road and rail from depots in France through Luxembourg and then into Germany. However, as we have seen, the French rail system had been so thoroughly worn out that it required significant repair. France desperately needed all available rolling stock to get its industrial base back on a peacetime footing. Therefore, the French Government requested the AEF consider another means of moving supplies to their occupation zone. This request meant that shortly after arriving in the occupation zone, Third Army had to rethink its logistic sustainment plan. They decided to bring what they could by truck from the AEF depots in France and to have the remainder of the supplies shipped from the United States to Antwerp or Rotterdam. From these ports, the cargo would be loaded onto river barges and towed down to the Rhine River ports in the American zone.

By Christmas 1918 most of the American occupation force was in

Not all of the units taking part in the occupation of the Rhineland were combat units. Some came from the SOS. In this picture from the 56th Engineers, the soldiers pose with their mess kits and canteen cups in Germany. Note that the soldier standing on the right is also showing his souvenir German army belt (author's collection).

place, either in the area between Trier and Coblenz or across the Rhine in a 30-kilometer-deep semi-circle. The Third Army set up its headquarters in Coblenz. Now that the Rhine had been reached and crossed, the problem facing the SOS and the Third Army logisticians was how to support and maintain these forces. Germany had been at war since 1914 and under blockade for much of that time. The German countryside had been stripped of anything that could produce food or be eaten, and the local population was close to starvation in some areas. Along with food, the occupying forces required massive amounts of replacement boots, overcoats, blankets, gloves and other cold-weather gear to help them survive the winter.

Facilities at Andernach and Coblenz-Lützel on the west bank of the river were designated as the support sites. Large ration dumps were added to the previously established depots at Andernach and Bendorf. All three of these sites were chosen for their proximity to the Rhine for receiving the inbound cargo and for the nearby road junctions and railheads that allowed easy onward movement of the supplies to the requiring units.

Knowing the SOS back in France was going to be busy supporting the rest of the AEF there, the logisticians in Germany knew they would have to solve a lot of their problems themselves. They set to work with some urgency and established a central salvage depot at Metternich in a two-story brick building situated next to a rail line. As carloads of salvaged American and German material arrived in the rail cars, it was unloaded and sorted for repair or reuse. As soon as a sufficient quantity of any item was obtained it would be packed and shipped out to the appropriate repair facility. During the first two months of operation, they processed thousands of coats, pants, overcoats and gas masks. They also handled abandoned enemy material such as saddles, caissons and wagon parts.

The logisticians looked around to see what else was available as anything obtained locally would relieve some transportation burden. The area around Coblenz had been a hub of support to the German army during the war. This worked greatly in the Americans' favor as the logisticians dug their way through great piles of abandoned German war matériel still in the area. In one warehouse, they found 140,000 blankets, which they placed in barges and shipped up the Rhine to Rotterdam for use by refugees in war-torn Belgium. They also found many bales of German army uniform cloth. These bales were sent to France for use in repairing the uniforms of the many German prisoners of war still being held there.[4]

While the Third Army was working to solve many logistics issues locally, the supply pipeline coming from the United States slowly started to deliver matériel. Supplies for the soldiers were first towed down the river on 23 March 1919 and continued to arrive at an average rate of 1,216 tons per week at Andernach and 1,912 tons per week at Bendorf. The depot at Coblenz-Lützel received 977 tons of quartermaster stores to be maintained as the Third Army's stocks. In a very short time, the Rhine River, control of which was the main reason for the Army to be in Germany, had become its support lifeline.[5]

United States Army remount units in Coblenz, Sinzig, Wengerohr, Trier and elsewhere in the U.S. zone did much to help German-American relations by successfully nursing the Third Army's 50,000 horses and mules back to health. With the motorizing of the artillery units and redeployment to the States of the other AEF divisions in France, many of these animals were no longer needed and they could be offered for sale by auction to the local population. Unfortunately, there was a problem with this pragmatic solution. A previous arrangement had been made with the French Government which called for the sale of any condemned horses to them for 450 francs apiece. This "French Option" was unacceptable, mainly due to the logistical headache of moving large numbers of sick animals back into France,

A branding iron in the shape of the Third Army/American Forces in Germany patch. It was used to mark the animals of the American occupation force (courtesy Alison Hutton).

and it did not address what to do with the healthy ones. Ignoring French complaints that selling horses to the local German populace was, in effect, aiding the enemy, the Americans made the animals available at a series of public auctions in the occupied zone. From March to May 1919, the Third Army auctioned more than 5,500 animals for farm work and another 192 for butchering.[6] The results were immediately positive. Germany had been stripped of draft animals to support its army in France, so local farmers were very eager to obtain healthy horses and mules. In one case, fervor ran so high the soldiers in the area's remount squadrons had to be called out of their barracks with weapons and field gear to maintain order among the overly enthusiastic buyers. These sales had an unexpected consequence; the now healthy animals brought premium prices and the Army actually made a profit by receiving more money than they had originally paid for them.[7]

Despite all their good work, the SOS and the Third Army logisticians were still falling short in some areas. Grantland Rice, the famous American sportswriter, was a 1st lieutenant in the Third Army and was a frequent contributor to the unit newspapers published there. One of his poems, a takeoff on the famous "Bingen on the Rhine" poem, was titled "Coblenz on the Rhine." Among the many verses were:

> A soldier of America lay starving in Coblenz;
> His government had made him live four months on thirty cents;
> A comrade stood beside him while his last Franc ebbed away,
> And bent with pitying glances to hear what he might say.
> "Tell my brothers and companions when they crowd around to get
> An earful of this bloody war that left us deep in debt,
> We didn't mind the fighting job, but slogging through the rain,
> Full many a bloke was starved to death along the Rhenish Plain."

After a number of similar verses detailing the failure of the Army pay and ration systems, he concluded:

> The starving soldier faltered in the Third Army Zone,
> His eyes put on a dying look—He had not strength to groan;
> His comrade bent to lift him, as he murmured softly: "Tell
> That Quartermaster when he comes I'll meet him down in hell."[8]

Ammunition handling and Ordnance Corps operations. Early in the occupation, in addition to salvaging German military equipment and monitoring war reparation efforts, Army logisticians had another important, and potentially dangerous, mission. When the Third Army arrived in the designated occupation zone, it found large quantities of ammunition left behind by German troops; shells of every caliber and large numbers of fuses, bombs, grenades, empty shell cases and small-arms ammunition. Large quantities of gunpowder, zinc, lead and brass used in the manufacture of ammunition were also found. Much of the ammunition was unserviceable and too dangerous to store or ship to the United States. Ordnance Corps soldiers quickly demilitarized or dismantled the most dangerous or unstable munitions. They were able to salvage some for future use, experimentation and static displays. They managed to recover 135,000 artillery shells, 400,000 fuses for artillery shells, more than 22 million rounds of small-arms and rifle ammunition, 3,000 heavy artillery brass cartridge casings, 36,000 naval shells and 2,000 tons of German gunpowder.[9]

SOS operations in France continue. Base Section Number 9 was established in Antwerp to support the Third Army while the largest part of the SOS was busy supporting the other divisions awaiting transportation back to America. At the same time, Spanish flu was still sweeping through Europe, although not as violently as in September and October 1918. By mid-1919, the occupation of Germany was logistically sound, most of the AEF's other soldiers were demobilizing back in the United States, and the SOS was able begin shutting down many of its operations. In retrospect, the statistics of the work accomplished by the SOS during the war and the redeployment is sometimes staggering: the forestry units milled 200,000,000 feet of lumber and cut four million railroad ties, one bakery produced 800,000 pounds of bread each day, SOS mechanics repaired 30,000 vehicles and the Advance Section depots maintained more than two million square feet of covered storage space. In fact, as one general noted, "practically everything we accomplished in the S.O.S. was unprecedented.... The imagination of a poet is required to visualize what we did."[10] Although no poets, both Johnson Hagood and James Harbord did attempt to quantify for the American public just what the SOS had accomplished. The story and accomplishments of each individual department of the SOS are certainly worthy of a short review.

The Engineer Department. The Engineer Department was particularly praiseworthy because so many of the functions they were performing had not even been conceived of as Army engineer missions prior to arrival in France. When the Armistice was signed, Engineering was the largest of the technical services in France with 174,000 engineer soldiers assigned. Serving in all three U.S. Armies and the combat divisions were 86,400 of these men while 43,000 were working on construction projects. Another 18,500 were in the forestry units and 7,600 were in supply units. The remaining 18,500 were either in schools or working in specialized shops.[11] Among their most important SOS work was the construction of the divisional training areas with barracks, mess halls, warehouses, hospitals, corrals and stables. They also provided these facilities with power and water.[12]

The Quartermaster Corps. Like the Engineer Corps, the Quartermaster Corps was reorganized several times in France and each time some functions were taken away and given to other departments. These changes were not so much an indictment on the quartermasters as a realization that such functions as veterinary services or military construction truly belonged in other departments. Two transportation functions, motor transport and ocean transport, were worthy of their own departments and required more oversight than was available through the Quartermaster Department. Even without these functions, the quartermasters were incredibly busy as they attempted to feed and clothe the two million soldiers in the AEF. By the end of the war, the quartermaster bakeries were making three million pounds of bread a day. The Quartermaster Corps was also responsible for receiving, storing and issuing 13,000,000 pairs of underwear, 25,000,000 pairs of socks, 10,000,000 wool shirts, and nine million pairs of trousers. Their salvage operation "reclaimed clothing and equipment to the value of $200,000 a day."[13] The Quartermaster Corps was responsible for "134 mobile disinfectors, 40 stationary disinfectors, 257 improvised disinfectors, 79 hot-air disinfectors, 545 stationary baths and 21 mobile baths" to delouse the soldiers of the AEF. Operating these critically important machines were more than 1,600 officers and enlisted men.[14]

The Transportation Department. As should be clear by this point, the problems with the Transportation Department seemed at times unsolvable. Managing the movement of the largest number of soldiers across an ocean in history was simply something no one knew how to do. Transportation industry leaders brought into the Army for their expertise were knowledgeable about their business, but this was unlike any business they had known. And, to make it more difficult, no one had ever been attempting to sink their commercial vessels while en route. Adding to the problem, the cargo on these ships also required food and sleeping space during the voyage.

The problems did not end with troops and supplies arrival in France. Port operations of the scale necessary to offload and move further inland all the arrivals were also of a scale unknown in the U.S. Army and the problems seen in the early days reflected it. Fortunately, through the efforts of men such as Hagood, Harbord and Smedley Butler and the massive construction effort in the base sections, some of the problems were being overcome by war's end.

Less well known but of a more positive nature was the Transportation Corps' inland waterway operation. Making use of the French canal and river system, the SOS was able to borrow French and British barges to move significant amounts of matériel through the area behind the American sector. Among the most commonly shipped commodities on this mode of transportation were coal and wood; both of which would have required significant rail or motor vehicle transportation had the barges not been used.[15]

The Motor Transport Corps. Due to the U.S. Army's experimentation and use of motor vehicles in the 10 years before the war, there was a wide variety of makes and models by 1917. As Hagood clearly pointed out in *The Services of Supply*, the Quartermaster Corps, the Ordnance Department, the Medical Department and even the newly formed Air Service all sent vehicles to France. Among the first Army units to arrive in France in June 1917 were four motor truck companies and a maintenance unit for them.[16] However, without commonality of design, each branch required different tool sets and repair parts. Mechanics for one type of vehicle were unable to fix or maintain the other kinds. Aware of the confusion, the AEF released an order in July 1918 requiring all vehicles to be consolidated in the newly formed Motor Transport Corps (MTC).

There were problems inherent with the MTC. The biggest of these was that there simply were not enough cars and trucks to go around. The Army's Table of Organization and Equipment did not allow for enough drivers, mechanics or vehicles to meet the need. Pushing back transport units on the shipping priority list to bring more infantrymen only made the problem worse. Giving perspective on how large the AEF was, Hagood wrote that on 11 November 1918, the Army had "24,055 cargo trucks, 4197 ammunition trucks, and some 4700 other trucks of special design."[17] Even this large fleet was less than half of what the AEF truly needed. Harbord, writing after the war, was still unhappy with how the motor transportation issues had played out with the War Department: "Suggestion had been made from Washington a few weeks before that we should substitute motor vehicles for animals-[in other words] substitute motors we could not get for animals we did not have."[18]

The Medical Department. The Medical Department was one of the largest departments or branches in the AEF, surpassed in number of enlisted soldiers only by the infantry, field artillery and engineers. Faced with supply shortages and overwhelming need for hospitals and beds, the Medical Department was very creative in using existing facilities such as hotels, apartment buildings and even monasteries as hospitals. By war's end, there were more than 200 base and camp hospitals or medical facilities, many clustered into hospital centers in order to pool their resources.

The Ordnance Department. The soldiers of the Ordnance Department received faint praise primarily because no one knew how to quantify their work efforts. It was recognized that the AEF generally never lacked for ammunition and that they fired five million artillery rounds and half a billion pistol and rifle rounds. It was also noted that while no American-made field artillery was used by American soldiers, a great deal of the other Allied armies' cannons had been made in the United States.[19]

The Chemical Warfare Service. Prior to the war, this function had been under the control of the Engineer Department and later was its own separate branch. Primarily a "combat arm" of the AEF, the only component of the Chemical Warfare Service in the SOS was the portion that received and issued chemical supplies and equipment. This service acquitted itself well and was able to maintain the stockage levels required by the AEF, in some cases even exceeding them by significant amounts.

The Signal Corps. Like the Chemical Warfare Service, the Signal Corps served in the combat zone but maintained a component assigned to the SOS. The Signal Corps initially leased their telephone and telegraph services from the French. This proved unsatisfactory because the French system was very limited and the equipment old. More importantly, the French did not have the capability to simultaneously carry telegraph and telephone traffic on the same network, a critical requirement when trying to reduce the amount of wire being strung. As a result, in autumn 1917 the Signal Corps began construction of a network dedicated to serving the AEF. Two Army Telegraph Battalions, the 406th and the 407th, received the mission and immediately began to build a network using the latest in American telecommunication methods and equipment. The network expanded to follow the shape of the AEF as it took over more training areas, base sections and front line sectors. In time, the network in the forward areas came under the control of the Advance Section. The Chief Signal Officer for the AEF moved in March 1918 to the SOS Headquarters at Tours.[20]

The Signal Corps later reported that it had built a network of 125,000 miles of phone and telegraph lines and of this, some 38,000 miles were actually in the front lines. Hagood also noted that "the Signal Corps handled nineteen million local telephone calls and one million long distance calls," as well as more than five million telegrams with 2,800,000 words per day.[21] Undoubtedly, many of these calls took place between French and American officers and were successfully coordinated by the Signal Corps' extremely efficient "Hello Girls." Ironically, although considered at the time to be Army Signal Corps members, these same women would have to wait until 1976 to be accorded veteran status by the United States government.

The Air Service. Just like the Chemical Warfare Department and the Signal Corps, the Army Air Service was really more of a combat force and only a small portion of its officers and enlisted men were considered to be in the SOS. Nevertheless, the basic "receive, store and issue" functions of supply as well as the construction of airfields and other aviation facilities were SOS responsibilities. Therefore, the Air Service aviation-specific supply and repair parts depots were considered to be part of the SOS, and most of these were located in the Advance Section. There were also Air Service units serving in England and Italy.

The Provost Marshal's Service. The Provost Marshal's Service was very lucky in the officers that were assigned, particularly Brigadier General Harry H. Bandholtz. Bandholtz had already established a solid reputation in the Army for his exploits in the Philippines. He arrived in France as the commander of the 54th Infantry Brigade in the 29th Division and led them through their early training and combat on the Lorraine Front before being assigned as the AEF's Provost Marshal. As a result of his reorganization of the Provost Marshal Service and his establishment of training and operational standards, Bandholtz is considered the "father of the modern Military Police Corps." A Pennsylvania State Trooper, Colonel J.C. Groome, also received high praise for his management of the German POW camp at Saint-Pierre des Corps. Hagood considered this camp to be the only part of the Provost Marshal's Service that was actually a part of the daily operation of the SOS, and he judged it to be an excellent operation.[22]

The War Risk Bureau. Tasked with maintaining the records that would provide information on the individual soldier's status and war insurance selections, the War Risk Bureau received high ratings from most who observed its operation. Although certainly not the most important department in the SOS for supporting the war effort, the recording of appropriate payment of insurance claims to soldier's families was critically important to the soldiers themselves. In time, this insurance was also extended to the war correspondents covering the AEF because many of them followed the Doughboys into the trenches and sometimes even accompanied their attacks.[23]

The Rents, Requisition and Claims Service. Nominally a service of the Judge Advocate General Corps, the officers of the Rents, Requisition and Claims (RRC) Service in France were placed under the command of the SOS. The mission for this organization was to investigate, assess and settle any monetary claims against the U.S. Army by any of the Allied nations or their citizens.[24] This was later extended to include property damage claims generated by Germans in the U.S. Army's occupation zone. The RRC also oversaw the massive sale of equipment that would not be transported back to the United States after the war.

The Army Service Corps. The Army Service Corps was another organization built from the ground up by the AEF in France. Serving as a key component of the SOS, the ASC provided the specialized workers required to operate the Base Sections, Hospital Centers and depots. These included specialists such as carpenters, cooks and bakers, mechanics, stenographers, blacksmiths, shoemakers, photographers, wheelwrights, etc., as well as a number of other SOS functions.[25]

The General Purchasing Board. Although the functions of the General Purchasing Board under General Dawes were discussed earlier, it is important to understand the ultimate success of this operation. In his book *Sinews of War*, James A. Huston wrote:

> Procurement in Europe reached substantial proportions. How important it was in saving ocean tonnage may be seen in the fact that the AEF actually obtained a greater percentage of supplies from European sources than ... from the United States. Through December 1918 the AEF received 7,675,000 ship tons of supplies from the United States, while it received the equivalent of over 10,000,000 ship tons from European procurement.[26]

Not mentioned by Huston was the important duty of the Purchasing Board to coordinate all the purchases made by the different branches of the SOS. This was critical. It ensured the branches weren't bidding against each other and driving up the cost of services and supplies. Maintaining offices in France, the British Isles, Spain, Switzerland, Portugal and Italy, the Board staff continually hunted for matériel that could be purchased, negating their requirement for shipment from America. These included lumber, draft animals, canned goods and even sheet metal for fabricating other items. The portion of the Purchasing Board that dealt with hiring local workers ended up employing some 29,000 laborers including some from North Africa, China, Malta, Italy, Belgium, Greece, France, and Senegal.[27]

Shutting down the SOS in France. The end of the SOS in France, when it came, came swiftly and on a large scale. In early May 1919 the *New York Times* reported that in a one-week period some 100,000 SOS soldiers had been relieved of duty and sent home. Another 200,000 were expected to be gone by the end of June. The announcement that Antwerp was to be the new SOS headquarters also included information that Base Sections Number 4 and 7 were closed. It also reported the schedule for closing the other sections: Base Sections Number 3 and 6 on 25 June; Base Section Number 2 on 10 July; Base Sections Number 1 and 8 on or around 20 July and Base Section Number 5 on 30 July. These closings would leave only the new Base Section in Antwerp as an active operation. All supply sections in the Advance and Intermediate Section were closed on 1 June. It was also announced that the U.S. Third Army would officially be renamed The American Forces in Germany (AFG).

Yet, with all this carefully scheduled shut down of facilities, there was still one more joker in the deck to be played. It was a true wild card and very nearly undid all the peace negotiations and the redeployment of the AEF back to the United States.

Restarting the war? Everything seemed to be going well until May of 1919 when reports filtered out from the Paris peace negotiations indicating the German government representatives were hesitant about signing the final surrender documents. Many German officials considered the surrender documents and the peace treaty being negotiated in Versailles to be a second capitulation to the Allies. Fearing for their reputations and their lives in an increasingly angry and violent postwar Germany, they were understandably reluctant to sign the documents. Their strategy appeared to be to drag out the negotiations, hoping to obtain less harsh terms.

This foot-dragging became apparent to the Allies. Just the opposite of Germany, they wanted to settle the treaty quickly so they could demobilize their armies that continued to consume many of the resources necessary to restore their war-weakened economies. They also needed to focus efforts on reshaping the map of Europe due to the dissolution of the Austro-Hungarian Empire and the Imperial Russian Empire. Hungary, Romania, Yugoslavia, the newly merged country of Czechoslovakia, Lithuania, and Poland were among the countries in question. All sought more land and population at the expense of their neighbors. Border clashes were frequent. Several of these incidents required the deployment of Allied troops to separate the warring factions. Clearly then, for the Allies, something had to be done quickly before their own military strength melted away. By this time almost half of the American occupation force in Germany had departed for home, leaving only the 1st, 2nd, 3rd and 4th Divisions and the 5th Division in Luxembourg. On 20 May 1919, Marshal Ferdinand Foch, overall military commander for the Allied Armies, directed the staffs of the French, British, Belgian and United States Armies to prepare operational plans that would move their forces out of their occupation zones and attack into unoccupied Germany.[28] Pershing's headquarters acknowledged the order and instructed Third Army Headquarters, located in Coblenz, to begin their planning phase. By 22 May, each of the American divisions had received instructions which included the wording:

> Should the enemy refuse or decline to sign the Treaty of Peace presented to him, the Allied and Associated Powers will renounce the present Armistice and resume the march of their armies into the enemy's territory.... The purpose of this advance would be: to separate northern and southern GERMANY by the occupation of the valley of the MAIN; to reduce the enemy's resources by the seizure of the RUHR industrial district; and to threaten his seats of government—WEIMAR and BERLIN....[29]

The basic operational plan for the Americans was simple in design. Since the 1st and 2nd Divisions were already occupying the bridgehead on the east side of the Rhine, they would lead the American forces through the 10-kilometer-wide neutral zone into unoccupied Germany. The 3rd Division, staged near Andernach on the west side of the Rhine, would move by foot, horse, motor vehicle and rail over the Rhine. The 4th Division would remain on the west bank of the Rhine to maintain security of the river crossings. A French Cavalry Division would pass through the American Zone and cross the Rhine to act as the link between the British army and the American forces.

A sign of the meticulous planning for this operation, posters were designed, printed and issued to the troops expected to advance into unoccupied Germany. The posters informed all German railroad workers and government officials in the newly occupied areas they were expected to remain on the job while anyone leaving "his post will be court martialed." They also included the ominous warning that "Any house, from which civilians have fired on Allied troops, will be burnt."

On 9 June 1919, the Third Army received another message indicating the rising tension between the Allies and the Germans:

> The enemy has refused to sign the Treaty of Peace presented to him. The Armistice has been renounced by the Allied and Associated Powers, effective at H

11. Closing the Accounts 201

h[our] of D day. The enemy occupies with one corps of approximately 10,000 second class troops, the territory through which this army will advance. His forces are scattered and are not prepared to offer an organized resistance. Resistance from stubborn detachments of a battalion or less may be expected.[30]

For the soldiers of Third Army, many of whom had fought their way through the Argonne against German soldiers, the statement from higher headquarters that they would be facing only 10,000 second class troops was probably greeted with some skepticism. They had learned the hard way what a few German soldiers behind a Maschinengewehr (MG 08) machine gun could do to advancing American troops.

As German hesitance continued to deadlock the peace treaty signing, Marshal Foch finally determined a date for the operation to commence. On 17 June, the Third Army received notification that D-Day would be 20 June 1919.[31] Prior to this, the Allied forces had been told that the day three days before the actual operation would be known as J-Day which would then let all participants know that they were now in the three-day window and to proceed with their troop movements. This planning information was so important in ensuring the transportation requirements were met that French Lieutenant Colonel Jean Marcel Guitry, senior member of the Inter-Allied Railway Commission, personally telephoned the French liaison officer in the Coblenz office on 16 June to ensure that he and his American counterpart were aware of the impending announcement. At this point, however, H-Hour had not yet been determined and while the subsequent J-Day (17 June) Third Army message provided further movement instructions for the American units, the exact time for the attack remained a mystery.

The very next day, 18 June 1919, Third Army received a change; D-Day was now set as 23 June 1919. Simultaneously as this message was sent, the roads in the American Zone on the east side of the Rhine were filled with trucks and horses as the soldiers and Marines of the 1st and 2nd Divisions moved to their jumping off points near the Neutral Zone. By 19 June, even the artillery regiments were in place and ready to support the advance with either fire or further maneuver. The Third Army reported that "concentration of our troops having been completed this date, the American Third Army is prepared to advance eastward."[32] It also informed its subordinate units that H-hour was now set for 7 p.m. on 23 June.

The Americans received word that the British forces to the north and the French to the south were ready. With this notification all eyes turned to watching the clock. Rations, gasoline and forage for the animals in the combat units were scheduled to be delivered to designated forward railheads. Ammunition was to be supplied from stockage maintained at the ammo depot in Neuwied. Evacuation hospitals were loaded on trains and staged at the Coblenz railhead awaiting movement orders. Resumption of the war was now less than 36 hours away.

Tensions increased on 21 June when the crews on the warships of the German fleet, interned at Scapa Flow in the Orkney Islands after the Armistice, scuttled their own ships rather than have them taken over by the Allies. Very quickly 74 German warships were sitting on the bottom of the sea. The next day in Versailles, the German delegation indicated they might be willing to sign the treaty except for the clauses that held Germany responsible for starting the war and asked for an extension to the signing deadline. Angry about the German warships being scuttled, the Allies rejected this request and informed the Germans that the deadline remained 23 June.

At 6 p.m. on 22 June, the Third Army reported, "The American Third Army is awaiting orders for forward movement."[33] War was now only 25 hours away. With possibility of war looming, events outside the occupation zones now took a sudden turn. In Berlin, the German cabinet and its leader, *Reichs* Chancellor Philipp Scheidemann, resigned from office. They were quickly replaced by a new coalition government formed under former trade union leader Gustav Bauer. When the senior German army leaders were summoned by the new government and asked if they could defend Germany from an attack by the Allies, their only reply was that the situation was "hopeless." In light of this revelation the German government notified the attendees at the Paris Peace Conference of their intention to sign the peace treaty as written. As a result, at 10 a.m. on 23 June, the Third Army sent a message to its units:

From: Chief of Staff, Third Army
To: Commanding General, III Corps
1. The preliminary operations directed by letter June 19, to begin at 19 h., June 23, are suspended until further orders.[34]

War had been averted with just nine hours to spare. The actual signing ceremony for the Treaty of Versailles took place on 28 June. Ironically, while the main participants accepted and signed, President Woodrow Wilson was unable to convince the United States Congress to ratify the treaty due to political infighting and a growing isolationist movement in the States. As a result, the U.S. would remain technically at war with Germany until the Treaty of Berlin was signed by both countries in August of 1921.

American Forces in Germany. In July 1919, the Third Army furled its flag and was replaced by the American Forces in Germany. In the United States, the 1920s were starting to "roar," and with the postwar economic boom and the growing sense of isolationism, no one really cared much

11. Closing the Accounts

Not every voyage back to the United States was a happy one. In this photograph, a row of flag-draped caskets are on deck. Written on the back: "Bringing a few of our boys home, 2 August 1920" (private collection).

about the German Rhineland. The U.S. congressional enthusiasm to maintain a force on the Rhine dwindled with time, causing the size of the AFG to shrink as the occupation ran its course. With the continued drawdown, every month brought more sales of excess equipment no longer needed. All AFG aviation activities shut down in April 1922, and all aviation equipment, including 24 DeHavilland DH-4 aircraft, several brand-new Liberty engines and other spare parts at the flying field near Weissenthurm, was sold.[35]

In January 1923, with its strength down to a thousand men, the AFG received orders to lower its flag and return home. Faithful to the very end to the cause of innovation and salvage, all matériel that could not be carried away was disposed of through local auctions and sales. Even the AFG's unofficial newspaper, *The Amaroc News*, supported completely by local subscriptions and advertising, sold off all its office equipment and donated the proceeds to buy milk for the children of poor German families in Coblenz. By February 1923, with only a few scattered Graves Registration officers remaining in France, the once two-million-soldier AEF remained only in memory.

Congressional hearings. Back in the States, the congressional hearings into wartime spending had already begun. A number of senior-

After the League of Nations is a Fact. (Maybe)

From the May 1919 edition of *The Skirmisher*, the 4th Division's newspaper in Germany, comes this drawing that spoke to the hopes of many that the weapons of war would be sold as junk. Sadly, the hoped-for "League of Nations" proved to be inadequate and a second world war would follow the first in just 20 years (private collection).

ranking officers of the SOS were called on to testify in 1921 including the most articulate of them, Charles Dawes. After many days of hearings, Dawes finally lost his patience with the congressmen and lashed out:

> We didn't dicker. Why man alive, we had to win the war. We would have paid horse prices for sheep if the sheep could have pulled artillery to the front....

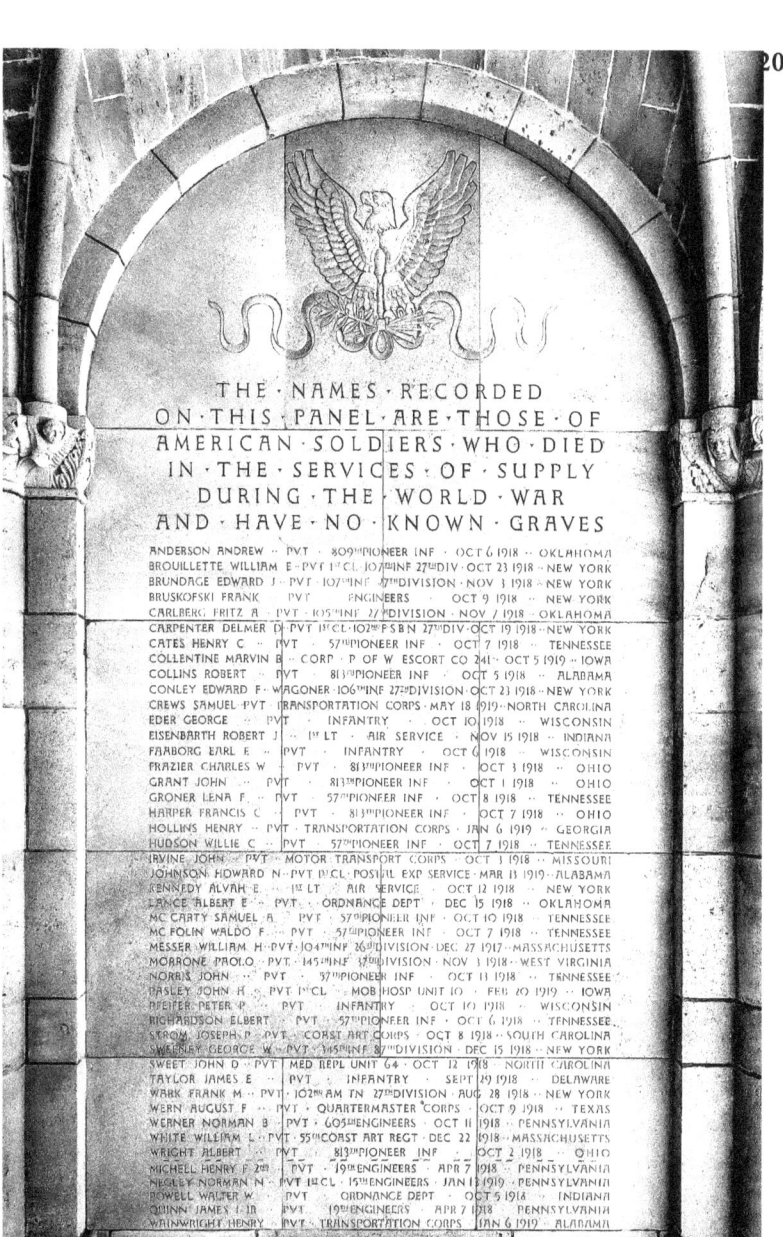

Unique among the many World War I memorials, the Services of Supply memorial in the Meuse-Argonne displays a list of dead SOS soldiers whose bodies were never identified. It's interesting that the names are listed alphabetically, completely without regard to the soldier's race or color (photograph by Brian Grogan, copyright 2016).

> Oh, it's all right now to say we bought too much ... but we saved the civilization of the world.[36]

Dawes was right. In recent years it has become fashionable to denigrate the American contribution to ending the war. Stopping the German attacks along the Marne in the summer of 1918 had proven that the AEF could fight. Ultimately it was that knowledge and the fact the Americans were landing thousands more of these fighters every day in France that brought the Germans to the negotiating table. American units played an important role in the British army's last offensive and the U.S. First Army's Meuse-Argonne Offensive broke the German lines decisively, although at terrible cost. Truly it was the AEF and its loyal, hardworking support force, the SOS, which "saved the civilization of the world."

Chapter Notes

Preface

1. Hagood, *The Services of Supply*, p. 154.

Chapter 1

1. Goedeken, "Charles Dawes and the Military Board of Allied Supply," p. 5.
2. The term LOC has remained in vogue today although the term "Zone of the Interior" has been replaced by "Continental United States" or more commonly CONUS.
3. Harbord, *The American Army in France, 1917–1919*, pp. 373–374.
4. *Ibid.*, pp. 372–373.
5. Dalessandro and Knapp, *Organization and Insignia of the American Expeditionary Force, 1917–1923*, pp. 29–30.
6. Harbord, *The American Army in France, 1917–1919*, p. 376.
7. *Ibid.*, p. 379.
8. *Ibid.*, p. 373.
9. Dalessandro and Knapp, *Organization and Insignia of the American Expeditionary Force, 1917–1923*, p. 33.
10. U.S. Department of the Army, *American Representation in Occupied Germany, 1920–1921, Volume II*, pp. 366–368.
11. Harbord, *The American Army in France, 1917–1919*, p. 377.
12. *Ibid.*, pp. 376–377.
13. Chaikin, "Quartermaster Supply in the AEF, 1917–1918."
14. Hagood, *The Services of Supply*, p. 42.
15. *Ibid.*, p. 186.
16. Harbord, *Leaves from a War Diary*, pp. 343–344.
17. *Ibid.*, p. 376.
18. Lieutenant Naumann, records and documents, private collection.
19. Hagood, *The Services of Supply*, pp. 52–53.
20. U.S. Army, *United States Army in the World War 1917–1919, American Occupation of Germany, Volume 11*, p. 33.
21. Dawes, *A Journal of the Great War*, pp. 172–173.
22. Max Brakebill, letters from France, 1918–1919, private collection.
23. Stallings, *The Doughboys*, p. 375.
24. Fredericks, *The Yanks Are Coming*, p. 134.
25. Stallings, *The Doughboys*, p. 25.
26. Thompson, *Trench Knives and Mustard Gas*, pp. 26–30.
27. *New York Times*, 28 April 1918.
28. Hagood, *The Services of Supply*, p. 57.
29. *Ibid.*, p. 107. Sadly, the LOC has no monopoly on this sort of problem. In 2004, one of the authors witnessed large shipments of plywood and Humvee tires on trucks returning from Iraq to Kuwait. These exact same items had been transported north just days earlier, on very dangerous convoy routes, only to be sent back as unneeded. When asked, one Transportation Corps officer said that he had seen this happen repeatedly and had taken to marking some shipments with small colored sticky labels so he could verify it was the same matériel he had shipped. Unfortunately, the headquarters guiding the operation had insisted these items were needed in Iraq and continued to press for their priority movement north. In Iraq there was no secure storage space for the bulky items and so back they came. And the sticky labels multiplied.

30. *Ibid.*, p. 51.
31. *Ibid.*, p. 271.
32. *Ibid.*, pp. 79–82.
33. *Ibid.*, p. 55.
34. *Ibid.*, p. 343. Statement to Hagood by 33rd Division Commander on 27 July 1918.
35. *Ibid.*, pp. 232–233.
36. *Ibid.*, pp. 138–141.
37. *Ibid.*, p. 157. Note: The term "Service of Supply" was also commonly used.
38. *Ibid.*, pp. 208–210.
39. Lawrence, *Doughboy's Diary*, p. 8.
40. Ayres, "The War with Germany: A Statistical Summary," p. 48.

Chapter 2

1. Hagood, *The Services of Supply*, p. 211.
2. *Ibid.*, p. 237.
3. Gleaves, *A History of the Transport Service*, p. 22.
4. Hirrel, *Supporting the Doughboys*, p. 68.
5. Fleming, *The Illusion of Victory*, p. 173.
6. Beaver, *Newton D. Baker and the American War Effort, 1917–1919*, p. 85.
7. Gleaves, *A History of the Transport Service*, p. 69.
8. *Ibid*
9. *Ibid.*, pp. 68–69.
10. Palmer, "German Raiders in Hampton Roads," pp. 2–3.
11. Beaver, *Newton D. Baker and the American War Effort, 1917–1919*, pp. 85–86.
12. Ruth Wright Kaufman, unpublished article, April 1919, p. 3. Archives and Special Collections, Library of the Marine Corps, Quantico, VA.
13. Ayres, "The War with Germany: A Statistical Summary," p. 36.
14. *Ibid.*, p. 48.
15. Gleaves, *A History of the Transport Service*, p. 18.
16. *New York Times*, 20 December 1917.
17. Hagood, *The Services of Supply*, p. 183.
18. Harbord, *The American Army in France, 1917–1919*, p. 398.
19. "Base Ports of AEF Return to France," *Stars & Stripes*, 28 February 1919.

Chapter 3

1. Baker, *Doughboy's Diary*, p. 120.
2. Dienst, *History of the 353rd Infantry Regiment, 89th Division National Army, September 1917 to June 1919*, p. 21.
3. U.S. Army, *Posts, Camps, and Stations Volume 3*, p. 748.
4. *Ibid.*, pp. 753–754.
5. *Ibid.*, p. 791.
6. Charles Etzweiler, letter to father Edward Etzweiler, 24 November 1918.
7. Ford, *The Medical Department of the United States Army in the World War, Vol. II*, p. 468.
8. Hagood, *The Services of Supply*, p. 184.
9. McClellan, *The United States Marine Corps in the World War*, pp. 107–109.
10. *Ibid.*, p. 109.
11. Citation: Butler's Army Distinguished Service Medal in *ibid.*, p. 106.
12. Marshall, *Memoirs of My Service in the World War, 1917–1918*, pp. 194–195.
13. Ford, *The Medical Department of the United States Army in the World War, Vol. II Army*, pp. 465–466, and Dalessandro and Knapp, *Organization and Insignia of the American Expeditionary Force, 1917–1923*, p. 32.
14. New Mexico Military Records, Ancestry.com.
15. *Ibid.*
16. Kaufman, unpublished article.
17. Ford, *The Medical Department of the United States Army in the World War, Vol. II*, pp. 469–470.
18. Baker, *Doughboy's Diary*, p. 121.
19. *Ibid.*, p. 122.
20. *Ibid.*, pp. 121–122.
21. Max Brakebill, letters from France 1918–1919, private collection.

Chapter 4

1. Ayres, "The War with Germany: A Statistical Summary," p. 51.
2. Harbord, *The American Army in France, 1917–1919*, pp. 380–381.
3. *Ibid.*, pp. 390–391.
4. Hagood, *The Services of Supply*, pp. 264–266.
5. Hirrel, *Supporting the Doughboys*, p. 68.
6. *The CRO*, 8 June 1919.

7. Brady, *History of the Ordnance Repair Shops, Mehun-sur-Yevre, France*, pp. 1–5.
8. "Women Increase Shop Production," *Mehun News*, February 1919.
9. "178 Bullets for every A.E.F. Shell," *AMAROC News*, date unknown.
10. *The CRO*, 8 June 1919.
11. Davies, *Twentieth Engineers, France, 1917-1918-1919*, unpaginated.
12. New Mexico Service Records, Ancestry.com.
13. *Ibid*. Hucks' sense of humor comes through on his New Mexico war service questionnaire. He was unmarried, and when asked to indicate whether he had any children, Hucks wrote: *"Jene sui pas"* ("I don't know"). For the question "Reason for discharge," Hucks wrote: "For cutting too much lumber."
14. Hagood, *The Services of Supply*, pp. 340–341.
15. *Ibid.*, pp. 193–195.
16. All information on Wallis is from New Mexico Service Records and New Mexico Death Records, Ancestry.com.
17. Hagood, *The Services of Supply*, p. 196.
18. U.S. Department of the Army, *American Military Government of Occupied Germany, 1918–1920, Report of the Officer in Charge of Civil Affairs, Third Army and American Forces Germany*, p. 39.
19. Barnes, *In a Strange Land*, p. 48.
20. Chaikin, "Quartermaster Supply in the AEF, 1917–1918."
21. U.S. Army Quartermaster Corps, *American Salvage Depot—Intermediate Number Eight*, pp. 1–3.
22. Harbord, *The American Army in France, 1917–1919*, p. 500.
23. Hagood, *The Services of Supply*, pp. 290–292.
24. Wayne Keith, diary, private collection.
25. Hagood, *The Services of Supply*, p. 211.
26. *Ibid.*, pp. 232–233.
27. *Ibid.*, pp. 149–150.
28. *Ibid.*, pp. 245–246.
29. Harbord, *The American Army in France, 1917–1919*, pp. 413–414.
30. Hagood, *The Services of Supply*, p. 274.
31. New Mexico War Service Records, Ancestry.com.
32. Hagood, *The Services of Supply*, pp. 165–167.
33. *Ibid.*, pp. 176–178.
34. *Ibid.*, p. 275.
35. Dawes, *A Journal of the Great War*, p. 45.
36. Cockfield, *With Snow on Their Boots*, pp. 202–237. Another option for returning the Russians to their homeland was explored. Instead of sending them northward through the Baltic, the French asked if the Americans would be willing to ship them from France westward across the Atlantic, cross country by train, and then again by ship to Vladivostok. The American response was an immediate "no."
37. Hagood, *The Services of Supply*, p. 286.
38. Harbord, *The American Army in France, 1917–1919*, p. 412.
39. Hagood, *The Services of Supply*, p. 313.
40. Dawes, *A Journal of the Great War*, pp. 103–105.
41. U.S. Army, *United States Army in the World War 1917–1919, American Occupation of Germany, Volume 11*, p. 33.
42. Hagood, *The Services of Supply*, p. 315.
43. *Ibid.*, pp. 317–318.
44. Dawes, *A Journal of the Great War*, pp. 174–175.
45. Cutchins, *An Amateur Diplomat in the World War*, pp. 85–86.
46. U.S. Department of the Army, Quartermaster Corps School, *Operations of the Quartermaster Corps U.S. Army During the World War*, Monograph No. 9, pp. 90–105.
47. Lawrence, *Fighting Soldier*, p. 105.
48. *Ibid.*, p. 115.
49. Nenninger, "Tactical Dysfunction in the AEF, 1917–1918," p. 180.
50. Bert A. Fidler, oral history, 1918–1919, private collection.
51. "178 Bullets for Every A.E.F. Shell," *AMAROC News*, date unknown.

Chapter 5

1. "The Rose of No Man's Land" by Jack Caddigan and James A. Brennan.
2. Hagood, *The Services of Supply*, pp. 344–345.

3. U.S. Army Medical Department, *Administration American Expeditionary Force, Volume 2*, Tables of Organization.
4. Reynolds, Evacuation System of a Field Army.
5. U.S. Army Medical Department, *Administration American Expeditionary Force, Volume 2*, Tables of Organization, No. 101.
6. *Ibid*.
7. Wadhams, Report of G-4-B, medical group, fourth section, general staff, G.H.Q., A.E.F., December 31, 1918.
8. U.S. Army Medical Department, *Administration American Expeditionary Force, Volume 2*, Tables of Organization, No. 320, 3–1.
9. Letter, Commander in Chief, A.E.F., to Chief, French military mission, September 27, 1917. Subject: Program for hospitalization.
10. 1st endorsement from Commander in Chief, G-4, general staff, G.H.Q., A.E.F., June 1, 1918, to the Commanding General, S.O.S.
11. Letter, Commander in Chief, A.E.F., to Chief, French military mission, September 27, 1917. Subject: Program for hospitalization.
12. *Ibid*.
13. Riddell, Report of the Activities Camp Hospital No. 26, St. Aignan-Noyers, as of January 1, 1919, and Buck, Report of Activities of Camp Hospital No. 52, Le Mans, as of January 1, 1919.
14. MacDonald, *The Roses of No Man's Land*, pp. 268–269.
15. Report from Chief Surgeon, AEF, to Surgeon General, U.S. Army, dated 1 May 1919. Subject: Activities of the Chief Surgeon's Office to May 1, 1919.
16. Wadhams and Tuttle, "Some of the Early Activities of the Medical Department, A.E.F.," p. 636.
17. For details concerning shortage of Medical Department personnel, see U.S. Army Medical Department, *The Medical Department of the United States Army in the World War: Volume VIII, Field Operations*, Chapt. I.
18. Crane, *The Medical Department of the United States Army in the World War, Vol. XIII*, p. 93.
19. Stallings, *The Doughboys*, p. 381.
20. *Ibid*.
21. Crane, *The Medical Department of the United States Army in the World War, Vol. XIII*, pp. 233–234.
22. Stanley Nasilowski, letter, to his friend Helen Bialkoswka, private collection. This letter was extremely difficult to get translated because of the archaic version of Polish/Russian in which it was written. Our thanks to Captain Ulyana Pivovarova, VANG, for helping us find a translator.
23. *New York Times*, 27 September 1918 and 5 October 1918.
24. Koehn, collection of letters, 1918–1919, from the 83rd Division, private collection, and Crane, *The Medical Department of the United States Army in the World War, Vol. XIII*, p. 462.
25. Crane, *The Medical Department of the United States Army in the World War, Vol. XIII*, pp. 462–463.
26. *Ibid*., pp. 462–463.
27. "Congressman Borland Dies Suddenly," *The CRO*, 1 March 1919.
28. MacDonald, *The Roses of No Man's Land*, p. 289.
29. *Ibid*., p. 290.
30. Cushing and Stone, *Vermont in the World War*, pp. 7–8.
31. Baker, *Doughboy's Diary*, pp. 111–114.
32. Deuel, diary entry, 18 December 1918, private collection.
33. Stallings, *The Doughboys*, p. 370.
34. Crane, *The Medical Department of the United States Army in the World War, Vol. XIII*, pp. 485–486.
35. *Ibid*., p. 505.
36. *Ibid*.

Chapter 6

1. Shanks, *As They Passed Through the Port*, p. 221.
2. Hirrel, *Supporting the Doughboys*, pp. 49–50.
3. "American War Locomotives for France," *American Machinist*, p. 856.
4. Harbord, *The American Army in France, 1917–1919*, pp. 373–374.
5. Hagood, *The Services of Supply*, pp. 340–341.
6. Huston, *The Sinews of War*, pp. 378–379.
7. *An Historical and Technical Biography of the Twenty-First Engineers, Light*

Railway, p. 28. This unit history provides an enlightening look at how U.S. Army railway operations were conducted in France.
    8. Hagood, *The Services of Supply*, pp. 340–341.
    9. New Mexico War Service Records, Ancestry.com.
    10. *Ibid*.
    11. *Ibid*.
    12. *Ibid*.
    13. *An Historical and Technical Biography of the Twenty-First Engineers, Light Railway*, p. 21.
    14. *Ibid.*, p. 51.
    15. Quoted in Stallings, *The Doughboys*, p. 40.
    16. Jackson, *Fall Out to the Right of the Road*, p. 148.
    17. U.S. Army Quartermaster Corps, *Operations of the Quartermaster Corps*, Monograph No. 2, p. 51.
    18. *54th Pioneer Infantry with the Army of Occupation, Third U.S. Army*, p. 13.
    19. *Ibid.*, p. 55.

Chapter 7

    1. Hagood, *The Services of Supply*, p. 90.
    2. *Ibid.*, p. 86.
    3. American Library Association homepage.
    4. Berry, *Make the Kaiser Dance*, p. 86.
    5. Hagood, *The Services of Supply*, p. 88.
    6. Roosevelt, *Day Before Yesterday*, p. 93.
    7. Hart, letter, 5 April 1919, Brest, France, Charles G. Thomas collection.
    8. Hunton and Johnson, *Two Colored Women with the American Expeditionary Forces*, p. 157.
    9. Schneider and Schneider, *Into the Breach*, pp. 174–176.
    10. *Ibid.*, p. 123.
    11. *Ibid*.
    12. Hagood, *The Services of Supply*, p. 89.
    13. Schneider and Schneider, *Into the Breach*, pp. 139–143.
    14. Hart, letter, 5 April 1919, Brest, France, Charles G. Thomas collection.
    15. Schneider and Schneider, *Into the Breach*, p. 120.
    16. *Ibid.*, pp. 149–152.
    17. *Ibid.*, p. 124.
    18. Beaver, *Newton D. Baker and the American War Effort, 1917-1919*, p. 223.
    19. Hagood, *The Services of Supply*, p. 90.
    20. Beaver, *Newton D. Baker and the American War Effort, 1917-1919*, p. 223. Peabody is best known today for the use of his name for the award for distinguished and meritorious public service by radio and television stations, networks, producing organizations, and individuals: the Peabody Award.
    21. Mayo, *That Damn Y*, pp. 413–416.
    22. "RC Finishes in France," *The CRO*, 10 June 1919.
    23. Sprenger and Edmonds, *The Leave Areas of the American Expeditionary Forces, 1918-1919*, p. 107.
    24. Cutchins, *History of the Twenty-Ninth Division "Blue and Gray," 1917-1919*, p. 249.

Chapter 8

    1. Dawes, *A Journal of the Great War*, preface.
    2. United States Military Academy, *Alphabetical Locator of Graduates and Former Cadets, Vol IX*, p. 55.
    3. U.S. Army Military Police School homepage, http://www.wood.army.mil/usamps.
    4. USMC History Division homepage, https://www.usmcu.edu/.
    5. Musicant, *The Banana Wars*, pp. 188–207.
    6. McClellan, *The United States Marine Corps in the Great War*, pp. 105–111.
    7. USMC History Division homepage, https://www.usmcu.edu/.
    8. Rinaldi, *The United States Army in World War I*, p. 177.
    9. "Not Taking Office Says Gen. Dawes," *New York Times*, 3 February 1921.
    10. United States Military Academy, *Alphabetical Locator of Graduates and Former Cadets, Vol IX*, p. 66.
    11. Hagood, *The Services of Supply*, 72.
    12. Hagood, *Caissons Go Rolling Along*, xviii–xix, and https://alumni.westpointaog.org/memorial-article.
    13. Pershing, *My Life Before the World War, 1860-1917*, pp. 524–525.
    14. United States Military Academy, *Alphabetical Locator of Graduates and Former Cadets, Vol IX*, p. 44.

15. Hagood, *The Services of Supply*, p. 8.
16. Eisenhower, *Yanks*, pp. 179–181.
17. Arlington National Cemetery website, http://www.arlingtoncemetery.mil/.
18. United States Military Academy, *Alphabetical Locator of Graduates and Former Cadets, Vol IX*, p. 177.
19. U.S. Army CASCOM website, http://www.cascom.army.mil/.

Chapter 9

1. Jesse Garner, 79th FA, New Mexico Service Records, Ancestry.com.
2. Lee, *Letters from Roger I. Lee, Lt. Colonel, U.S. Army Medical Corps, 1917–1918*, pp. 69–70.
3. Hagood, *The Services of Supply*, p. 169.
4. *Ibid.*, pp. 168–169.
5. Max Brakebill, letters from France, 1918–1919, private collection.
6. Koehn, collection of letters, 1918–1919, private collection.
7. Dawes, *A Journal of the Great War*, p. 21.
8. *Ibid.*
9. Chamberlain and Weed, *The Medical Department of the United States Army in the World War, Vol. VI, Sanitation*, pp. 615–616.
10. *Ibid.*
11. Dawes, *A Journal of the Great War*, p. 72.
12. *Ibid.*, p. 102.
13. *Ibid.*, p. 165.
14. U.S. Army Quartermaster Corps, *Operations of the Quartermaster Corps*, Monograph No. 2, p. 123.
15. *Ibid.*
16. *Ibid.*, p. 124. In the last half of the 19th century, some U.S. Army troops stationed in remote areas in the trans–Mississippi West had cultivated vegetable gardens for much the same reasons that their military "grandsons" were doing in France.
17. *Ibid.*, p. 125.
18. *Ibid.*, p. 126.
19. Pennsylvania Service Records and Army Transport Manifests, Ancestry.com.
20. U.S. Army Quartermaster Corps, *Operations of the Quartermaster Corps*, Monograph No. 2, p. 125.
21. Dawes, *A Journal of the Great War*, pp. 98–99.
22. U.S. Army Quartermaster Corps, *Operations of the Quartermaster Corps*, Monograph No. 2, pp. 24–25.
23. *Ibid.*, p. 25.
24. Army Transport Manifests, Ancestry.com.
25. Various WWI Service Record databases, Ancestry.com.
26. U.S. Army Quartermaster Corps, *Operations of the Quartermaster Corps*, Monograph No. 2, p. 26.
27. *Ibid.*, p. 27. As an example of the SOS's thorough practice of salvaging useful materials, the cloth bags used at the coffee plants had previously been used to store goods such as flour or sugar. The bags were sent to a salvage plant where they were cleaned and deodorized before being shipped to the coffee plants for reuse. French civilian women were employed to sew the bags shut once they were filled.
28. *Ibid.*, pp. 26–27.
29. AEF, Order of Battle of the AEF.
30. Hagood, *The Services of Supply*, p. 63.
31. Harbord, *The American Army in France, 1917–1919*, p. 384.
32. *The CRO*, 3 May 1919.
33. "Tours Sergeant Killed by Tram," *The CRO*, 10 May 1919.
34. "Frank A Styert, Veteran Soldier, Meets Glorious End," *The Cootie*, 19 April 1919.
35. "CRO Man Badly Hurt in Fall," *The CRO*, 26 April 1919.
36. Barbeau and Henri, *The Unknown Soldiers*, p. 89.
37. Rinaldi, *The United States Army in World War I*, p. 54.
38. Barbeau and Henri, *The Unknown Soldiers*, pp. 108–109.
39. Harbord, *The American Army in France, 1917–1919*, p. 391.
40. Hagood, *The Services of Supply*, p. 106, and Barbeau and Henri, *The Unknown Soldiers*, p. 108.
41. Barbeau and Henri, *The Unknown Soldiers*, p. 107.
42. *Ibid.*
43. *Ibid.*, pp. 165–166.
44. The rosters of men in the detachments are from Army Transport Manifests, civilian occupations are from World War I Draft Registrations and 1920 U.S.

Census, Ancestry.com. In a few cases, it was impossible to determine a man's pre-war or immediate postwar occupation.
45. Pennsylvania Service Records, Ancestry.com.
46. *Ibid.*
47. *Ibid.*
48. Connecticut Service Records, Ancestry.com.
49. Some of the men in the Stateside-bound Headquarters, Band Instrument and Typewriter Repair Detachment were found listed in one of the earlier, France-bound detachments.
50. Connecticut Service Records, Ancestry.com.
51. *Stars & Stripes*, 17 January 1919.
52. "Yankee Girls Primp Up for General's Inspection," *The CRO*, 9 March 1919.
53. "Tours Ordnance Dept. Employs 50 Yankee Girls," *The CRO*, 15 February 1919.
54. Harbord, *The American Army in France, 1917-1919*, p. 377.
55. "Hun Propaganda No Worse Than Liquor Curse," *The CRO*, 8 March 1919.
56. "Forestry Men Are Getting After Jobs," *The CRO*, 10 May 1919.
57. AEF Headquarters, District of Paris, France, 18 December 1918.
58. "Division Markings Barred in States," *Stars & Stripes*, 20 February 1919.
59. "Insignia to Stand," *Stars & Stripes*, 28 February 1919.
60. Cutchins, *History of the Twenty-Ninth Division "Blue and Gray," 1917-1919*, pp. 260-261.
61. Barbeau and Henri, *The Unknown Soldiers*, p. 104.
62. "Personnel Searchers Return from Coblentz," *The CRO*, 29 March 1919.
63. "Soldiers Trapped in Big MTC Fire," *The CRO*, 22 February 1919.
64. "270,000 Francs Damaged at Fire," *The CRO*, 1 March 1919.
65. "American Firemen Fight French Fire," *The CRO*, 8 June 1919.
66. "Heroic SOS acts recorded in GO," *Stars & Stripes*, 31 January 1919.
67. Dawes, *A Journal of the Great War*, p. 18.
68. *Ibid.*
69. "Yankee Girls Are Policing Wicked Paris," *The Gangplank*, 13 June 1919. It's important to note if you refer back to Chapter 5 to the card providing prophylactic information, one of the sites mentioned in this story, the *Boulevard des Italiens*, is located close to the "Pro Station" on the card. Coincidence?
70. "Ice Plant Company Is Losing Patience," *The York Dispatch*, York, Pennsylvania, 10 February 1919, and "Refutes Complaint of Ice Plant Unit," *The Gazette and Daily*, York, Pennsylvania, 11 February 1919, Newspapers.com.
71. "Refutes Complaint of Ice Plant Unit," *The Gazette and Daily*, 11 February 1919, Newspapers.com.
72. "No Unfair Treatment of Ice Plant Company," *The York Dispatch*, 28 March 1919, Newspapers.com. The name H.D. Clements does not appear on the Ice Plant Company No. 301 rosters on the Army Transport Manifests for the company's shipment to France (transport No. 1, 18 January 1918) or for the Company's return to the United States (USS *Nebraska*, 10 June 1919); see Army Transport Manifests, Ancestry.com.
73. *Ibid.*
74. Scott, *The American Negro in the World War*, pp. 326-327.
75. AEF Headquarters, District of Paris, Special Order Finding #256, private collection.
76. *New York Times*, 30 July 1919.
77. *Ibid.*
78. *New York Times*, 18 July 1918.
79. *New York Times*, 10 December 1919.
80. *New York Times*, 10 December 1919.
81. *New York Times*, 31 December 1919.
82. *New York Times*, 7 February 1920, and Garland, "Army Officer Accused of Prisoner Abuse," pp. 13-14.

Chapter 10

1. Hagood, *The Services of Supply*, p. 54.
2. "CRO Not Part of the SOS," *The CRO*, 22 February 1919.
3. "2,000,000 Tales in Master Cards," *The CRO*, 10 May 1919.
4. "Seven Marines Are Sent Home," *The CRO*, 14 April 1919.
5. "No Plans for CRO," *The CRO*, 26 April 1919.
6. Beurket, *Postal Service for a Field Army in [the] Theater of Operations*. Beurket, a West Point graduate from Pennsylvania, served as the officer in charge

of the Central Post Office. Unless otherwise specified, much of the information in this section comes from this document.
7. Hagood, *The Services of Supply*, pp. 82-83.
8. Ibid., p. 83.
9. *The Battle of Bourges, 1918-1919*, p. 42; and Beurket, *Postal Service*, p. 14.
10. *Stars & Stripes* (Paris Edition), 28 February 1918.
11. Hagood, *The Services of Supply*, pp. 84-85.
12. Ibid., p. 54.
13. Beurket, *Postal Service*, pp. 10-11.
14. Ibid., p. 20.
15. Ibid.
16. Ibid., p. 21.
17. *Oroville Daily Register*, 11 November 1918.

Chapter 11

1. Lt. Gen. Hunter L. Liggett, Commander, U.S. First Army, "Praises Service of Supply," *Stars and Stripes*, 22 November 1918.
2. Ibid.
3. Kirby, *How Me and Amos Won WWI*, p. 61.
4. U.S. Department of the Army, Quartermaster Corps School, *Operations of the Quartermaster Corps U.S. Army During the World War*, Monograph No. 9, undated, pp. 28-31.
5. U.S. Department of the Army, *American Military Government of Occupied Germany, 1918-1920, Report of the Officer in Charge of Civil Affairs, Third Army and American Forces Germany*, p. 60.
6. Lockett, *Report of the Military Commander, Coblenz, Germany from December 8, 1918, to May 22, 1919*, pp. 101-111, 118-120, 129, and U.S. Army Quartermaster Corps. *United States Army in the World War*, 1:341; *Report of Remount Service, A.E.F.*, pp. 82-85.
7. Barnes, "Great Coblentz Horse Sale," pp. 41-43.
8. *Die Wacht Am Rhine* 1, no. 3 (1 April 1919).
9. U.S. Department of the Army, *American Representation in Occupied Germany, 1920-1921*, Volume II, p. 200.
10. Hagood, *The Services of Supply*, p. 336.
11. Harbord, *The American Army in France, 1917-1919*, p. 497.
12. Ibid., p. 498.
13. Hagood, *The Services of Supply*, pp. 341-342.
14. Harbord, *The American Army in France, 1917-1919*, pp. 500-501.
15. Huston, *The Sinews of War*, p. 369.
16. Ibid.
17. Hagood, *The Services of Supply*, p. 344.
18. Harbord, *The American Army in France, 1917-1919*, p. 442.
19. Hagood, *The Services of Supply*, pp. 346-347.
20. Raines, *Getting the Message Through*, pp. 176-178.
21. Hagood, *The Services of Supply*, p. 348, and 86th Anniversary Signal Corps, U.S. Army pamphlet, p. 4.
22. Hagood, *The Services of Supply*, pp. 349-350.
23. Pershing, *My Experiences in the World War, Volume II*, p. 88.
24. Harbord, *The American Army in France, 1917-1919*, p. 509.
25. Ibid.
26. Huston, *The Sinews of War*, pp. 370-371.
27. Harbord, *The American Army in France, 1917-1919*, pp. 489-91.
28. Order, General Headquarters, Allied Armies, 20 May 1919, DGCRA No. 8618.
29. Chief of Staff, Third Army, to Commanding Generals, III Corps and 3d Division, 22 May 1919, "Directive for the High Command Only." It was forwarded to Third Army via G-3, GHQ.
30. U.S. Third Army, Plans in Case Germany Refuses to Sign Peace Treaty, Field Orders 193-32.1, No. 9 (Third Army, AEF, 17 June 1919).
31. U.S. Third Army, Plan of Communication, Supply and Evacuation, Annex No. 3, Trèves, France (Third Army, AEF, 19 June 1919).
32. U.S. Third Army, June 14 to 18 [Extract] Estimate of the Situation, Operations Report 193-33.1, Folder No. 47 (Third Army, AEF, 19 June 1919).
33. U.S. Third Army, June 14 to 18 [Extract] Estimate of the Situation,

Operations Report 193-33.1, Folder No. 50 (Third Army, AEF, 22 June 1919).

34. U.S. Third Army, Third Army to CO III Corps, June 1919, Folder No. 27923.

35. U.S. Army, *American Representation in Occupied Germany 1922-1923*, p. 272.

36. "Not Taking Office Says Gen. Dawes," *New York Times*, 3 February 1921.

Bibliography

Official Documents and Reports

AEF. Order of Battle of the AEF. Printed by the First Section, G-1, General Staff, GHQ AEF, 1918.

AEF Headquarters, District of Paris. Special Order Finding #256, 11 October 1918. Private collection.

AEF Headquarters, District of Paris, France. Memo dated 18 December 1918. Signed by L.S. Edwards, Adjutant General.

American Military Government of Occupied Germany. Notes on Army, Corps and Division Quartermaster Activities in the American Expeditionary Forces—France. Schuykill Arsenal, Philadelphia, undated.

Ayres, Leonard P. "The War with Germany: A Statistical Summary." *Source Records of the Great War, Volume VII*. Edited by Charles H. Horne. Indianapolis: The American Legion, 1931.

Beurket, Maj. George S. *Postal Service for a Field Army in [the] Theater of Operations*. Fort Leavenworth: The Command and General Staff School, 1933.

Buck, Maj. William J., M.C. Report of Activities of Camp Hospital No. 52, Le Mans, as of January 1, 1919. Historical Division, SGO.

Chamberlain, Col. Weston, and Lt. Col. Frank Weed. *The Medical Department of the United States Army in the World War, Vol. VI, Sanitation*. Washington, D.C.: U.S. Government Printing Office, 1926.

Chief of Staff, Third Army. To Commanding Generals, III Corps and 3rd Division, 22 May 1919. Author's verbiage: Commander-in-Chief, Allied Armies, G.Q.G.A., May 20, 1919, General Staff. 1st Section, No. 2583, "Directive For The High Command Only."

Committee on Classification of Personnel in the Army. *The Personnel System of the United States Army, Vol. I, History of the Personnel System*. Washington, D.C.: U.S. Government Printing Office, 1919.

Crane, Maj. A.G. *The Medical Department of the United States Army in the World War, Vol. XIII*. Washington, D.C.: U.S. Government Printing Office, 1927.

Cushing, John T., and Arthur F. Stone. *Vermont in the World War*. Burlington, VT: Free Press Printing Company, 1928.

Ford, Col. Joseph H. *The Medical Department of the United States Army in the World War, Vol. II*. Washington, D.C.: U.S. Government Printing Office, 1927.

Hirrel, Leo P. *Supporting the Doughboys: U.S. Army Logistics and Personnel During World War I*. Fort Leavenworth: Combat Studies Institute Press, U.S. Army Combined Arms Center, 2017.

Huston, James A. *The Sinews of War: Army Logistics 1775–1953*. Army Historical Series. Washington, D.C.: Office of the Chief of Military History, United States Army, 1966.

Lockett, Lt. Col. James M. *Report of the Military Commander, Coblenz, Germany from December 8, 1918, to May 22, 1919*. Fort Leavenworth: General Service Schools Press, 1921.

MacDonald, Charles B. *American Military History*. Army Historical Series, Volume 1. Washington, D.C.: Office of the Chief of Military History, United States Army, 1989.

McClellan, Maj. Edwin N. *The United States Marine Corps in the Great War*. Washington, D.C.: Headquarters, U.S. Marine Corps, Historical Branch, G-3 Division, 1920 and updated 2014.

Order, General Headquarters, Allied Armies. 20 May 1919. DGCRA No. 8618.

Pershing, Gen. John J., U.S.A. Commander in-Chief, American Expeditionary Forces. Report Cabled to the Secretary of War, November 30, 1918. Corrected 10 January 1919.

Raines, Rebecca R. *Getting the Message Through: A Branch History of the U.S. Army Signal Corps*. Washington, D.C.: Center for Military History, United States Army, 1996.

Reynolds, Col. C.R., M.C. Evacuation System of a Field Army. Undated, Historical Division, SGO.

Riddell, Col. William C., M.C. Report of the Activities Camp Hospital No. 26, St. Aignan-Noyers, as of January 1, 1919. Historical Division, SGO.

Special Committee on Charges of Alleged Executions Without Trial in France. *Hearings Before a Special Committee on Alleged Charges of Executions Without Trial in France: United States Senate*. Washington, D.C.: Government Printing Office, 1923.

U.S. Army. *United States Order of Battle of the United States Land Forces in the World War (1917-1919) Zone of the Interior: Territorial Departments Tactical Divisions Organized in 1918 Posts, Camps, and Stations*, Volume 3, Part 1 and 2. Washington, D.C.: Historical Division, United States Army, 1949.

U.S. Army Medical Department. *Administration American Expeditionary Forces, Volume 2*. Tables of Organization, No. 28, War Department, 1918.

U.S. Army Medical Department. *Manual for the Medical Department, U.S. Army*. 1916, Article XIII.

U.S. Army Medical Department. *The Medical Department of the United States Army in the World War: Volume VIII, Field Operations*. Washington, D.C.: Surgeon-General's Office, Government Printing Office, 1925.

U.S. Army Quartermaster Corps. *American Salvage Depot—Intermediate Number Eight*. Adjutant General Printing Plant, SOS, October 1918.

U.S. Army Quartermaster Corps. *Operations of the Quartermaster Corps, U.S. Army During the World War*, Monograph No. 2, undated. Extracts from the *Historical Report of the Chief Quartermaster, A.E.F., France*, undated.

U.S. Army Quartermaster Corps. *United States Army in the World War*, 1:341; *Report of Remount Service, A.E.F. Operations of the Quartermaster Corps, U.S. Army, during the World War*. Philadelphia: Quartermaster Corps School, Schuylkill Arsenal, 1929.

U.S. Department of the Army. *American Military Government of Occupied Germany, 1918-1920, Report of the Officer in Charge of Civil Affairs, Third Army and American Forces Germany*. Washington, D.C.: United States Government Printing Office, 1943.

U.S. Department of the Army. *American Military History, Vol I*. Richard W. Stewart, Chief Editor. Washington, D.C.: Army Historical Series, 2005.

U.S. Department of the Army. *American Military History, Vol II*. Richard W. Stewart, Chief Editor. Washington, D.C.: Army Historical Series, 2005.

U.S. Department of the Army. *American Representation in Occupied Germany, 1920-1921, Volume II, American Forces in Germany*. Compiled by the Assistant Chief of Staff. G-2, 1921.

U.S. Department of the Army. *American Representation in Occupied Germany, 1922-1923, American Forces in Germany*. Compiled by the Assistant Chief of Staff. G-2, 1923.

U.S. Department of the Army. *The Army Lineage Book, Volume II: Infantry*. Washington, D.C.: Government Printing Office, 1953.

U.S. Department of the Army. *United States Army in the World War, 1917-1919, American Occupation of Germany, Volume 11*. Washington, D.C.: U.S. Army Historical Division, 1948.

U.S. Department of the Army. *United States Army in the World War, 1917-1919, Military Operations of the American Expeditionary Forces, Volume 9*. Washington, D.C.: U.S. Army Historical Division, 1948.

U.S. Department of the Army. *United States Army in the World War, 1917–1919, Reports of the Commander-In-Chief, A.E.F., Staff Sections and Services, Volume 12*. Washington, D.C.: U.S. Army Historical Division, 1948.
U.S. Department of the Army, Center for Military History. *American Armies and Battlefields in Europe*. Washington, D.C.: Government Printing Office, 1995.
U.S. Department of the Army, Historical Division. *United States Army in the World War 1917–1919, American Occupation of Germany*. Washington, D.C.: Government Printing Office, 1948.
United States Military Academy. *Alphabetical Locator of Graduates and Former Cadets, Volume IX*. 1950.
U.S. Third Army. June 14 to 18 [Extract] Estimate of the Situation, Operations Report 193-33.1, Folder No. 47 (Third Army, AEF, 19 June 1919).
U.S. Third Army. June 14 to 18 [Extract] Estimate of the Situation, Operations Report 193-33.1, Folder No. 50 (Third Army, AEF, 22 June 1919).
U.S. Third Army. Plan of Communication, Supply and Evacuation. Annex No. 3, Trèves, France (Third Army, AEF, 19 June 1919).
U.S. Third Army. Plans in Case Germany Refuses to Sign Peace Treaty, Field Orders 193-32.1, No. 9 (Third Army, AEF, 17 June 1919).
U.S. Third Army. Third Army to CO III Corps, June 1919, Folder No. 27923.
Wadhams, Col. Sanford H., M.C. Report of the activities of G-4-B, medical group, fourth section, general staff, G.H.Q., A.E.F., December 31, 1918. Historical Division, S.G.O.
Wadhams, Col. Sanford H., M.C., and Col. Arnold D. Tuttle, M.C. "Some of the Early Activities of the Medical Department, A.E.F." *The Military Surgeon* XLV, no. 6 (1919), 636.
War Department. *Order of Battle of the United States Land Forces in the World War. Vol. 2*. Washington, D.C.: U.S. Government Printing Office, 1931–1949.
War Department. *Order of Battle of the United States Land Forces in the World War. Vol. 3*. Washington, D.C.: U.S. Government Printing Office, 1931–1949.

Published Sources

"American War Locomotives for France." *American Machinist* 47, no. 20 (2 August 1917).
Baker, Chester E. *Doughboy's Diary*. Shippensburg, PA: Burd Street Press, White Mane, 1998.
Barbeau, Arthur E., and Florette Henri. *The Unknown Soldiers: Black American Troops in World War I*. Philadelphia: Temple University Press, 1974.
Barnes, Alexander F. "Great Coblentz Horse Sale." *Army Logistician*, July–August 1993.
Barnes, Alexander F. *In a Strange Land: The American Occupation of Germany, 1918–1923*. Atglen, PA: Schiffer, 2011.
The Battle of Bourges, 1918–1919. Bourges, France: American Expeditionary Forces, 1919.
Beaver, Daniel R. *Newton D. Baker and the American War Effort, 1917–1919*. Lincoln: University of Nebraska Press, 1966.
Berry, Henry. *Make the Kaiser Dance*. Garden City, NY: Doubleday, 1978.
Chaikin, Dr. William. "Quartermaster Supply in the AEF, 1917–1918." *Quartermaster Review*, May–June 1950.
Cockfield, Jamie H. *With Snow on Their Boots*. New York: St. Martin's Press, 1998.
Cutchins, John A. *An Amateur Diplomat in the World War*. Richmond: The Commanders Committee, The American Legion, 1938.
Dalessandro, Robert J., and Michael G. Knapp. *Organization and Insignia of the American Expeditionary Force, 1917–1923*. Atglen, PA: Schiffer, 2008.
Dawes, Charles G. *A Journal of the Great War*. Boston: Houghton Mifflin, 1923.
Eisenhower, John S.D. *Yanks: The Epic Story of the American Army in World War I*. New York: Simon & Schuster, 2001.
Fleming, Thomas. *The Illusion of Victory: America in World War I*. New York: Basic Books, 2003.

Fredericks, Pierce G. *The Yanks Are Coming.* New York: Bantam, 1964.
Garland, Patrick V. "Army Officer Accused of Prisoner Abuse." *Military Police,* 22 September 2009.
Gleaves, Albert. *A History of the Transport Service: Adventures and Experiences of United States Transports and Cruisers in the World War.* New York: George H. Doran, 1921.
Goedeken, Edward A. "Charles Dawes and the Military Board of Allied Supply." *Military Affairs* 50, no. 1 (January 1986).
Greenwood, John T. *John J. Pershing and the American Expeditionary Forces in World War I, 1917–1919: April 7—September 30, 1917, Volume 1.* Lexington: University Press of Kentucky, 2021.
Grotelueschen, Mark E. *The AEF Way of War: The American Army and Combat in the First World War.* PhD dissertation, Texas A&M University, August 2003.
Hagood, Gen. Johnson. *The Services of Supply.* Cranbury, NJ: The Scholar's Bookshelf, 2006.
Hagood, Maj. Gen. Johnson. *Caissons Go Rolling Along.* Edited by Larry A. Grant. Columbia: University of South Carolina Press, 2010.
Harbord, James G. *The American Army in France, 1917–1919.* Boston: Little, Brown, 1936.
Harbord, James G. *Leaves from a War Diary.* New York: Dodd, Mead, 1925.
Hunton, Addie W. and Kathryn Johnson. *Two Colored Women with the American Expeditionary Forces.* New York: AMS Press, 1920 and 1971.
Jackson, Edgar B. *Fall Out to the Right of the Road.* Verona, VA: McClure Printing Company, 1973.
Kirby, Dr. Lelias E. *How Me and Amos Won WWI.* Birmingham: Commercial Printing Company, 1976.
Lawrence, Joseph D. *Fighting Soldier: The AEF in 1918.* Edited by Robert H. Ferell. Boulder: Colorado Associated University Press, 1985.
Lee, Roger I. *Letters from Roger I. Lee, Lt. Colonel, U.S. Army Medical Corps, 1917–1918.* Brookline, MA: Privately printed, 1962.
Lengel, Edward G. *To Conquer Hell: The Meuse Argonne, 1918.* New York: Henry Holt, , 2008.
MacDonald, Lyn. *The Roses of No Man's Land.* New York: Macmillan, 1980.
March, General Peyton C. *The Nation at War.* Garden City, NY: Doubleday, Doran, 1932.
Marshall, George C. *Memoirs of My Service in the World War, 1917–1918.* Boston: Houghton Mifflin, 1976.
Mayo, Katherine. *That Damn Y: A Record of Overseas Service,* Boston: Houghton Mifflin, 1920.
Musicant, Ivan. *The Banana Wars.* New York: Macmillan, 1990.
Nenninger, Timothy K. "Tactical Dysfunction in the AEF, 1917–1918." *Military Affairs* 51, no. 4 (October 1987).
Palmer, Elijah. "German Raiders in Hampton Roads." *The Daybook* 17, Issue 4 (undated). Published by the Hampton Roads Naval Museum.
Pershing, John J. *My Experiences in the World War, Volume II.* New York: Frederick A. Stokes Company, 1931.
Pershing, John J. *My Life Before the World War, 1860–1917.* Edited by John T. Greenwood, Association of the United States Army. Lexington: University Press of Kentucky, 2013.
Rand McNally & Company. *U.S. Army Facts and Insignia.* Chicago: Rand McNally & Co., 1918.
Rinaldi, Richard A. *The United States Army in World War I: Orders of Battle: Ground Units, 1917–1919.* Takoma Park, MD: Tiger Lily Publications, 2005.
Roosevelt, Eleanor. *Day Before Yesterday: The Reminiscences of Mrs. Theodore Roosevelt, Jr.* Garden City, NY: Doubleday, 1959.
Schneider, Dorothy, and Carl J. *Into the Breach: American Women Overseas in World War I.* New York: Penguin, 1991.
Scott, Emmett J. *The American Negro in the World War.* Chicago: Homewood, 1919.
Scully, C. Alison. *The Course of the Silver Greyhound.* New York: G.P. Putnam and Sons, 1936.

Shanks, Maj. Gen. (Ret.) David C. *As They Passed Through the Port.* Washington, D.C.: The Cary Publishing Company, 1927.
Sprenger, Albert James, and Franklin Spencer Edmonds. *The Leave Areas of the American Expeditionary Forces, 1918-1919.* Philadelphia: The John Winston Company, 1928.
Stallings, Laurence T. *The Doughboys: The Story of the AEF 1917-1918.* New York: Harper & Row, 1963.
Thompson, Hugh S. *Trench Knives and Mustard Gas: With the 42nd Rainbow Division in France.* Edited by Robert Ferrell. College Station: Texas A&M University Press, 2004.

Unit Histories

Brady, Maj. George S. *History of the Ordnance Repair Shops, Mehun-sur-Yevre, France.* Printed at Government Shop by Ordnance Troops, Mehun-sur-Yevre, France, 1919.
Cutchins, John A. *History of the Twenty-Ninth Division "Blue and Gray," 1917-1919.* Philadelphia: McCalla and Company, 1921.
Davies, Alfred H. 1920. *Twentieth Engineers, France, 1917-1918-1919.* Portland, OR: Twentieth Engineers Pub. Assn.
Dienst, Capt. Charles F. *History of the 353rd Infantry Regiment, 89th Division National Army, September 1917 to June 1919.* Wichita: The 353rd Infantry Society, 1921.
86th Anniversary Signal Corps. U.S. Army pamphlet, 3 March 1949.
English, George H. *History of the 89th Division U.S.A.* Denver: War Society of the 89th Division. 1920.
54th Pioneer Infantry with the Army of Occupation, Third U.S. Army. Coblenz, Germany, 1919.
An Historical and Technical Biography of the Twenty-First Engineers, Light Railway, United States Army, Presenting Their Part in the World War. New York: The McConnell Printing Company, 1919.
The 308th Engineers Veterans Association. *With the 308th Engineers from Ohio to the Rhine and Back.* Cleveland: Premier Press, 1923.

Newspapers and Periodicals

Agamemnon Daily News. The official newsletter published for the soldiers and sailors aboard the USS *Agamemnon* (formerly *Kaiser Wilhelm II*), 1919.
AMAROC News. The official newspaper of the American occupation of Germany. Published in Coblenz, Germany, 1919-1922.
The CRO. The newspaper published for members of the Central Records Office at Caserne Carnot, Bourges, France, 1918-1919.
Die Wacht am Rhein: A Journal of Truth. Published by the G-2-C, Third Army, Coblenz, 1919.
The Gangplank. The official news magazine of the SOS ports, 1919.
The Gazette and Daily. York, Pennsylvania, 1919.
Mehun News. The newspaper published for soldiers assigned to the Mehun Ordnance Camp at Atelier de Mehun-Sur-Yevre, France.
The Messkit. Published in France for the AEF, 1919.
New York Times, 1918-1922.
The 9th Infantry Regiment Cootie. Published at Bendorf, Germany, by the soldiers of the 9th Infantry Regiment, 2nd Division, 1919.
The Octagon. Published at Montigny-sue-Aube, Franc,e by the U.S. Army XIII Corps.
Oroville Daily Register. Oroville, California, 11 November 1918.
The Skirmisher. Published by the 4th Division, 1917-1919.
Star and Stripes. French edition, 1918-1919.
The York Dispatch. York, Pennsylvania, 1919.

Unpublished Sources

Brakebill, Max. Collection of letters while serving with the 40th Division, 1918–1919. Private collection.
Deuel, Irving M. Personal diary, 17 December 1918 to 24 July 1919. Private collection.
Etzweiler, Charles. Collection of letters, souvenirs and ephemera collected while serving with a Railroad Regulating Station in France, 1918–1919. Private collection.
Fidler, Bert A. Oral history, 1918–1919. Compiled by Matthew R. Fidler. Private collection.
Hart, Private Raymond Jay. Letters. Aviation cadet, U.S. Army Air Service, Casual Co. #6. Charles G. Thomas collection.
Kaufman, Ruth W. Unpublished article April 1919. Archives and Special Collections, Library of the Marine Corps, Quantico, VA.
Keith, Wayne. Wartime diary of service in the States and in France with the 37th Division. Private collection.
Koehn, Robert. Collection of letters, 1918–1919, from the 83rd Division. Private collection.
Nasilowski, Stanley. Letter from Stanley Nasilowski to his friend Helen Bialkoswka. Private collection.
Naumann, 2nd Lt. Louis J. Collection of letters, official documents, souvenirs and ephemera collected while serving with in the District of Paris in the AEF, 1918–1919. Private collection.
Roseberry, Clyde B. Souvenir scrapbook of the war and his service in the 21st Engineer Regiment. Private collection.

Official Websites

The American Battle Monuments Commission Homepage and website: http://www.abmc.gov.
The American Library Association homepage: https://www.ala.org.
The Arlington National Cemetery official website: http://www.arlingtoncemetery.mil/.
The Army National Guard homepage and website: http://www.nationalguard.com/.
Army Transport Manifests via Ancestry.com.
Connecticut Service Records via Ancestry.com.
New Mexico War Service Records via Ancestry.com.
Pennsylvania War Service Records via Ancestry.com.
The U.S. Army Center for Military History website: http://www.history.army.mil/.
The U.S. Army Combined Arms Support Command (CASCOM) website: http://www.cascom.army.mil/.
The U.S. Army Medical Department, Office of Medical History website: http://history.amedd.army.mil/booksdocs/wwi/.
The U.S. Army Military Academy website: https://alumni.westpointaog.org/memorial-article.
The U.S. Army Military Police School homepage: http://www.wood.army.mil/usamps.
The U.S. Army Quartermaster Museum website: https://www.qmmuseum.lee.army.mil/.
The U.S. Marine Corps History Division (U.S.M.C. HD): https://www.mcu.usmc.mil/historydivision/.

Index

Numbers in ***bold italics*** indicate pages with illustrations

Abbeville Agreement 77, 88
Abeyta, Adolph 112, 113, ***113***
Advance Section 8–10, 15, ***16***, 17, 21, ***61***, 68, 73, ***89***, ***100***, ***103***, ***107***, 136, 194, 197
USS *Aeolus* 32
African-Americans ***3***, 7, 10, ***11***, ***20***, 72, 102, 120–121, 127–128, 152, ***166***, 169; Labor Battalions 154, 165; *see also* racism
USS *Agamemnon* 32, 33, 40
Air Service 11, 13, 25, 78, 157, 159, 173, 195, 197
alcohol 161, 162, 173
Allerey 89, 105
AMAROC News 61, 203
USS *America* 32, 33
American Forces in Germany (AFG) 202–203; *see also* Third Army
USS *Antigone* 32
army prison 18, 141, 173, 174–176
Army Service Corps (ASC) 13, 63–64, ***64***, 65, ***65***, 140, ***140***, 198
Army, U.S.: Andernach 191, 200; Bendorf 191; Coblenz 140, 165, 190–193, 200–203; First 19, 78, 188; horse auctions 192, 203; Rhine River ***190***, 191–192, 200–201, 203; Third (Army of Occupation) 13–14, 41, 122, 158, 162, 165–166, 179, 188–191, ***192***, 193, 199–202; *see also* American Forces in Germany
Arrington, Harriet 90
Atterbury, William W. 106, 154

Baker, Newton 29, 31, 35, 77, 128, 174
USS *Baltic* 28
Band Instrument and Typewriter Repair Detachment 158
Bandholtz, Harry Hill 131–132, ***132***, 197
base hospital 87–89, ***89***, 90, ***90***, ***99***, 100, ***103***, 141
Base Sections: 1 (St. Nazaire) 10, 15, ***24***, ***38***, 41, 45, 50, 55, ***101***, 109, 169, 180; 2 (Bordeaux) 11, ***11***, ***12***, 15, ***18***, 41, 199, 50, 53, 56, 59, 89, 120, 148; 3 (Great Britain) 11; 4 (Le Havre) 12, 13, 40–41 47, 59, 148; 5 (Brest) 4, 12–13, 32, 39, 41, 46, ***46***, 49–50, 56, 59, 70, 89, 98–99, 102, 115, 122, 134, 158, 169, 199; 6 (Marseilles) 13, 40, 49, 59, 153; 7 (la Rochelle) 13, 41, 49–50; 8 (Genoa) 13; 9 (Antwerp) 13–14, 41, 125, 179, 189, 193, 199
Beau Desert 50
Beck, Albert ***88***
Beresford, Charles 28
Bessens 50
Bliss, Tasker 31, 35
Blois 17, 91
Borland, William 100
Boston 33
Bourges 128, 166–168, ***178***, 178, 180–182
Brakebill, Max 19, 56, 144
British ships 37, 77
Butler, Smedley Darlington 47, 50–51, ***51***, ***52***, 52–53, 133, ***133***, 134, ***134***, 195

Camp Pontanezen ***46***, 46–47, 50–55, ***51***, ***54***, ***55***, 70, 102, ***133***, 134; duckboards ***52***, ***55***, 134, ***134***; inadequate water supply 52–53; sanitation report 47
camps (National Army): Devens (Ayer, Massachusetts) 97; Dix (Wrightstown, New Jersey) 52, 97; Funston (Fort Riley, Kansas) 39, 43, 97; Grant (Rockford, Illinois) 97, 99; Lee (Petersburg, Virginia) 44, 70; Meade (Admiral, Maryland) 70, 97; Pike (Little Rock, Arkansas) 39, 97; Sherman (Chillicothe, Ohio) 97; Travis (San Antonio, Texas) 39; Upton (Yaphank, New York) 44
camps (National Guard): Beauregard (Alexandria, Louisiana) 39; Bowie (Fort Worth, Texas) 39; Cody (Deming, New Mexico) 39; Doniphan (Lawton, Oklahoma) 39; Sevier (Taylor, South Carolina) 39; Sheridan (Montgomery, Alabama) 70; Wheeler (Macon, Georgia) 138

Index

camps (specialized or technical training): Humphreys (Belvoir Virginia) 97; Johnston (Jacksonville, Florida) 64; Merritt (Dumont, New Jersey) 44; Mills (Garden City, New York) 45; Stuart (Hampton, Virginia) 45
cavalry units (U.S. Army) 17, 73, 137, 150, *150*, 153
Central Records Office (CRO) *121*, 128, 152, 161, 167, 177–178, *178*, 179, *179*, *180*, 183–185, 187
Chaikin, William 15
Château-Thierry 26, 27, 90, 152
Chemical Warfare Service 169, 196–197
China 17, 134, 184, 199; Chinese workers 60, 74, 146, 169
Coffee Blenders Detachment (QMC) 2, 148, 149
Cole, Eli K. 47, 49
convalescent camps 64, 87, 89–91, 93, 95
Coolidge, Calvin 133, *135*, 136
USS *Covington* 32, 35
The CRO *128*, 161, 165
Czech Legion *122*, 199

Dawes, Charles Gates 71–72, 75–76, 80, 135, *135*, 136, 144–146, 148, 169, 198, 204, 206
USS *DeKalb* 33
Depot Divisions 20, 39, 64, 69, 81, 92; 1 (41st Division) 69, 82, 91; 2 (83rd Division) 82; 3 (76th Division) 82; 4 (85th Division) 82; 5 (39th Division) 81; 6 (40th Division) 56, 82, 173; 7 (31st Division) 81
Detzer, Karl W. 174–176
District of Paris 17–18, *90*, *120*, *129*, 163, 173
Divisions (US Army): 1st 19, 21, 27, *124*, 141, 177; 2nd 19, 26–27, 47, *120*, 138, 150, 200–201; 3rd 26, *50*, 83, 159, 200; 4th 14, 26, 83, 166, 200, *204*; 5th 200; 26th 19, 24, *83*, *111*, *125*, 177; 27th 27, 77; 28th 26, 55, 77; 29th 13, 82, 115, 130–131, 164–165, 197; 30th 27, *66*, 77; 31st 81, 138; 32nd 81, 115; 33rd *18*, 24, 27, 77; 35th 77; 37th 69–70, *120*, *125*; 38th 81; 39th 81; 40th 56, 82, 173; 44th 41st 20, 45, 49, 69, 82; 42nd 19–22, 35–36 *36*, 45, 53, *88*, 177; 76th 82; 77th 77, 125; 78th 27, 77; 80th 27, 77; 82nd 77; 83rd 82; 84th 77, 82, *125*; 85th 82; 86th 82; 87th 81–82; 89th 43–44, 140; 92nd 72, 152; 93rd 7, 72, 152

Engineer Regiments 10, 11, *20*, 39, 47, 62–63, 67, 72–73, 76, 78, 81, 86, 94, 106–110, 144, 161, 169, 194, 196; 10th 62; 11th 113; 17th 135, 169; 15th 140, 168; 19th 10, 109; 20th 62–63; 21st 110–111, *112*, 112–113; 22nd *84*; 23rd 168; 26th 52; 35th 13; 56th *190*; 69th 98; 101st *111*

females (U.S. Military) 160–161; *see also* "Hello Girls"
Field Hospital 86–87, 93–94, 117

first AEF fatalities 141–142
Fisher, Charles N. *65*
foreign laborers 146
Forestry Section/Service 17, 62–63, 95, 107, 162, 193–194
French rail cars 46, 114
French railroads 21, 106, 108, 189
French ships 37
French women workers 60, *67*, *68*, 74, 121, *123*, 124

Garden Service (QM) 2, 146–147, 148
General Purchasing Board 136, 144–145, 198–199
USS *George Washington* 33
German prisoners of war (POW) 1, 4, 10, 69, *110*, 120, 143, *143*, 144, *145*, 146, 154, 163–164, 171, 191, 197
German ships name changes 32–33
German submarines 13, 28–29, 35, 63; *see also* U-boat
Gièvres *14*, 15, 49, 161, 174–175
Gleaves, Albert 38
Goethals, George 27, 76
Graves Registration Service 64, 165, 203
USS *Great Northern* 34, 149
Griffin, Louis G. 111, *112*
Guantanamo Bay, Cuba *126*
Gunther, Elise 74

Hagood, Johnson 17, 22, 25–27, 39, 65, 71–77, 94, 128, 136–137, *137*, 143, 154, 182, 194–197
"Haller's Army" 165
Harbord, James Guthrie *12*, 27, 58–59, 61, 63, 69, 73, 76–77, 79, 94, 136–138, *138*, 139, 148, 150–154, 161, 194–196
headquarter staff sections: G-1 (personnel administration) 19, 25; G-2 (military intelligence) 25; G-3 (operations) 25; G-4 (logistics) 25, 140; G-5 (training) 25
"Hello Girls" *125*, 197; *see also* females (U.S. Military)
Hoboken 31, 44–45, 98, 149, 156, 158
Hoover, Herbert 35
horses 8, 16, 22, 24, *24*, *37*, *38*, 73–74, 79, 110, *111*, 114, 169, 172, 189, 191–192, 200–201, 204
hospitals and hospital centers 10, 13, 64, 86–105, 111, 117, 127, 135, 141–143, 147, 151, 174, 178–179, 184, 194, 196, 198, 201
Hough, Francis Olney *49*
Hucks, Albert Sidney 63
USS *Huron* 33

Ice Plant Company 301 170–172
Intermediate Salvage Depot Number Eight 67–68
Intermediate Section 8–10, 14–15, *15*
Into the Breach 124
Issoudun 49

Index 225

Is-sur-Tille 15, 46, 161, 175
Italian ships 37

Keith, Wayne A. 69–70
Kenly, Robert G. *180*
Kernan, Frances Joseph 22, 26–27, 63, 138–139, *139*, 151
Knight, George *47*
Koehn, Robert 144
Krebs, Adam H. *164*
USS *Kroonland* 13, 39, 99

La Pallice 13, 41, 49–50
Le Mans 55, 70, 90, 174
USS *Leviathan* 13, *32*, 33, *34*, 39, 70, 102
lines of communication (LOC) 10, 17, 19, 21–22, 25–26, 71, 136
Little, Clinton 74

USS *Madawaska* 33
mail problems/process 181–187
March, Peyton Conway 76–77, 97–98
Marine Brigades: 4th Marine Brigade 20, 47, 138; 5th Marine Brigade 43, 45–49, *49*, *50*, *133*, 134, 150, 179
Marine Regiments: 11th 47, 49; 13th 47, 49–50, 134
Mars-sur-Allier Hospital Center 64, 89
Marshall, George C. 51, 189
Master Card Division/Locator Card Section 117–179, 184
McAllister sisters *124*
McAndrew, James W. 80, *80*
Medical Department 52, 90–92, 105, 117, 156, 195–196; Dental Corps 92, 156; Prophylactics Station *96*; Veterinary Corps 74, 92, *93*, 194
Mehun 15, 40, 49, 60–62
USS *Mercury* 33
The Messkit 166
Meuse-Argonne Offensive 72, *80*, 81–82, *81*, *84*, 92, 102, 111, *112*, 115, 136, *145*, 188–189, *205*, 206
Montoir 50
Motor Transport Corps 184, 195
USS *Mount Vernon* 33, 35
mules *37*, *38*, 73, 189, 191–192

Nantes 10, 50, 89
Nasilowski, Stanley 97
National Army 17, 39, 81, 182
National Guard 19, 20, 27, 39, *46*, *49*, 56, 64, 70, 72, *81*, 81, 131, 165, 175, 182
New York City 28, *30*, 33, 43, 70, 140, 149, 157–158, *164*, 174, 184
non-combat injuries and diseases 53, 54, *54*, 95, 96, 102; *see also* pneumonia; Spanish flu
Norfolk 33
USS *Northern Pacific* 34

USS *Olympic* 102
Operation Enduring Freedom 73
Operation Iraqi Freedom 73
Optical Repair School, Ordnance 60, 157, 158
Ordnance Corps 60, 83, 157–158, 161, 185, 193
overseas stripes *120*, 160

Panama Canal Zone 57, 122
Peabody, George Foster 128
Philadelphia 33, 108, *108*, 134–135, 156
Philippines 33, 133, 136, 138–139, 197
Pioneer Infantry Regiments 2, 66, 72, 78, 153; 1st 97; 54th 66, 115; 56th 66; 57th 102; 808th 102
pneumonia 13, 39, 95–100, 102
USS *Pocahontas* 33, 55
Port of Embarkation Command *30*, 70
Postal Express Service (PES) 25, 63, 100, 177–183, *183*, 185–187; Central Post Office 100, 182
Powers, Clifford *157*
USS *Powhatan* 33
USS *President Grant* 33
USS *President Lincoln* 33, 35, *36*
USS *Princess Matoika* 33
Provost Marshal General Department/ Provost Marshal's Service 17, 63, 72, 131, 150, 163, 170, 175, 197

Quartermaster Corps 14, 17, *47*, 140, 146–147, 159–160, 172, 182, 194–195
Queen Mary's Army Auxiliary Corps (QMAAC) 75, *178*, *186*

"Race to Berlin" 59, *61*, 153–154
racism 141, 152, 165; *see also* African American
railroad 14–16, 25, 34, 67, 71, 73, 78, 80, 105, 106–112, *112*, *113*, 114–115, 184, 193, 200,
Rents, Requisition and Claims Service 198
replacement uniforms 16, 22, 190
restarting the war 199–202
Rice, Grantland 192–193
Richard, Charles 98
Roosevelt, Archie 21
Roosevelt, Eleanor (Mrs. Teddy Roosevelt, Jr.) 119
Roosevelt, Franklin Delano 137
Roosevelt, Theodore "Teddy" 21, 119
Roosevelt, Theodore "Teddy," Jr. 119
Rotterdam 14, 41, 189, 191
Russian soldiers/prisoners of war 4, 7, 75–76, 164–165

St. Mihiel 66, 78, 80–81, 115, *145*
St. Sulpice 11, 174
salvage recovery operations 2, 10, 63, 65–66, *66*, 67–68, *68*, 69, 104–105, *110*, 114, 155, 191, 193–194, 203,

USS *Seattle* 41
Service of Utilities 106; Construction Department 107; Light Railways and Highways 107, 109; Motor Transportation 107, 167, 195–196; Transportation Department 17, 22, 25, 71, 107, 195
service organizations: American Library Association (ALA)/Library War Service (LWS) 116, *126*, 126; hospitals 87, 90–91, 117; Jewish Welfare Board 116, *121*, 125; Knights of Columbus (K of C) 116, *121*, 124–125, *125*; Red Cross 74, *87*, 87, 90–91, 95, 104, 116–117, *119*, 122, 127–128, 144, 170; Salvation Army 97, 116, 122, 124, *124*, 128; Young Men's Christian Association (YMCA) 70, 97, 116–117, 119–120, *120*, 121–122, *122*, 127–128, *129*, 140, 155, 170; Young Women's Christian Association (YWCA) 116, 119, 121–122, *123*, 127
Services of Supply (SOS) 1, *2*, *3*, *4*, 17, 59, 94, 136–138, *138*, *139*, 139, 141, 152 195, *205*; command philosophies 26; establishment 25–25, 94; naming 25
Siberia 78, 122
Signal Corps 14, 72, 178, *125*, 157, 196–197
Smith, Frank H. "Hardboiled" 173–176
Somalia 16
Somervell, Brehon Burke 139, 140, *140*
Spanish flu 30, *34*, 39, *40*, 43, 86–105, *98*, 115, 151, 193
Stallings, Laurence 104
Stars & Stripes 159, 163, 168, 184
Surgical Instrument and Typewriter Repair Unit 156–158
USS *Susquehanna* 33

Taylor, H.K. 154
Theater of Operations: Forward Zone 8; Rear Zone 8
Thornton, Cornelia Elizabeth *99*
tours *9*, 10, 15, 25, 49, 58, 67, 70, 76, 103, 122, 150–151, 160, 188, 197
Transportation Department 17, 22, 25, 71, 107, 195
Treaty of Brest-Litovsk 7
Tugo, Oscar C. 141–143, *142*, 143

U-boats 7, 35, *36*; *see also* German submarines
United States Air Force (USAF) 3
United States Marine Corps (USMC) 3–4, 7, *18*, 19–20, 27–28, 37, 39, 43, 47, 49, *49*, *50*, 78, 90, 97, 104, 121, *126*, 133, *133*, 134–135, 138, 150, 152, 169, 179–180, *180*, 201

veterinary hospitals 74, 92, *93*, 194
USS *Von Steuben* 33, 35,174

Wallis, Raymond K. 64, *64*, 65
War Risk Bureau 63, 197, 198
Whitlow, James A. 52, 53
USS *Wilhelmina* 98
Wilcox, Ella Wheeler 172, 173
Wilson, Woodrow 5, 29, 35, 56, 72, 202
Women's Army Auxiliary Corps (WAAC) 75, 146, 160, 178

Zammuto, Angelo *153*
Zone of the Interior 8

www.ingramcontent.com/pod-product-compliance
Lightning Source LLC
Chambersburg PA
CBHW041439300426
44114CB00026B/2941